Positive Parenting
in the
Muslim Home

D1616415

POSITIVE PARENTING
IN THE
MUSLIM HOME

NOHA ALSHUGAIRI

MUNIRA LEKOVIC EZZELDINE

FOREWORD BY DR. JANE NELSEN

ISBN-13: 978-0-9742950-5-3
ISBN-10: 0-9742950-5-1
Library of Congress Control Number 2016931850

Printed and bound in the United States of America
Izza Publishing, PO Box 50326, Irvine, CA, 92619-0326
www.izzapublishing.com

Cover design by Ramsey Nashef

www.positivemuslimhome.com
www.positivedisciplinemuslimhome.com

To my mom, Afaf Ali, and dad, Mazin Alshugairi:
for raising us with Positive Discipline even before it was born.

~ Noha

To my sons, Yusuf, Zayd, and Ali:
for helping me gather wisdom on this parenting journey.

~ Munira

A strong family for a strong community.
Be There. Connect. Encourage. Love.

CONTENTS

FOREWORD

In recent decades the field of psychology has begun to acknowledge the beneficial role religion plays in the lives of people. What may surprise many is that Alfred Adler had posited such sentiments, "There have always been people…who knew that the meaning of life was to be interested in the whole of humankind and who tried to develop social interest and love. In all religions, we find this concern for the salvation of humankind. In all the great movements of the world, people have been striving to increase social interest, and religion is one of the greatest strivings in this direction." Children raised with a sense of purpose who are oriented to service and contribution are more likely to become adults who lead a rich, fulfilled life.

In this book, Noha and Munira present the timeless principles of Positive Discipline for the Islamic context. They have done a remarkable job of weaving the principles of Positive Discipline into the daily lives of Muslim families. Their synthesis is yet another testament to the universality of Positive Discipline principles.

There is no doubt that parents love their children. Unfortunately, some current parenting practices lean toward permissiveness in an effort to avoid the use of punishments. While disregarding punitive parenting measures is commendable, permissiveness is creating a generation of children who are spoiled and entitled. Noha and Munira have observed this alarming trend in their community. They have done such an excellent job in this book of conveying the importance of using both kindness and firmness to teach children the desire and skills for contribution to the family and society to balance the need for belonging. Children need to learn to give as well as to receive. Young adults raised with excessive love and no skills for contribution struggle in life. Noha and Munira have also warned against the exact opposite: a controlling parenting style stemming from the fear that children might fail to adopt and adhere to their parents' values and traditions. In their book, Noha and Munira invite the Muslim community to shift toward parenting with kindness and firmness at the same time—the Positive Discipline way.

When I first published the Positive Discipline book in 1981, I did not imagine it would become the seed of a global movement that currently spans cultures and faiths in many countries. I am delighted to offer this book for the global Muslim community. It is my hope that, together, with our children, we will all be united in creating peace in the world beginning with ourselves, within our homes, schools, and communities.

Dr. Jane Nelsen
www.positivediscipline.com
August 24, 2016

ACKNOWLEDGMENTS

We praise Allah (God) for empowering us with courage, patience, and wisdom to bring this book to life. He is the Sustainer and the Granter of *Tawfiq* (divine success). To Him we owe the greatest gratitude.

Without our lived experience, this book would not be authentic. Our families, both nuclear and extended, are where we learned the hard realities of parenting. Without their love, support, and constant belief in our abilities, we would not have been able to share this journey with you. Our deepest gratitude to our parents (Mazin Alshugairi & Afaf Ali; Halil Lekovic & Kaja Lekovic), siblings (Rula Alshugairi, Ismail Alreshq, Ahmad Alshugairi, & Roula Dashisha; Edina Lekovic & Tarek Shawky), spouses (Amer Zarka; Omar Ezzeldine), and children (Omar Zarka, Maryam Amir, Hisham Zarka, Kinza Benali, Mona Zarka, Amr Hafez, & Lemiece Zarka; Yusuf Ezzeldine, Zayd Ezzeldine, & Ali Ezzeldine).

Special thanks and gratitude to Dr. Jane Nelsen, the founder of Positive Discipline, for her unwavering enthusiasm and encouragement. For Mary Hughes who envisioned this book before we did. For our teachers who initially trained us, Jane Nelsen, Lynn Lott, Jody McVittie, Lois Ingber and all the Positive Discipline Associates who continue to spread and expand this beautiful philosophy.

Sincere appreciation goes to our editors who took the time to read, point out details, make suggestions, and share their honest feedback: Omar Ezzeldine for critiquing ideas and concepts, Mona Zarka for her sharp attention to the manuscript voice and grammar, Hanaa Eldereiny for evaluating the book as a fellow mental health professional, and Kathleen Farrell for efficiently and thoroughly doing the detailed work of copyediting.

We are especially grateful to our guest writers—Ahmed Younis, Tarek Shawky, Saleh Kholaki, Dina Eletreby, Metra Azar-Salem, Hina Khan-Mukhtar, and Ohood Alomar—for contributing invaluable wisdom and insight.

Finally, our heartfelt gratitude goes out to all the families who opened their hearts, shared their struggles and successes, and taught us humility and resiliency. For all of you, we are grateful.

ALLAH IS OUR GUIDE AND SUPPORTER

Nothing is better on the parenting journey than invoking the guidance and support of Allah. We invite you to recite these verses following daily prayers. May Allah Grant you *qurat ain* (serenity) in your spouses and your children.

"رب هب لي من لدنك ذرية طيبة إنك سميع الدعاء"

"My Lord! Bless me with offspring that are among Your good, pious descendants; You are one who accepts supplications."

(Quran, 3:38)

"رب اجعلني مقيم الصلاة ومن ذريتي. ربنا وتقبل دعاء. ربنا اغفر لي ولوالدي وللمؤمنين يوم يقوم الحساب"

"My Lord! Make me one who continually performs prayers and make my offspring the same. Our Lord, accept our supplication. Our Lord, forgive my sins and those of my parents and all the believers on the day of reckoning."

(Quran, 14:40)

"ربنا هب لنا من أزواجنا وذرياتنا قرة أعين واجعلنا للمتقين إماما"

"Our Lord! Grant to us from our spouses and children comfort and contentment, and make us leaders for the God-conscious."

(Quran, 25:74)

"رب أوزعني أن أشكر نعمتك التي أنعمت علي وعلي والدي وأن أعمل صالحا ترضاه وأصلح لي في ذريتي. إني تبت إليك وإني من المسلمين"

"My Lord! Grant me the ability to give thanks to You for Your Blessings that You have Bestowed upon me and upon my parents. And Grant me the ability to do righteous good deeds which please You. And make righteous my children. I have repented to you and I am among the Muslims."

(Quran, 46:15)

GEMS FROM OUR TRADITION

To further support you in your parenting journey, here are some sayings from our Islamic tradition.

"Train your children with a different methodology than yours, for they were born for a time different than yours."
(Ali bin Abi Talib or al-Hasan al-Basri)

"He is not amongst us who does not treat our youngsters with mercy nor respects our elders."
(Hadith, Abu Dawood, Tirmizi)

"To discipline one's child is better than to give a provision in charity."
(Hadith, Tirmizi)

"A child should have other children whose manners are good and whose habits are acceptable because a child learns much faster and is more willing to take from another."
(Ibn Sina)

"Piety is from Allah. Good Manners are from parents."
(Omar bin Abdul Aziz)

"Endeavor to converse with your children, in case others who transgress and disobey get to them before you."
(Jafar al-Sadiq)

PREFACE

Our Story

Noha Alshugairi

When I was pregnant with my first born, Omar, may Allah Bless him, my husband was keen on me preparing for parenting. I, on the other hand, did not see the point. My parents did not study child psychology and I thought at the time they did a decent job. (Later on I discovered they actually did an amazing job!). However, just to please my husband, I did enroll in child psychology during my last semester at Rutgers University. Since I wanted to finish all my coursework before my due date, my last semester was a heavy load with 21 units. I assumed, since my biological science classes were easy for me, that a psychology class would be simple to master. I certainly overestimated my command of the English language at that time. While I was proficient in biological terms and concepts, psychology was a new field for me with many unfamiliar terms and ideas that I was supposed to know from a Psychology 101 class. The class revolved around concepts I had never heard of before. In summary, I was lost. Add to that the fact that I did not see the point of taking the class in the first place, and you can guess that I dropped the class with no regrets at all.

What follows is a period of time when I had my four kids and was consumed with mothering. I subscribed to *Parents* magazine and, throughout the years, I learned very valuable tips on how to handle difficult challenges such as tantrums and picky eaters.

However, it did not cross my mind during those wonderful 12 years that I needed to take a class or read a book about parenting. I reasoned that since my childhood was filled with love, joy, and security and I wanted the same for my kids, there was no need to pursue a different way than that of my parents. For the most part, I followed in their footsteps with some minor tweaks here and there.

As Omar was about to become a teenager, I started wondering if I knew how to raise a teen in the U.S. My children's era and culture were drastically different from the era and environment I grew up in, and I wanted reassurance that I could handle the supposedly rebellious teen years to come. It is a blessing from Allah that I lived in Huntington Beach, CA, where a wide variety of classes were available, including a class on how to parent teenagers. I enrolled, and that was the beginning of a journey into *conscious intentional parenting*.

The class was based on the Adlerian school of psychology and was monumental for my shift from a slightly authoritarian parent to a more authoritative parent. I am certain that taking the class eased the trials of the teen years because of some critical insights that I gained: the ability to see issues from my kids' point of view, having family meetings, listening more than talking, engaging the children in solutions, and giving them space to face the consequences of their actions. This shift in my style of parenting garnered the nickname amongst my friends of "extra-large" (a reflection of my above-average tolerance for teens' whims and moods) for what was perceived as a less controlling way of dealing with my teens.

Years passed and I encountered the question of parenting philosophies again following the completion of a Master's degree in Counseling. One of my goals as a therapist was to help parents better interact with their children. I believed that working on this primary relationship between parent and child would mitigate many of the problems I saw in my office. I knew how to parent my kids, but how could I teach that to other parents? I wanted a framework for teaching the concepts in a way that would not be inundated by theory rendering the information impractical. Again, Allah Granted me a wonderful learning opportunity: I came across a workshop for "Teaching Parenting the Positive Discipline Way." I had not heard of the concept, but I was willing to explore. That first class in how to teach Positive Discipline was facilitated by Jane Nelsen herself and it was the beginning of my Positive Discipline journey. I left the training that weekend determined to spread this message in our community because it aligned very well with Islam and because the concepts and tools were understandable and practical. Positive Discipline in a nutshell is a hands-on application of Islam with our children in our homes.

Munira Lekovic Ezzeldine

I realized that I viewed parenting very differently around the time my first son was 16 months old. One evening when I had friends over for a dinner party and I was in the kitchen preparing coffee, a friend happened to notice a poem I had posted on my refrigerator. It was a poem by Kahlil Gibran entitled "On Children":

> *"And a woman who held a babe against her bosom said,*
> *'Speak to us of Children.' And he said:*
>
> *Your children are not your children.*

They are the sons and daughters of Life's longing for itself.

They come through you but not from you, And though they are with you, yet they belong not to you.

You may give them your love but not your thoughts.

For they have their own thoughts.

You may house their bodies but not their souls.

For their souls dwell in the house of tomorrow, which you cannot visit, not even in your dreams.

You may strive to be like them, but seek not to make them like you.

For life goes not backward nor tarries with yesterday.

You are the bows from which your children as living arrows are sent forth.

The archer sees the mark upon the path of the infinite, and He bends you with His might that His arrows may go swift and far.

Let your bending in the archer's hand be for gladness;

For even as he loves the arrow that flies, so He loves also the bow that is stable."

As my friend read the poem she looked up at me and said blankly, "I really don't like that poem; how can you view children like that?" I was astonished by her reaction because the poem spoke so deeply to me and served as a personal reminder to me of my goals as a parent. I proceeded to explain to her my views and, needless to say, she couldn't understand. She ended the conversation by telling me my son was young and once he was older, like her own children, I would come to my senses. She went on to say I would realize that the world is a scary place and I just had to protect my child and keep him safe.

That conversation was a pivotal moment for me because, as a new parent, it was the first time I discussed my views about parenting and I was immediately criticized and dismissed. Yet, in that vulnerable moment, my heart was at peace because I truly believed being a parent was a spiritual journey, and I had no intention of parenting from a place of fear and control. I believed that my son did come through me but was not my possession; rather, he was a gift given to me by God to nurture into adulthood. Through raising my children, I continued to learn from them as well as teach them about the world and their purpose on this earth, reaffirming my own journey.

A couple of years after the birth of my second son, I pursued my Master's degree in Counseling. This was when I formally learned about child development and counseling practices. This is also where Noha and I met as students in the Master's program, and she introduced me to the principles of Positive Discipline. I remember my immediate reaction was: *It's just common sense.* The principles captured the long-term views I held when raising my children and the relationship I wished to have with them. I learned more, read more, and used more of the Positive Discipline tools as my sons progressed through the toddlerhood and early school years. Many tools came naturally to me, and many tools I implemented for the first time.

What I most appreciated about the Positive Discipline philosophy was that it was not about being the perfect parent or never making mistakes. Rather, it was an authentic way of interacting with my children and learning through the process. At a conference I attended once, Jane Nelsen said, "If you are able to implement at least half of the Positive Discipline tools, you are doing pretty well." This felt encouraging, and I invite you to remember this advice as you learn about the tools in this book.

Today I have three children. My two oldest are in secondary school and my youngest is in elementary. The parenting journey for me thus far has been one filled with stress and growth, success and failures, and every step of the way, an affirmation of the relationships I have built with each of my children. Parenting has been hard work and has required a lot of emotional investment and sacrifice of time, but it has also created a space for me to nurture and teach these three people—who continue to amaze me every day by their energy, wit, and compassion—that relationships are the most important elements of this life. Parenting has changed me for the better, and I continue to pray that God guides me. This book is the parenting book I wished I had when I became a new parent. May the words in this book inspire you to connect and build strong relationships with your children too.

Our Lens

To fully benefit from this book, dear reader, let us share with you the lens from which this work has sprung. We are both American Muslims. We were both raised in Muslim homes with values and cultural practices associated with our family heritage. I (Noha) am a first generation American who immigrated to the U.S. in my early twenties. My formative years were in Saudi Arabia where I made the conscious decision to be a practicing Muslim at the age of 14. I was raised with a Pan-Arab identity. My parents focused on instilling the values of integrity, responsibility, and respect to all. I (Munira) am a second generation American who was born in Europe and raised in Southern California from the age of two. I was raised in a Balkan Muslim home by immigrant parents navigating the American context. I struggled to reconcile my ethnic, religious, and cultural background as a child. My intentional commitment to Islam occurred during my college years.

Our varied life experiences infuse this book with richness and depth. Our community in Southern California - a microcosm of the global Muslim *umma* (community) with over 30 ethnic groups—has introduced us to diverse family practices and norms. We have come to appreciate the myriad ways Islam is practiced all over the world. Our context in the U.S. continually shapes how we navigate practicing Islam in a non-Muslim majority culture. Hence, we present a pluralistic worldview just as Islam is. Our view of the world is of coexistence, inclusiveness, and tolerance. Accordingly, we raise issues and challenges that Muslims who live in Muslim-majority countries may not struggle with. However, with a world that has become borderless via the Internet, we believe that our lens is a reflection of the emerging global culture.

The goal of this book is to empower you in your parenting journey. It is about you, not about creating the perfect or ideal Muslim child. There is no guarantee that your children will turn into your vision of who you would like them to become; Allah is the only One who knows their destiny. However, we believe that the insights and tools discussed in this book will build the foundation for a well-connected family using research-based parenting practices. We believe that a strong family connection is the most critical factor ensuring continued influence in the parent-child relationship. We pray that your family will be blessed with connection, love, and respect.

This book is our way of sharing this beautiful message with the global Muslim community beyond the boundaries of Southern California. We pray you will find the book beneficial and practical in your journey to become the best parent you can be. May Allah bring us benefit from that which we learn.

This Book

Our focus is to nurture a strong bond between parents and children, which we believe is the cornerstone to lifelong parental influence. Part I covers foundational concepts: parenting in the Islamic paradigm; the Positive Discipline philosophy; and a basic psychological understanding of parents and children. In Part II, Positive Discipline tools are explained in depth with real-life examples. Part III is separated into the four phases of development, from baby through early adulthood. Specific challenges for each age group as well as the Positive Discipline tools most effective for each challenge are described in this section. Lastly, in Part IV, we share a collection of essays addressing different aspects of Islamic parenting in the 21st Century.

PART I

FOUNDATION

INTRODUCTION

Steven Covey's second habit, in *The 7 Habits of Highly Effective Families,* states: "Begin with the end in mind" (1997, p. 70). Take a moment and reflect. What is your parenting goal? Are you cognizant of what you are working toward in your efforts to raise your children? In our years asking parents this question, we have discovered that many of them do not have an answer. For the few who have a clear answer, their response is: "Why of course I want my kids to be good Muslims!" or "I want my kid to be the best." What is missing is the connection between their long-term goals and current parenting strategies. Many times what is happening in the family is in fact working against the stated goals. Some parents have the goal of wanting their children to "be happy," but don't understand the skills and characteristics children need to be happy from the inside out. Thus, they "spoil" their children in order to make them "happy" and then wonder why they become selfish adults who think others should make them happy.

Thus, we ask the question to invite you to begin your own journey of conscious intentional parenting. Knowing your long-term parenting goals will inform the why, what and how of your parenting practices. Write your goal here and date it. It is always a good idea to date your self-reflections so you can gauge how far you have come when you read them later on.

My parenting goal is:

Date:

Many parents become overwhelmed by their children's behavior throughout each stage of development. Especially in moments of stress and frustration, they may focus on short-term results (How can I get this behavior to stop?) rather than on their long-term goals (How can I use this to teach responsibility?). Such parents are swept into a constant flurry of life problems because they react instead of problem-solve. They miss key opportunities to teach children how to become responsible and capable adults. When parents shift to a long-term parenting mindset, daily parental challenges become focused opportunities to teach valuable life skills that align with parenting goals. Always keep your parenting goal in mind.

Here is an example that articulates this point: A toddler spills a glass of milk on the counter, and the frustrated parent yells at the child while quickly cleaning up the mess. In this instance, the parent is focused on the short-term goal of quickly cleaning up the mess and expressing disappointment in the child. A parent with a long-term mindset realizes that the spilled milk can be an opportunity to teach about fixing mistakes and taking responsibility. This parent instead would explain to the child where the paper towels are so the child can clean up the mess and ask the child to think of a solution to help prevent the problem in the future (putting a lid on the cup). In this scenario, the parent didn't get caught up in the small problem of spilled milk, but instead focused on the bigger picture of learning from a mistake thereby helping the child feel capable by participating in problem solving.

Here is another example for older children: A teenager tells his mother he just got a parking ticket at school for parking in the wrong space. The frustrated mother yells at her son and scolds him for being irresponsible. She then takes the keys away for the weekend and pays for the ticket. What is the son learning? "Mom will take care of problems when they occur. She will yell and scream a bit but then she will fix it." On the other hand, a mother with a long-term mindset realizes that the parking ticket is an opportunity to teach. She invites the son to reflect on how he would take care of the current ticket and what solutions he has to avoid another ticket. She would not pay for the ticket herself. What is the son learning? "When problems arise, I need to find a solution. I am responsible for my actions." The mother in this scenario remained loving while allowing her son to face life, be responsible, and learn from his own mistake.

This is our invitation to you: parent your children today with an eye toward how you would like to see them as adults. Take a moment and write down what characteristics you would like your children to exhibit as adults. Keep these in mind as you interact with your children on a daily basis.

I would like to see the following characteristics in my adult children:

1.

2.

3.

4.

5.

6.

7.

8.

9.

10.

11.

12.

13.

14.

15.

Take a look at the parenting goal you wrote earlier. Does it fit with your long-term goals? If not, how would you change it?

CHAPTER 1

ISLAM AND PARENTING

Many readers of this book will identify their source of authority as Islam. The goals of raising children in Islam generally fall under the concept of *tarbiya*. *Tarbiya* is an Arabic word that comes from the root *r-b-b* (ربب) meaning to supervise and manage. From this root is the word *arrab* (الرب) which is a descriptor of Allah, the Supreme executive of the universe. Also, from the same root is the word *rabba* (ربى) in relation to children, which means to take care of and to maintain. *Tarbiya* of children, as explained by the famous 13th century lexicographer of the Arabic language Ibn Manzour, means "to oversee, support, and supervise children until they pass childhood" (as cited in Hijazi, 2008, p. 13). We are in our children's lives as Allah is for us in the universe: caretakers, supporters and certainly not coercers.

When you look at how different societies achieve the goal of *tarbiya*, it immediately becomes apparent that there are many methods for parenting, some of which seem completely at odds with each other. However, at the core of each method is a unique framework of values particular to that group. These values govern the group's worldview including the parent-child relationship. Simply put, what determines a *tarbiya* philosophy are the values of a specific family or community.

Accordingly, for Muslims, the goals of *tarbiya* are determined by Islam. Abdurrahman O. Hijazi, the contemporary Lebanese philosopher and educator, states that "*tarbiya* is a collection of behaviors and verbal exchanges that are either directly taken or extrapolated from the Quran and Sunnah and whose aim is to achieve goals defined by Islam for the growth and happiness of Muslims in this *dunya* (worldly) and *akherah* (afterlife)" (2008, p. 24). This posits the question: What are those goals that Islam defines for a satisfactory life? They are the core of the faith; the purpose of creation.

Allah the Almighty created mankind for the purpose of worshiping Him The Lord of the Universe. "And I (Allah) created not the *jinn* (unseen beings) and mankind except that they should worship Me" (Quran, 51:56). He also ordained that humans' worship, distinct from the ritualistic worship of Angels, is performed through their daily actions. It is done through building, cultivating, and establishing civilizations on Earth. "Worship Allah; you have no other *ilah* (deity) but Him. He brought you forth from the earth and settled you therein" (Quran, 11:61).

As such, a Muslim's earthly endeavors are transformed into acts of worship as long as the intention is to seek Allah. Habits become acts of worship through intentions. Hence, parenting becomes a critical piece of life, because the family home is where values and worldviews are transmitted. Muslim parents view *tarbiya* as a vehicle for teaching their children Allah's purpose of creation. *Tarbiya* becomes the cradle from which their children know, love, and connect with Allah.

For parents seeking to raise children who are conscious of

Allah, Abdullah Alwan (1981) a 20th century Syrian scholar known for his seminal book, *Raising Children in Islam*, proposed that *tarbiya* includes the following domains of life:

- Religious: teaching the tenets of Islam.
- Moral: inoculating with Islamic character.
- Healthy body: fostering a healthy lifestyle.
- Intellectual: encouraging critical thinking skills.
- Psychological: nurturing a healthy sense of self, others, and the world.
- Social: engendering a sense of community.
- Sexual: understanding and managing natural desires and urges.

We believe *tarbiya* is relationship-based. Hence, in this book we focus on developing a parent-child bond as the strongest foundation to transmit values. Since we respect that Muslim families will differ in the knowledge and practices they follow in their own homes (in all the domains stated above), we focus on the family connection rather than a specific way of being. We offer a framework for nurturing a strong Islamic identity, while recognizing that the application of this structure will vary from one family to another. This is our invitation to you: focus on your connection with your children. It is in your mundane daily interactions that your values will be imprinted in their hearts.

Positive Discipline Philosophy

Positive Discipline is a parenting philosophy established by Jane Nelsen (www.positivediscipline.com) and added to by Lynn Lott (www.lynnlott.com) and other Positive Discipline associates over the years. Jane Nelsen self-published her seminal book, *Positive Discipline*, in 1981 (and published in 1987 by Ballantine of Random House) from which she started a movement toward cooperative, respectful parenting. What first began as Jane Nelsen single-handedly teaching the philosophy to parents and teachers has since blossomed into an organization (www.positivediscipline.org) focused on training parents and teachers to utilize its principles at home and school.

Positive Discipline is based on the general principles of the Adlerian school of psychology. The latter is a school of thought formulated by Alfred Adler (1870-1937) and continued after his death by his colleague Rudolf Dreikurs (1897-1972). Alfred Adler was a contemporary of Sigmund Freud with whom he worked for 8-10 years. However, Adler disagreed with Freud's deterministic (sexual) view of human nature and began espousing a resilient view of human nature based on the need to belong and to contribute in a social context. Corey (2005) defined the following as key principles of Adlerian psychology:

1. Individuals are Holistic and are Part of Systems

While Freud focused on biological drives and childhood experiences, Adler believed in the critical importance of an individual's social and moral contexts while highlighting the present and the future instead of the past. In doing so, Adler saw humans as free to choose how they want to live their lives rather than being lifelong prisoners of the conclusions they formed from their childhood experiences. Adler created the process of using Early Recollections to help his patients see how some of their conclusions were no longer useful to their successful living today.

2. Behavior is Goal-Directed

Despite the fact that behavioral goals may be unconscious, Adler believed that humans seek to satisfy the basic need to belong in a social context, and that "misbehavior" occurs when children (and adults) find "mistaken" ways to belong. He advocated understanding a child's "mistaken" goal in order to use "encouragement" to help the child find "useful" ways to belong.

3. Striving for Significance

Adler believed that all human beings experience a sense of inferiority in their lives that invites them to compensate in different ways. He believed that the need to gain mastery over an aspect of one's life is innate and is necessary for people to overcome obstacles. Adler emphasized the need to move "from a felt minus to a felt plus" (Corey, 2005, p. 97). Simply stated, individuals often need help (encouragement) to move in life from a discouraging perception of themselves to one that is positive. Adler also posited that during this striving toward mastery, people choose either socially productive or useless, destructive behaviors depending on the individual's perceived goal and path to mastery.

4. Need to Belong

Adler believed that an integral piece of the human experience is that individuals are embedded in communities. Belonging is feeling connected to one's family, society, and humanity which is necessary for a grounded sense of self. Adler believed that those who are connected to others tend to direct their behaviors toward the more useful spectrum of activities and are less likely to feel inferior and worthless.

5. Universal Life Tasks

Adler believed that individuals strive to master critical life tasks: "building friendships (social task), establishing intimacy (love-marriage task), contributing to society (occupational task)" (Corey, 2005, p. 99).

From these general Adlerian principles and others, Jane Nelsen established the Positive Discipline framework for parenting. In the following section we will explore how Positive Discipline principles align with Islam.

Congruence Of Positive Discipline And Islam

Why did we choose Positive Discipline as our guiding parenting philosophy? We have been blessed with adopting Islam as our way of life. For us to adopt a new idea, we have to believe it aligns well with Islam. We discovered in Positive Discipline a parenting philosophy that strove toward goals inherently Islamic. Here are eight areas of alignment between the Positive Discipline philosophy and Islam.

1. Building Social Interest

As stated earlier, Adlerian psychology believes that social consciousness is a measure of mental health. The more an individual is engaged in activities focused on the betterment of society, the better that individual is able to deal with the ebb and flow of life. Recent research on happiness validates this earlier view. In her groundbreaking book, *The How of Happiness*, Sonja Lyubomirsky (2008), presents research correlating a higher level of happiness with social connections, whether with family, friends, or strangers. In addition, her research highlighted that random acts of kindness boost an individual's level of contentment and satisfaction.

This growing body of research has highlighted the significance of Islamic teachings that encourage social responsibility and community development. Among those are teachings targeting a higher sense of responsibility toward family, neighbors, friends, and strangers. The examples are numerous and beyond the scope of this book. However, consider the following hadith traditions as a sample of how fostering social connection is a foundational piece in Islam:

> "Whoever eases the tribulation of someone, Allah will Ease his tribulations on the day of Judgment." (Hadith, Muslim)

> "The relation of the believer with another is like the bricks of a building, each strengthens the other." (Hadith, Bukhari, Muslim)

> "…reconciling a conflict between two people is a charity, helping another with a burden is a charity, a good word is a charity, with every step you take toward the mosque is a charity, and removing harm from the road is a charity." (Hadith, Bukhari, Muslim)

2. Fostering Belonging and Contribution

In Positive Discipline, families and schools work toward ensuring that members gain a sense of belonging while contributing in useful ways. Positive Discipline perceives interdependence as essential to the human experience and hence, children are encouraged to be empathic and of service to others. The Islamic view is no different. Rituals and activities involve the community. The concept of the *umma* or global Muslim community empowers Muslims with an instant sense of belonging that permeates borders, cultures, and ethnicities. It is enough for someone to say the Islamic greeting, "*Assalamu Alaikum*" (peace be upon you), for a person to feel connected without the need for an introduction. "We have created you in tribes and nations so you may know one another, the noblest amongst you in the sight of Allah is the most pious," (Quran, 49:13).

3. Understanding the Belief Behind the Behavior

Adlerian psychology views behavior as a result of seeking connections with others and not as a passive response to biological drives. While sometimes the way a person connects is destructive and unhealthy, it still reflects a response to either a conscious or unconscious desire to connect. Accordingly, Positive Discipline views a child's misbehavior as an unproductive way to connect with the parent. By utilizing Positive Discipline tools, the misbehavior can then be transformed through a teaching moment, to encourage a strength, a new understanding, or a new life skill that creates a sense of capability, etc.

This idea of beliefs behind behavior and the ability to refine both is an integral part of Islam. One of the early lessons a Muslim learns is the concept of motives and intentions. Muslims are taught to bring intentions into awareness, assess them, and then either go forth or adjust them. In Islam the ultimate goal is the connection with Allah, Lord and Sustainer. Life is transformed into a primary journey of connecting with the Only One, Allah. As Muslims travel this life seeking Him, they redirect both acts of worship and the mundane acts of life solely toward Allah. "Deeds are considered by the intentions behind them, and a person will earn based on what was intended," (Hadith, Bukhari, Muslim).

4. *Encouragement*

In Adlerian psychology, encouragement is the primary motivator for change. It is a powerful concept. Yet its potency can be easily dismissed because encouragement is a gentle and subtle force. The example of the life of our beloved Prophet Muhammad, peace be upon him (pbuh), illustrated that he was as an encourager rather than an enforcer of law and rules. "And by the Mercy of Allah, you dealt with them gently. And had you been severe and harsh¬hearted, they would have dispersed from around you" (Quran, 3:159).

5. *Mutual Respect*

Positive Discipline operates on the basis of respect for oneself and others. Respect means the ability to see oneself and others as separate entities deserving of their own opinions, feelings, and decisions. This requires healthy boundaries. It is this ability to see others as they are, rather than as one wants them to be, that is critical in fostering positive healthy relationships in all areas of life. Parents who are able to see their children as separate entities empower them to become responsible, capable, and proactive individuals.

The story of Prophet Muhammad (pbuh) with Ibn Abbas is a beautiful example of mutual respect. Narrated in the Hadith books of Muslim and Bukhari, Ibn Abbas (who was a young boy at the time) was in a gathering that included the Prophet (pbuh) and the elders of the Companions. Ibn Abbas was seated to the right of the Prophet (pbuh) and, according to the prophetic tradition, he would be the first to drink from a cup that the Prophet (pbuh) had drunk from. But the prophetic tradition also states respecting the elders in the gathering by allowing them to go first. The Prophet (pbuh) turned to Ibn Abbas and asked his permission to hand the cup to the elders first. In response, Ibn Abbas refused, stating that he would not miss the opportunity to drink immediately after the Prophet (pbuh). What followed was a beautiful example in granting children choices and then respecting these choices. The Prophet (pbuh) respected Ibn Abbas's choice and the cup was handed to Ibn Abbas. In this illuminating story, the Prophet (pbuh) recognized the conflict in priorities in this incident (beginning with the one seated to his right vs. the respect owed to elders present), verbalized them, acknowledged Ibn Abbas's right to the cup after him, and then respected the latter's decision even when it superseded the rights of the elders present. This is a prophetic example highlighting respect for the rights of individuals no matter who holds the right.

If this story similarly were to occur today, a father might not even consider asking permission from his son. If the father did ask and the son demanded his right, the father would likely cajole him into changing his mind. The father might even scold the son for being disrespectful. However, through this poignant story, the Prophet (pbuh) exemplified mutual respect at the same time by understanding the needs of the child, the people involved, and the situation.

6. Kindness and Firmness at the Same Time

At first, the idea that one can be kind and firm at the same time may seem paradoxical. Many people believe that a parent can either be firm (have rules, be strong and powerful, control what the child does, etc.) or kind (loving, caring, warm, nurturing, attentive to child, etc.). There are some who oscillate between these two states depending on the situation. So, if the child is being nice, the parent is kind; and when the child goes out of line, the parent moves into firmness. Positive Discipline challenges this notion by inviting parents to be kind and firm at the same time. This is made possible by the parent addressing the needs of the child (kindness) while also addressing the needs of the situation (firmness).

The Prophet (pbuh) was a great model of kindness and firmness at the same time. Our tradition is filled with examples of the Prophet (pbuh) maintaining boundaries while at the same time being gentle and kind. For example, appreciate the Prophet's (pbuh) response when he commanded the companions to break their *ihram* (the sacred state of being ready for pilgrimage) during the Treaty of Hudaybiyah. The companions, in anger and sadness over the perceived unjust terms of the treaty, did not immediately heed the Prophet's (pbuh) command. Following the advice of his wife, Umm Salamah, the Prophet (pbuh) silently (without repeating his command) proceeded to break his *ihram*. His actions were louder than his words. The companions immediately followed suit. His firmness was evident in acting without talking, while his kindness was in avoiding the denigration of the companions for their lapse in response.

7. Short-term versus Long-term

In Positive Discipline, parents work toward building the character of their soon-to-be adult children. This Positive Discipline concept means that what parents do with their children in the moment is focused on what kind of adults they envision their children becoming. Interactions are not centered on changing the behavior of the moment but rather utilizing teachable moments to empower and nurture children to become the best adults they can be. This is one of our most important Islamic concepts. Muslims know that their actions in this life determine their afterlife; "He who does an atom's worth of good will reap it, and he who does an atom's worth of evil will face it" (Quran, 99:7-8). Muslims "begin with the end in mind" (Covey, 1997) and so does Positive Discipline. "Indeed you exhibit preference for this life, when the hereafter is better and everlasting" (Quran, 87:16-17).

8. Focus on Solutions

One of the major contributions of Jane Nelsen to parenting practices is the shift toward focusing on solutions rather than consequences. Before Positive Discipline, parents were instructed to punish and/or use logical consequences as a means of teaching children lessons from their misbehaviors. Such interventions led to parent-child disconnection and alienation, as we will discuss later in the book. Jane Nelsen invited parents to see mistakes and challenges as opportunities to teach life lessons and proposed that children learn better if they are engaged in the process of finding solutions.

The story of the Bedouin who urinated in the mosque is a beautiful example of how the Prophet (pbuh) sought solutions. It is narrated that a Bedouin entered the holy mosque of Madina and urinated while the Prophet (pbuh) and his companions were in the mosque. In shocked reaction, the companions started scolding the Bedouin. The Prophet (pbuh) in his wisdom, directed them to calm down, allow him to finish, pour water over the area to purify it, and then teach the Bedouin the etiquette of the mosque. The Bedouin was not punished nor scolded. He was taught what to do to fix the problem and how to behave in the future.

Parenting is an interaction between parent and child. Both influence the process. In the next chapter, we begin exploring aspects of the parent that impact the parent-child relationship.

CHAPTER 2

Understanding Ourselves

The way parents discipline is influenced by their personalities, levels of education, cultural values, lived experiences, and emotional responsiveness. Before we can implement Positive Discipline, we must have a deeper understanding of ourselves as parents. Are there different ways of parenting? How do people decide how to parent? What is a parenting style? In this chapter, we highlight observations by social scientists explaining some of the current parenting trends. We also share our own observations of parenting practices found in Muslim homes.

Trends in Parenting

The past century has seen various historical trends in parenting practices and philosophies in the U.S. Hulbert (2004) explains that from the 1920s to the 1940s, psychologists like John Watson encouraged a hands-off approach to raising children with little nurturing or physical contact. Mothers were discouraged from cuddling their children for fear of spoiling and creating "weak" American children. After World War II, mothers were encouraged to trust their instincts by pediatricians like Benjamin Spock who suggested parents be more flexible and affectionate with their children. He encouraged parents to treat children as individuals, which was in direct conflict with what the previous generation had been advised about parenting.

By the 1970s, families had various choices and were making their own parenting decisions depending on what best suited their families. Some families choose for both parents to work outside the home and some children were sent to daycare or had caregivers other than their own parents. In the 1990s, pediatrician William Sears became a proponent of attachment parenting, which encouraged parents to be their child's primary caregiver in order to strengthen the emotional bond between parents and children. The 2000s was a do-it-yourself era where parents sought to do the best for their children by doing it on their own. Parents did not trust institutions and experts and relied on their own instincts. Families increasingly chose home births, homemade pesticide-free baby food, homeschooling, and ensuring their child's success by enrolling in activities like music lessons, sports, or academic tutoring. The current phenomenon in parenting includes buzzwords like helicopter parenting, tiger-mom parenting and most recently, growth-mindset and mindful parenting. Today, many parents are left feeling confused and filled with anxiety as the pendulum of parenting trends swings in reaction to the previous generation's parenting style.

In the American Muslim community, we found that parenting practices are not only impacted by parenting trends, but also differ by changing personal, social and cultural norms. Some American Muslims parent in alignment with or contrary to how their own parents raised them, while still others parent based on expectations of their culture, community, and relatives. Some immigrant parents find parenting practices in their home country do not translate well in the U.S., and so create a hybrid style. Some homes consist of multi-generational families living together where elders act as co-parents with their own styles. Ahmed (2011) found that some American Muslim converts change their parenting practices all together steering away from how they were raised and altering their family traditions and rituals. These various approaches all highlight that parenting practices are diverse within each Muslim community both geographically and ethnically. The family, however, is central regardless of style in Muslim homes.

Parenting Styles

Renowned developmental psychologist and researcher Diana Baumrind (1967) posited that all parenting practices fall into three main parenting styles: Authoritarian, Permissive, and Authoritative. These three approaches are philosophically very different and elicit drastically different reactions from children. As you read through the following styles, remember that the parent-child dynamic is nuanced. It is rarely as extreme as presented. Some parents may identify with a few negative parenting practices. These are opportunities for growth and change.

1. Authoritarian Style

This style of parenting is one in which the parent makes all the decisions that direct the family. Authoritarian parents view children as inherently ignorant and incapable of thinking rationally. They expect children to follow without asking any questions. Authoritarian parents feel a great responsibility to manage all aspects of their children's lives. They have specific ideas and high expectations of who they want their children to become and they are on a path to create those children. Compliance and control of children is sought with the threat of punishment for misbehavior and praise or rewards for doing what the parent wants. When children question parental ideas, parents feel indignant and may say, "How dare you disobey me? I have done so much for you!" They do not feel they have any responsibility to nurture a child's emotional well-being, but, rather, the child owes them blind respect and obedience. Some Muslim families adopt this style because they feel this is the only way to raise obedient children who would ultimately be "good Muslims." This style is strengthened with the erroneous belief that, since Allah rewards and punishes believers, parents must adopt the same attitude with their children.

Example: An 8-year-old child is watching TV and has chosen not to wash the dishes in the sink. The authoritarian parent walks into the room and yells, "How dare you watch TV right now? You should be washing the dishes!" The child responds, "I just started watching this show." The parent responds, "I don't care what you are doing, turn off the TV right now and go to the kitchen. If you don't get up right now, you will be grounded from TV for a week!"

Children of these parents feel oppressed and lack any influence and control in their lives. The constant threat of punishment from the parent breeds resentment, rebellion, revenge and/or retreat within the child. It does not lead to a healthy, functioning adult who feels responsible and accountable for their life. The message a child receives from the authoritarian parent is,

"I am loved if I do it your way and that is the only way I am loved."

2. Permissive Style

Permissive parents follow a non-traditional style of parenting in which they are lenient and free spirited. Permissive parents do not wish to impose rules on their children and they go to great lengths to avoid confrontations with their children. These parents find it difficult to establish any boundaries with children. The child's happiness is central to all decisions in the parenting process as they seek to satisfy their child's demands. Permissive parents do not want to be the "bad guy" or feel like their children hate them, so these parents prefer that the children make all the decisions and establish their own rules. Permissive parents love their children and expect to be loved by their children because they are nice to them.

Example: An 8-year-old child is watching TV and has chosen not to wash the dishes in the sink. The permissive parent walks into the room and says, "Honey, you were supposed to wash the dishes. What happened?" The child whines, "But, I am going to miss this show. I can't." The parent responds, "Ok, I guess it is fine today. But promise me that tomorrow you will do the dishes. I will do them today."

The reaction permissive parents receive from their children may be misbehavior. Since parents have no rules, children feel lost and unsure of how to behave. They usually adopt the belief that love means "treat me like I am the center of the universe." Typically misbehavior occurs because these children have not learned how to work within the limits at home and school. They may push any boundaries that are set since they have learned early on that adults will give in. Some of these children flourish when routines and structures are established in the classroom or with other caregivers. The message a child receives from a permissive parent is, "I am loved if I get my way. As long as I am the boss, the people around me love me."

3. Authoritative Style

This is the Positive Discipline style. This style of parenting is democratic where both parent and child have a voice. Authoritative parents seek to hear the views and opinions of their children when problem-solving and making big decisions while at the same time maintaining their parental authority. When a child fails to meet the parents' expectations, parents react in a nurturing way and seek to jointly solve the problem with the child. Authoritative parents believe that mistakes are wonderful opportunities to learn. They empower their children to develop self-discipline and personal responsibility for their actions. They believe that respect is mutual between the parent and the child, and parents become positive role models for children. Parents are consistent in their rules, and children know what is expected of them. Children feel they belong to a "team" and seek to cooperate and contribute. The authoritative parenting style requires much more work from parents than any of the other styles. It is an intentional approach to parenting with long-term goals in mind.

Example: An 8-year-old child is watching TV and has chosen not to wash the dishes in the sink. The authoritative parent walks into the room and sits down next to the child, looks the child in the eye, and asks, "What was the agreement we made about the dishes?" The child responds, "Wash them before I sit down to watch TV." The parent responds, "What do I expect you to do right now?"

The children of these parents feel they can make decisions and that their actions have an impact on themselves and others. They feel responsible and accountable to others, and they know they are safe and loved by their parents. The family atmosphere invites mutual respect and dignity, which allows children to learn from mistakes. The message a child receives from the authoritative parent is, "I am loved even when I make mistakes, and I am responsible for my actions. I have a voice and we work together as a family to solve problems in ways that are respectful to everyone."

In addition to parenting styles, children's inborn temperaments (p. 39) impact the family dynamics. Children with different temperaments react differently which, in turn, accentuates or curbs the impact of parenting styles. While we strongly believe that authoritative parenting is the best style for a well-connected parent-child relationship, we have seen examples of children who were able to weather the negative ramifications of permissive and authoritarian styles. In these situations, the temperaments of these children align with their parents' styles. For example, a structured child may thrive with an authoritarian parent but struggle to find balance with a permissive parent. Conversely, a free-spirited child would suffer greatly with an authoritarian parent because they would feel misunderstood and dismissed in the family. The same child may find nurture with a permissive parent. Family dynamics are rarely simple and straightforward. There are many factors that influence the family.

However, with Positive Discipline, families are better equipped to deal with these varied factors providing the best environment for nurturing and empowering their children.

The Dance

Parenting styles are not as simple or linear as we have presented them above. It's true that there are households where one style of parenting is prevalent, but there are many households where a hodgepodge of styles exist.

Some parents "dance" between the authoritarian and permissive style depending on their tolerance and energy levels. In such households, parents are permissive, giving their children everything they ask for until they become exhausted and drained. When they reach the high point of disgust with how their children are behaving they switch to an authoritarian mode. They become demanding, commanding, saying no, punishing, lecturing, etc. Then they reach the high point of fear of losing the love of their children and go back to being permissive. In these households, parents are unpredictable. Life swings between the two extremes randomly. Children learn behaviors and reactions that work to pull their parents back into the permissive zone. In the process they lose trust in the parents' abilities to maintain structure and order. Needless to say, such households are characterized by strife and chaos.

Another "dance" that I (Noha) have observed amongst American Muslim parents is a paradoxical pairing of both permissiveness and authoritarianism. On the one hand, these parents are very exacting and demanding when it comes to religious practices and/or school expectations while very lenient when it comes to material things, routines, and responsibilities. Their rationale for such a dichotomy is that they live in a society where children are permitted to do or behave in ways that do not fit the Islamic paradigm. Accordingly, these parents feel the need to compensate for that deprivation. However, their choice of compensation (buying the latest gadgets, video games, and brands; not expecting them to help around the house; letting go of routines and rules) robs children of essential opportunities to develop life skills. When children come to expect instant gratification, they miss the opportunity to learn patience, perseverance, and delay gratification. Unfortunately, these children grow into adults who struggle greatly as they navigate both work and family life. Sadly, these parents miss the fact that training for life occurs during childhood, utilizing the daily acts of living.

When Parents Disagree Over Parenting Styles

Positive Discipline would be most effective if both parents were on the same page. However, it is common to hear a couple lament the fact that they don't see eye-to-eye on parenting. The issue becomes further complicated when arguments over how to parent occur in front of the children. Each parent usually expresses frustration that the other is not willing to "get on board." It is also equally common to find each parent leaning toward a different parenting style. Usually one is permissive while the other is authoritarian. The tendency toward different polarities by both parents is typically a compensatory mechanism to counteract the parenting style shortcomings of the other parent.

The first step in such a situation is for parents to learn about authoritative parenting. Reading this book is a step in that direction. Certainly if both were to learn and implement it together, that would be ideal. However, just because a co-parent is not willing to get on board does not negate one's ability to effect change. The second step is the process of inviting the other parent to shift, keeping in mind that change is a slow process. Change occurs only when it comes from within: coercing, forcing, imposing, or nagging a co-parent to change and do things one way will not yield good results. Alternately, sharing books and articles is a gentle invitation to change. However, the most effective action a parent can take is simply modeling Positive Discipline at home. Commonly, when a parent focuses on doing the best parenting (instead of getting caught up in the partner's "wrong" parenting), the co-parent will inevitably be influenced.

Children are also very adept at adjusting to each parent's style. They will learn early on that Mom's approach is different than Dad's and they will adjust accordingly. This also extends to other people in their lives, such as grandparents, relatives, and teachers. Rather than attempting to control how others deal with your children, focus on utilizing the mismatch as another opportunity to teach life lessons.

Parenting is a bidirectional process. In the next chapter, we discuss how children impact the parent-child relationship through the biologically and socially driven process of child development. While children are influenced by their environment, they imprint the family dynamic through their inborn temperaments and innate strengths.

CHAPTER 3

Understanding Our Children

After shedding some light on the significance of parenting styles, in this chapter we will explore how children wield personal power from the moment they are born. Parents will recognize that parenting involves their efforts as well as those of their children. Effective parenting requires an understanding and acceptance of the influence children exert. Positive Discipline provides a road map for transforming what potentially could be an adversarial relationship into a beautiful synergy empowering both the parent and the child.

Temperament

All children are born with distinct traits that define their personalities. For example, some children are slow to warm up to new people while others may be loud and boisterous. Every child is different. There isn't one "good" or "bad" way of being. These inborn qualities are what make each person unique. Psychologists call these inborn traits of being temperaments. It is important for parents to discover, understand and accept their children's temperaments. By doing so, parents will have fewer struggles because they will be able to anticipate how their children react to the environment and, in turn, will know how they can best guide them.

Temperament styles fall on a spectrum. This means that people vary in the degree to which they exhibit each style. That degree is usually inborn with the potential for modifications as the child matures and gains self-awareness. The discovery of temperament characteristics is attributed to Drs. Stella Chess and Alexander Thomas (as cited in Nelsen, Erwin, Duffy, 2007, p. 99) who, in the 1960s and 1970s, conducted longitudinal studies assessing how infants' characteristics change with time. They found that certain characteristics were inborn and, despite environmental adaptability, remained constant throughout the lifespan. Some commonly observed temperament styles include the following ten traits:

1. Activity Level

This temperament describes how prone the child is for physical activities. Some children are happiest when they are active and moving about, while others are happiest when they are engaged in quiet activities or are simply observing what is going on around them.

2. Rhythmicity

This describes how routine-oriented a child is in life. Children who are prone to rhythmicity are comfortable with routines and knowing what to expect. These children tend to become upset if their routines are disrupted. They also tend to react intensely when things they are expecting do not take place as planned. So a planned outing to the playground that was cancelled last minute becomes a trigger for a tantrum. On the other hand, children low on this spectrum tend to be more spontaneous. Lack of routine and structure does not faze them, and their reactions to surprises are low-key. They may also struggle with an environment that is highly structured and does not allow for spontaneity.

3. Approach or Withdraw

This temperament spectrum describes the initial reaction to new situations, people, and events. Someone who responds to newness with smiles and energy is someone who is high on the spectrum of this temperament. Someone who has a negative reaction to newness and withdraws on initial contact with an unexpected change is low on this spectrum.

4. Adaptability

This style describes a child's long-term reaction to change. So, after the initial response to a change (#3 above), how does the child adapt to the new circumstance? Some adapt rather quickly even if they initially had a negative reaction. Others take a long time to adapt. Exhibiting low adaptability indicates resistance to the new change given time, which could be seen as rigidity. Someone who is high on this spectrum is able to adapt to change with less reluctance.

5. Sensory Threshold

This refers to the intensity of the stimulus needed to provoke a response. Children with a high sensory threshold are those who are capable of taking in a lot of stimuli before they need to react. Children with a low sensory threshold are those who are highly sensitive to the internal and external environment and will react to the slightest change. External stimuli include everything taken in through the five senses: sight, hearing, taste, touch, and smell.

Internal stimuli are the emotional and psychological reactions to external life events.

6. Quality of Mood

This spectrum describes the differences between children who are sunny in nature (high on the spectrum) compared to those who tend to be gloomy and sad (low).

7. Intensity of Reactions

This describes the energy put forth in reacting to a situation whether positively or negatively. Some children respond with a high level of intensity, while others are more subdued in how they respond.

8. Distractibility

This refers to how easily children can be distracted from what they are engaged in. Someone who remains focused despite distractions is someone who is low on this spectrum, while someone who gets easily distracted by their environment is high on this spectrum.

9. Persistence

High persistence indicates a tenacity to stick with a project or idea despite challenges and obstacles. Low persistence indicates lack of patience to see a project or idea through when challenges arise.

10. Attention Span

This refers to the amount of time dedicated to an activity without interruptions. Someone with a high attention span is capable of devoting long periods of time to a project or idea without the need to take a break or do something else. A child with a low attention span needs to take breaks often and devotes short periods of time on an activity.

Parents who share similar temperaments with their children may have positive interactions and peaceful relationships. On the other hand, parents and children who exhibit temperaments on the opposing ends of the spectrum may face conflicts and disappointments. For example, an extroverted parent who is outgoing and talkative may feel there is something "wrong" with an introverted child because the child does not engage with others. Conversely, an introverted parent may be annoyed and baffled by an extroverted child's behavior. When there is a mismatch in temperaments, parents may erroneously believe they have to change their children. However, parents that accept their children's inborn traits will focus on how best to interact with the children, leading to a more positive relationship.

It is critical to emphasize here that even though temperament styles are inborn, parents are able to help their children learn skills to complement their temperaments for a better life through awareness and practice. For example, a child who has a short attention span and has difficulty with homework can be told that this is an area of challenge and is encouraged to practice focusing on homework for short periods of time using a timer. A child who has a low threshold for stimulation is made aware of that dynamic and is taught how to establish boundaries to minimize undue exposure to stimuli. Through awareness and practice, children can utilize their inborn temperament styles as areas of strengths. Parents play a critical role in this process. Take a moment to reflect on where your child falls along the temperament spectra. Compare and contrast your child's ratings with yours. Following these reflections, what decisions would you make to help your child identify and manage temperaments? What decisions would you make to minimize the mismatch between both of your temperaments?

Innate Strengths

While the field of psychology may have begun with a focus on deficiencies and disorders, it is currently shifting toward a positive spin on human nature. Two ideas that have emerged in the late 20th Century and early 21st Century and are dramatically changing the understanding of psychology are: (a) the brain's plasticity in response to positive environmental changes (e.g. therapy, positive social interactions, physical activity, medications, etc.) and (b) everybody is born with innate strengths that, if nurtured well, can lead to productivity and life satisfaction. These ideas are reviving a dormant belief in the power of human resiliency to overcome life's challenges. They are also moving the field of psychology from a focus on pathology toward an appreciation of the multitude of ways we can impact our life course.

Observant parents have always noted the innate strengths of their children. It comes up when parents describe children as, "He can sit and read for hours!" "She started memorizing Quran at the age of 3 just by listening to the CD in the car," "He is the peace-maker in the family. He finds ways to get his siblings to quiet down and see eye-to-eye," "She is our computer expert at home." However, only in the late 20th Century did we begin to explore and categorize people's innate abilities and use what Adler called "encouragement" to nurture them.

One of the early researchers to explore the question of innate strengths was the developmental psychologist Howard Gardner. In 1983, he revolutionized the understanding of intelligence by extending the continuum of intelligence to areas of human abilities beyond those associated with math and science. For a long time, math-science aptitude was seen as the only measurement of "smarts." Innate abilities related to physical dexterity, artistic expressions, and social interactions were less valued than academic abilities. This narrow perception of brainpower was pervasive, especially in the West, until the advent of Gardner's theory of *Multiple Intelligence.*

Gardner posited that, "People have a wide range of capacities. A person's strength in one area of performance simply does not predict any comparable strengths in other areas...some children seem to be good at many things; others, very few" (1999, p. 31). These different areas of strengths are what make each child unique. Gardner postulated that these areas of strengths "arise from the combination of a person's genetic heritage and life conditions in a given culture and era" (1999, p. 45).

While psychologists currently do not use the term *intelligence* to describe an area of strength and, hence, reject the term multiple intelligences, Gardner's work focused attention on the various domains where human abilities and endeavors flourish. Accordingly, we will look at his work as a framework for categorizing innate strengths and abilities rather than intelligences. As with temperaments, these areas of strengths fall on a spectrum. Different individuals fall at different points on the spectrum of each strength, and each individual has a unique combination of strength points from all the domains.

Gardner stipulated seven main domains of innate strengths: linguistic, logical-mathematical, musical, bodily-kinesthetic, spatial, interpersonal, and intrapersonal. It is clear that his domains contain the diversity of excellence in human endeavors. Below we briefly describe each domain and highlight some prominent Muslims who excel in each area.

1. Linguistic

The ability to use language, either written or oral, for expression. This strength is seen in orators and teachers who easily explain ideas and information. This type of individual has well-developed auditory skills and can think in words. The collection of Hadith of Prophet Muhammad (pbuh) is an example of this domain. Not everyone had the Prophet's (pbuh) ability to use words succinctly and artistically to convey a message. Many Muslim scholars and religious leaders exhibit this ability such as Sheikh Hamza Yusuf, Professor Sherman Jackson, and Malcolm X.

2. Logical-mathematical

The ability to use logic to solve problems and the ability to comprehend and use mathematical operations to come up with solutions. This strength is highly cherished and valued in the Muslim community. Islamic tradition holds it in high regard, showcased by al-Khawarizmi who was the father of Algebra. In the last half century, Nobel Prize recipients Ahmed Zewail and Mohammad Abdus Salam demonstrated this domain through their contributions in science.

3. Musical

The ability to appreciate and create musical patterns. Gardner emphasized the critical role culture plays in the development of a particular strength. Due to the differing opinions about music in the Islamic tradition, Islamic history does not boast of musical legends. However, musical giftedness is apparent in the Islamic tradition as the science of recitation (*tajweed*) of the Quran. The ability to recite in a pattern that is melodic with the use of only a voice to create a pleasing and soothing sound is a unique ability. In early Islamic tradition, the Prophet Muhammad (pbuh) distinguished Bilal bin Rabah for his beautiful voice by assigning him the task of making the *athan* (call to prayer). In modern times there are many well-known American Muslim artists and musicians like Lupe Fiasco, Omar Offendum, Yasiin Bey, and Yassin Alsalman.

4. Bodily-kinesthetic

The ability to use the body to create or do something. Physical dexterity can be fine motor skills, such as the ability to cook or perform surgery, or it can be gross motor skills, such as the ability of an athlete or a horse trainer. There are numerous examples of prominent American Muslims who exhibit this strength, such as basketball player Kareem Abdul-Jabbar, boxer Muhammad Ali, Olympic fencer Ibtihaj Muhammad, and surgeon Mehmet Oz.

5. Visual-Spatial

The ability to appreciate and manipulate space. This involves the ability to visualize how a space would become or how an existing space can be manipulated. Artists, photographers, and engineers all exhibit this domain through their work, as do pilots and dancers. The Umayyad Mosque in Damascus and the Taj Mahal in India are beautiful examples of the work of Muslim architects. Famous Muslim architect Mimar Sinan is best known for designing the Blue Mosque in Turkey. The ancient heritage of Islamic Art includes: calligraphy, painting, glass, ceramics, tiles, and carpets. Contemporary examples include the calligrapher Haji Noor Deen and the architect Khaled Omar Azzam.

6. Interpersonal

The ability to be in-tune with others; detecting their emotions and understanding their points of view. People who are high on this spectrum are able to work with others effortlessly. This ability is a component of what is commonly called *emotional intelligence*. Many psychologists, mediators, doctors, educators, and coaches exhibit this strength. The Prophet's (pbuh) ability to lead the Muslim community was in part due to his high interpersonal strength.

7. Intrapersonal

The ability to detect one's own emotions, motives, and drives. This strength is the other half of emotional intelligence. Many contemporary Muslims dismiss this faculty and do not see the value of self-reflection and introspection. However, the Sufis in the Islamic tradition have long called for the development of this ability as part of the journey toward connecting with Allah. Imam Abu Hamed al-Ghazali (n.d.), the famous 11th Century Muslim philosopher, stated in his book, *The Alchemy of Happiness*, "Know yourself. Know Allah."

The main reason we share this beautiful concept is for the purpose of connection. Parents love their children deeply and want the best for them. Parents hope their children's lives will be better than theirs. Sometimes this love and hope become coercive and judgmental when children do not follow their parents' wishes. Parents who equate success in life with achievements along the math-science continuum may see secure livelihoods only in these fields. As a result, they may push their children into these academic areas and neglect other innate abilities their children may exhibit. These parents dismiss children's strengths in areas such as music and the arts as hobbies or talents rather than as unique qualities that can lead to fulfilling lives. We have come across many families who would ridicule their children's choices in the Arts and Humanities as stupid and worthless. Again, while this may stem from love and wanting a "better life for their children," the wound to the child's psyche can be deep. The loss of potential is grave, and ultimately such practices rob the global Muslim community of beautiful and creative contributions.

As seen from the examples above, the Muslim community needs all talents in order to build a thriving global community. Prophet Muhammad (pbuh) had companions with unique abilities, and he was able to utilize all of them. The talents of Hassan bin Thabit, the Prophet's (pbuh) poet, lay in using words (linguistic domain) to support and defend the message of Islam. In one famous story during the Battle of the Trench, it is narrated that Hassan bin Thabit was relegated to protect the women behind battle lines. An intruder was spotted and Hassan was asked to intercept, but he could not. It was Safiya, the Prophet's (pbuh) aunt, who ultimately intercepted the intruder and protected the group. Hassan's talent lay not in physical warfare.

His was of the spoken word. We invite you, as the Prophet (pbuh) recognized, celebrated, and utilized the talents of all his companions, to do the same with your children. Here are some ideas to consider:

- Appreciate the wide and diverse range of human strengths.
- Consider Gardner's seven strength domains and identify which ones you see in your children and which ones you see in yourself.
- Train yourself to notice your children's strengths early on. Talents can be detected in childhood by observant and engaged parents.
- Expose your children to different experiences to uncover their hidden potentials.
- Avoid lauding only the math-science aptitude. Encourage all of your children's efforts to excel in their areas of interests.
- If your children are unaware of their strengths, share your observations with them.
- Avoid pressuring children for standards that are beyond their abilities. With subjects or fields in which children struggle, focus on supporting and encouraging.
- When considering college majors, assess whether the choice fits the proven ability. Leave the final decision to your children.
- If your children choose majors or are heading toward career paths that are unpredictable, share your concerns about their future life plans without demeaning their choices.

Birth Order

Alfred Adler was one of the first psychiatrists to suggest that birth order influences personality. He believed that children's place in the family impacts their long-term friendships, romantic relationships, and occupation. Today, there is little consensus among researchers and psychologists about this idea. However, many families observe that first-born children compared to youngest and "onlies" (a child with no siblings) share many similar qualities.

Some common traits found amongst first-born children are that they are diligent, reliable, structured, cautious, and controlling. They may be natural-born leaders and may behave as mini-adults. They strive to work hard and be the best at whatever they do. Their traits usually follow them into adulthood.

Middle children amongst three siblings may feel lost in the middle. They may thrive on friendships outside of the family and have a temperamental attitude at home. They generally take the role of peacemakers and people pleasers, or rebels (with or without a cause). As adults, they may continue to work hard and prove themselves in whatever they do.

The last-born in a family tends to be easy-going, playful, and charming or a "speeder" who wants to surpass their older siblings. Their individuality stands out as they fight for their family's attention or bask in over-attention. They have an adventurous spirit and are willing to take risks, or decide they belong only when others are taking care of them. These early decisions impact the future "blueprint" for living.

Finally, onlies exhibit qualities of both the oldest and youngest. However, as firstborns like to be "first," onlies may like to be "unique." They are leaders and open to risk taking. Onlies generally connect better with other adults than with peers. As they enter adulthood their character of perfectionism and diligence is displayed in whatever they do.

Regardless of the birth order, it is important that parents accept their children's unique personality traits. In addition, letting go of comparing children to siblings or other children stems the tide of sibling rivalry.

Child Development

Human beings develop through a series of stages from birth to death. The different stages of development are not only physical but also include social and emotional development. Renowned psychologist and psychoanalyst Erik Erikson was the first to introduce a model for the psychosocial stages of human development. His insights and theory have become a cornerstone of psychology and social sciences.

Erikson's original model has been expanded by Newman and Newman (2005) to an eleven stage model. We will focus on the first seven stages, which encompass the most dramatic change and growth in an individual's life span. Every stage is characterized by the following: asset gained when stage is navigated effectively (Virtue); critical social relationships necessary for support (Significant Relationships); noteworthy milestones (Important Events); and common developmental trends (Psychosocial Development).

Infancy (0-1 year)

Virtue. Hope.

Significant relationship. Parent or primary care giver.

Important events. Feeding, attachment, playing, interacting with others.

Psychological development. Infants depend on their primary caregivers for food, care, and affection. These primary experiences are critical for fostering the basic sense of trust in the world. If infants' needs are met more often than not, they develop a strong attachment to their caregivers. They learn to trust their environment. If, however, infants are abandoned or neglected, they develop a pervasive mistrust that could gravely impact their life course.

Toddlerhood (2-3 years)

Virtue. Will.

Significant relationships. Parents, siblings, extended family, caregivers.

Important events. Grasping, walking, talking, toilet training, feeding & dressing themselves.

Psychological development. Children direct their energy toward the development of physical skills through which their self-control and self-confidence begin to develop. Children whose efforts and appropriate independence are encouraged will begin to believe in their abilities and skills. Overprotective parents may unwittingly send the message that mistakes are to be avoided at any cost, thus establishing seeds of shame in their children's world.

Early Childhood (3-5 years)

Virtue. Purpose.

Significant relationships. Nuclear and extended family, preschool, caregivers.

Important events. Toilet training, feeding & dressing themselves, exploring, using tools, making art, parallel play, engaging in make-believe and role-playing.

Psychological development. Children continue to become more independent as their motor skills are further developed. They begin to explore social relationships while learning to regulate their emotions. Preschoolers are intent on exploring the physical world and struggle with recognizing the limits of what they can and cannot do. Children whose parents are encouraging and consistent in their discipline will continue their novel exploration of the world while respecting boundaries and limits. Children who are disciplined harshly and inconsistently may develop a sense of guilt and become inhibited.

Middle Childhood (6-12 years)

Virtue. Competence.

Significant relationships. Nuclear and extended family, neighbors, friends, peers and teachers at school, as well as extracurricular team members and coaches.

Important events. Family bonds, friendships, academics, skill learning, self-evaluation, and team play.

Psychological development. Focus shifts from the home to the school environment as children begin the formal academic path. They struggle to learn new skills and face failures. Their social world expands as they develop peer friendships. Children feel competent when they gain mastery over some areas of their lives. This will vary depending on the child's innate strengths. If they do not feel successful and accomplished, they may begin to feel inferior and incompetent.

Early Adolescence (13-18 years)

Virtue. Fidelity to others.

Significant relationships. Nuclear and extended family, friends, peers and teachers at school, extracurricular team members and coaches, mentors, and role models.

Important events. Physical maturation, cognitive maturation, emotional regulation, membership in peer group, budding sexual interest, questioning personal identity, and exploring career and life paths.

Psychological development. Children transition into adolescence. They begin the process of individuation and separation where they recognize they are distinct entities from their parents. They struggle to answer the questions, "Who am I?" "Where am I going?" and "How will I get there?" In the process, they may develop stronger bonds with their peer group as they navigate their emerging individual and group identities.

Late Adolescence (18-24 years)

Virtue. Fidelity to values.

Significant relationships. Nuclear and extended family, friends, college peers, co-workers, instructors, managers, mentors, and role models.

Important events. Autonomy from parents, gender identity,

internalized morality, college graduation, career choice, significant relationships, marriage, and childbearing.

Psychological development. Adolescents continue to seek autonomy from their parents. Some continue the process of self-reflection as they formalize their identity and moral code. They consider their upbringing and establish their own opinions in areas ranging from culture, religion and politics to occupation and sexuality. Young adults who define who they are move forward with direction and purpose. Others struggle to figure out answers to life's questions and may be lost for some years to come.

Early Adulthood (24-34 years)

Virtue. Love.

Significant relationships. Partners, nuclear and extended family, friends, coworkers, and managers.

Important events. Romantic relationships, marriage, childbearing, career, lifestyle, college, professional schools, and activism.

Psychological development. Most young adults at this stage will focus on the need for intimacy. Forming close relationships and sharing with others takes center stage. They will seek to create a work and family lifestyle. If they are still uncertain of who they are, they may be reluctant to commit or depend on others which may lead to isolation and loneliness.

In Part I, we focused on expanding understanding of yourself and your children. In Part II, we will discuss how Positive Discipline tools are applied with real families.

PART II

POSITIVE DISCIPLINE TOOLS

CHAPTER 4

No Carrots And Sticks

One major distinction about Positive Discipline is that it does not ascribe to external behavior modification strategies such as punishments or rewards. Positive Discipline is **not** a carrot and stick framework in which children are trained to behave through pain or pleasure. Parents may be surprised to learn that Positive Discipline does not encourage the use of fear, threats, or bribes to get a child to comply. Instead, Positive Discipline offers a variety of tools that fosters an inner locus of motivation. Let's first discuss punishments and rewards and why Positive Discipline does not use these carrot and stick tools.

Punishment

What is the definition of punishment? Our definition includes the use of physical force to overpower the child (spanking, hitting with a hand or other objects), taking away privileges (spending time with friends, playing, or watching TV) or taking away property (allowance, cell phone, or computer).

Ask yourself the following questions. We invite you to write your answers down:

- What are my personal opinions about punishment?

- What has been my experience with punishment?

- What decisions have I made in my life based on my experience with punishment?

Jane Nelsen (2006, p. 13) shares the 4 results of punishment:

1. Resentment: "This is unfair. I can't trust adults."
2. Revenge: "They are winning now, but I'll get even."
3. Rebellion: "I'll do just the opposite to prove I don't have to do it their way."
4. Retreat:
   - Sneakiness: "I won't get caught next time."
   - Reduced Self-Esteem: "I am a bad person."

Do you see yourself in any of these scenarios? These results are usually evident when punishments are used as the sole strategy for discipline. When it's their turn to parent, individuals raised with punishment-based parenting tend to fall into one of the following three groups.

The first group includes parents who suffered from the pain of punishment as children but have not made the momentous decision to parent their own children differently. With this group, the cycle repeats itself. The new parents propagate the ways of previous generations. They typically have no awareness of other ways, so they utilize the same oppressive methods. The cycle of punishment-based parenting could continue until someone in the family becomes intentional about the parenting process. The main struggle for this group is developing self-awareness.

A second group of parents are those who made the conscious

decision to avoid using punishments. However, in their zeal to avoid what their own parents have done, they go to the other extreme and become permissive. As stated in Chapter 2 (p. 29), permissive parenting has its own problems. The main struggle for this group is learning how to be firm and consistent without the use of punishment. In their efforts to become authoritative parents, they may believe that any firmness they establish is alienating their children. Their fear of losing the love of their children may push them back to being permissive.

The last group is comprised of parents who abhorred the punishments of their parents and, as adults, are uncertain about how to handle their own children. These parents choose to actively learn and educate themselves about parenting. We are in awe of this group. We see many examples of this last group in second generation American Muslims. Many readers of this book fall into this group. May Allah Bless your efforts as you navigate the parenting challenges of your family and embrace a new way of engaging with your children.

There is a particular group of parents who adamantly share sentiments like, "Well, I was spanked and look at me, I am fine now. I deserved the spanking, and I learned my lesson. Punishment worked for me. Why are you telling me not do it with my child?" For this group it is important to understand that punishments were likely not used as the sole form of discipline. In these homes, there were also conversations, discussions, collaboration, mutual respect, etc. The end result is that these adults ultimately felt connected to their families of origin. Hence, the punishments do not hold the same heavy weight as they do for the groups mentioned above. We invite you to focus on utilizing the Positive Discipline tools as they will certainly build a stronger family connection.

When we ask parents why they use punishments, many say, "I do it because I want to teach my child the lessons of life." The irony is that punishment does teach lessons. However, they are oppressive and debilitating lessons. In fact, punishments used as the sole method of discipline scar the psyche. The child is wounded for life. Children scarred by punishment move into adulthood with unconscious dysfunctional theories about social interactions such as:

- The tester: an adult who won't trust others until they prove their mettle. This is a person who is initially aloof. Trust could be built with time, but it's usually a fragile trust fraught with doubts and suspicions.
- The avenger: an adult who is seeking revenge for childhood pain. This is an individual who reacts to the slightest provocation by attacking and insulting others.
- The meek: an adult who is subdued and submissive. This is a person who lacks self-confidence and seeks direction from others.
- The victim: an adult who believes the world is out to get him/her. This is an individual who does not believe he/she has control over his/her life.
- The bully: an adult whose mode of operation is to control others. This is a person who does not feel safe unless he/she is in control of a situation.
- The undercover: an adult who is not forthcoming and open. This is a person who hides his/her true feelings and

thoughts for fear of criticism and ridicule.

As you can see, long-term ramifications of the sole use of punishments vary dramatically. No one can predict how a child will turn out. However, one thing is clear. These ramifications are injurious. The life lessons parents believe they are teaching are in reality psychological shackles that trap children in unconscious dysfunctional social dynamics. This is why punishments limit and suffocate children's potential rather than act as an empowering force.

Punishments are distractions from the issue at hand. They do not invite children to think for themselves nor do they invite children to consider solutions to the challenge. Typically children ruminate over the punishment itself and are not even thinking of the issue. So the takeaway becomes: "How can I avoid this again?" "How can I do what I want without getting punished?" "How can I hide or sneak behind my parents' backs to do what I want?" What is very disheartening about these messages is that none of these options are good seeds for a productive adult life. (See Spanking in the Islamic Context, p. 379).

Rewards

Some parents may not need to be convinced of the negative impact of punishment but are baffled about why they should not use rewards, which they see as a positive strategy. So, why are rewards being equated with punishments and are left out of the Positive Discipline tools? While the negative impact of rewards is not as ruinous as those of punishment, they inflict their own share of psychological injuries.

Rewards are tangible material gains connected to desirable end results. Examples include: stickers on behavior or routine charts; prizes for memorization of the Quran; money for academic success; candy for behaving perfectly; extra video game time for finishing homework early, etc. In a nutshell, rewards are anything that is not related to the task at hand and are promised in return for the child fulfilling that task. It is a forced association between a goal and something completely unrelated. It is artificial. The parent creates the system, the connection, and the anticipation. The following discussion highlights our concerns about establishing a parenting system based solely on the abundance of rewards.

Rewards are effective short-term only. It's true that, specifically with young children, rewards are motivating and encouraging. However, as the child grows older it becomes difficult to find the right reward to motivate. "If there is nothing in it for me, why bother!"

Rewards are a distraction from the task. Energy and effort revolve around the details of the reward rather than the task. Parents believe rewards motivate their children to develop good habits or skills. In reality what a child learns is how to assess the value of the reward and bargain for more. When a child haggles the parent to amplify the reward, the targeted task becomes a bargaining chip and is sidelined in the process. More importantly, the child-parent dynamic shifts into who is going to "win."

Rewards have ceilings. In households where rewards are constantly negotiated, rewards tend to go up in quality and quantity. Rewards that were initially exciting gradually become lame and the child demands more or better. Typically parents give in to the demands, unaware of the danger. At some point, the child's demands reach an unreasonable limit, and the parent feels stuck.

Different children react to rewards differently. Some children engage in the reward system while others will not. I (Noha) still remember the moment when my son, as a second grader, told me, "I don't care!" in response to one of my rewards. I was stunned. What do you do when your child throws the reward back in your face? I was paralyzed and did not know what to do. I decided then and there to reassess my strategy. Looking back, I am grateful that my son enlightened me (unconsciously of course!) on the short-lived impact of rewards. Even though he was the only one of my children who resisted rewards, that was the last time I used rewards to work out my interactions with all my children.

Rewards foster dependency on others. The hidden danger in rewards lies in promoting an external locus of control. Growing up motivated by tangible gains or the accolades of others leads to a life driven by the opinions and goals of others. However, there comes a point in life when a person discovers the futility of such a drive. It could be that the reward is not incentivizing enough, the plethora of opinions is confusing, the competition is stiff, etc. The end result is a difficult period of reassessment and restructuring. During this time, rewarded individuals become stagnant as they search for a new motivating system.

Some parents resist letting go of rewards because they believe that if humans don't have something to work toward, then they won't work. We invite this group of parents to focus on fostering the joy that comes with a "job well done." That satisfaction is deeper and more enduring than the temporary pleasure of rewards. Recognize that when you focus on these material distractions, you inculcate what Allah Has described in the Quran as "life in this world is the pleasure of our egos," (57:20). By avoiding the use of incentives, you open the door to experiencing the simple pleasures of life and leading an authentic life that is better connected to Allah.

The Issue of Control

We have a simple question for you; "How much control do you believe you have over how your child will turn out?" We invite you to be honest. Take time to reflect.

To be candid with you, I (Noha) was one of those parents who arrogantly believed that it's up to me (100% my responsibility) for how my children turn out. I don't believe I was conscious of that belief but I certainly operated with that attitude. Of course, I knew that my children would have different personalities, but I naively thought I would simply have to figure out what works for each one of them, do it, and—voila!—change them.

We are definitely a critical piece that either empowers or inhibits our children. We have influence, a great deal of influence, in fact. But we are definitely not 100% responsible for the adults they become nor for the lives they lead. In addition to our parenting style and our connection with them, there are several other factors that contribute to who they become.

To begin with, their genetic makeup impacts many crucial areas in their lives: intelligence, temperament, anger threshold, etc. Then, there is the issue of the social environment, including the nuclear family and beyond. Every child is born into a different environment—even those born into the same family. Birth order and significant life events grant every child a different context. Outside the family unit, other people exert influence, including teachers, neighbors, and friends. Beyond the intimate social circle there is the subtle, yet very powerful, cultural imprint of the geographical location and era. Lastly, the free will that humans are created with is basically the freedom to think and choose from the myriad of choices available to all of us in the world.

The confluence of all these factors, including your parenting style and your connection with your child, impacts the adults that children become. It is important to reflect on your understanding of the limits of your control because it unconsciously colors your interactions with your children. Parents who believe they are 100% responsible for how their children turn out resort to strategies of control and coercion to mold their children into what they believe they "should be." Of the strategies to control, the most common are punishments and rewards. Usually these parents see their children as extensions of themselves. On the other hand, parents who accept the fact that they are not in full control of their children's destiny, collaborate with their children, see them as separate entities, and nurture them to be their best. Parents have dreams and wishes for their children. However, these dreams never become shackles that strangle and suffocate. These parents see their role as that of a gardener who tends the flowers with the best care but doesn't know for certain which way the stems will grow.

One of the main reasons we bring up this issue is that we see two common things amongst Muslim parents. They love their children very much. They take their responsibilities seriously. Such deep love and profound sense of responsibility lead some parents to manipulate every aspect of their children's lives. Usually these parents believe that their children don't know what is best for them and hence, control and coercion come into play. They do not see their children as capable of figuring things out on their own through the ebb and flow of life. Controlling is all done in the name of love. The earliest sign of such an attitude is food battles and the later signs of such suffocating and debilitating love are those related to career and marriage choices. Just to emphasize, we are not advocating abandoning your children to do whatever they want. Rather, we are inviting you to abandon a fixed vision of who you think they will become. Grant them space to learn the lessons of life while you are there by their side supporting and encouraging.

The first habit in *The Seven Habits of Highly Effective Families* (Covey, 1997, p. 27) is to "be proactive." Covey emphasizes that the essence of proactivity is to be responsible = response-able. He encourages us to shift our focus in our daily life to intentionally choosing responses and actions rather than obsessing over controlling other people in our life. My (Noha) work as a therapist has shown me time and again the value of his message. It has been my experience that when parents are able to focus on their actions and responses, their children were more likely to be influenced by them. On the other hand, when parents are fixated on how their children "should" behave, disconnection, rebellion, and alienation follow. If your goal is to continue to be an influence in your children's lives, collaborate with them instead of controlling them.

So ask yourself: Where do I stand? Are you and your child

partners in the journey to adulthood? Are you the commander who must be followed without question because you know what is best? Or are you both the co-pilots? Your answer here is critical because Positive Discipline is for parents who seek to collaborate, nurture, and empower.

Parenting Myths

In my (Noha) practice, I have come across many myths that trap parents in their parenting journey. These have led to anguish and pain. Table 4.1 highlights some of the common myths and recommendations for reading.

TABLE 4.1
Common Parenting Myths

Myth	Related Book Section
I simply have to teach them Islam and my children will be good Muslims.	Question of Faith (p. 268 & p. 288); Islam-the-Choice (p. 397).
My children are not going to be like..., they will be the best children.	Parenting Styles (p. 31); Why is My Teen In Serious Trouble? (p. 279)
If I am firm with my children, they will hate me.	Parenting Styles (p. 31); When Parents Disagree Over Parenting Styles (p. 37); The Dance (p. 36).
It's my responsibility to fix my children's emotions.	Effective Communication (p. 87); Mirroring (p. 180); Positive Time-out (p. 131).
I have to tell my children they are special so they will have good self-esteem.	Encouragement (p. 94); Fragile Adult Syndrome (p. 391).
I need to be there for my children all the time or else I am not a good parent.	Empowerment (p. 90); Exhausted Parents (p. 183); Get a Life (p. 105).
I tell my children so many "NO"s because of Islam, so I make up for it by giving them anything they ask for.	Parenting Styles (p. 31); Buy Me More (p. 170); Entitlement (p. 197).
If I am not on the same page with my spouse regarding parenting, all is lost.	Parenting Styles (p. 31); When Parents Disagree Over Parenting Styles (p. 37); The Dance (p. 36).
I am responsible for my children's happiness.	Buy Me More (p. 170); Entitlement (p. 197); Fragile Adult Syndrome (p. 391).

In the next chapter, we cover many of the Positive Discipline tools that will empower you—the parent—to replace punishments and rewards. We invite you to use the mundane activities of everyday living as teaching moments for lasting life skills.

CHAPTER 5

Positive Discipline Tools

In this chapter, we cover 49 Positive Discipline tools. Which tool a parent uses will depend on the situation, the temperaments of both the parent and child, and, of course, the age of the child. Some tools are applicable with all age ranges and some are age-specific.

All the tools discussed have been mentioned in other books including: *Positive Discipline, Positive Discipline A-Z, Positive Time-Out,* and *Teaching Parenting the Positive Discipline Way,* and the recently published *Positive Discipline Parenting Tools: The 49 Most Effective Methods to Stop Power Struggles, Build Communication, and Raise Empowered Capable Kids,* written by Jane Nelsen and two of her children, Mary Nelsen Tamborski, and Brad Ainge. We have described the tools and given examples based on our own understanding and experience. Tools marked with an * are not specifically Positive Discipline tools but align well with the philosophy. For easy referencing, tools are listed in alphabetical order.

In a nutshell, we invite you to focus on ***connecting*** with your children. We believe that connection is the foundation upon which the family unit will weather life challenges. There will be challenges, for that is how Allah ordained life; "We have created you in constant turmoil" (Quran, 90:4). Our invitation to connect is not for loving without limits. Our invitation is for loving your children while being able to set respectful boundaries. We believe that implementing Positive Discipline *consistently* leads to the following:

- Collaborative teamwork.
- Respect for all members, no matter how young they are.
- Every member having a voice that is heard.
- Children discovering their strengths.
- Children believing in their abilities.
- Children nurtured to be the best adults they can be.
- Children feeling comfortable coming to parents with problems and concerns.
- Children learning self-soothing strategies.
- Children capable of dealing with disappointments and failures.
- Parents who are less frazzled by daily life.
- Parents who direct their energy to what is effective and under their control.
- A positive family culture.
- Problems that are addressed through solutions.
- A family that enjoys the company of one other.
- A strong family connection even when children leave the nest.

Act Without a Word (Non-Verbal Signals)

This tool is about using gestures to communicate messages that have been already communicated through words.

Examples of Act Without a Word.

- Pointing to the child's backpack when it is thrown in the middle of the hallway.
- Sitting next to and silently hugging your teenage daughter when she is crying or sad.
- Pointing to the seat belt when your child has not put it on.
- Walking away when your child is yelling and screaming at you.
- Extending your hand, palm up, as you wait for your son to give you the cell phone.
- Sitting in the car waiting for your child to leave for school in the morning (without screaming, yelling, or threatening).
- When it is time for prayer, calling the *athan* (call to prayer) and starting the prayer without waiting for everyone to assemble (just as it's done in the mosque).

Agreed Upon Deadlines

This tool is commonly used as part of the tools Problem Solving (p. 134) and Follow Through (p. 104). However, it can be used alone, too. When parent and child both disagree on issues that involve time, this tool becomes useful. It is about being concrete and clear.

Examples of Agreed Upon Deadlines.

- At the end of a discussion about chore assignments, a parent asks the child: "When do you think you would do….?" If the time limit expressed by the child does not work for the family, the parent expresses and requests a different time limit.

- If bedtime is an issue, parent and child engage in a conversation until they are both clear on what time works for both.

- When the parent wishes to discuss an emerging issue, the parent asks the child, "When would be a good time to discuss…." and then Follow Through at the designated time.

- When going out together, the family discusses beforehand how long the trip will be and the deadline for leaving the house.

- When a young child is asking the parent to come and play, the parent hands the child a timer set for the designated time and Follows Through when the timer goes off.

Allowance

Teaching a child about the value of money is done through establishing an allowance system. Allowance is a stipend that a child receives regularly and is *not tied* to chores nor good behavior. By having "buying power," children learn how much things cost, become adept at comparison shopping, develop the patience for saving money, and enjoy spending money on things they really want.

Allowances mitigate money battles. A mother of a 13-year-old girl was lamenting her daughter's obsession with brand-name clothing. She described how shopping had turned into a constant battle of wills over how much and what to buy. I (Noha) listened and empathized. I inquired if she was willing to try something new. When she was ready to take in a new idea, I invited her to give her daughter an allowance. She was intrigued but skeptical. However, a few weeks later I got a call from the delighted mother who shared her amazement at what happened the first time her daughter went shopping with her allowance. The same daughter who refused to look at sales racks before the allowance was now the first to check them. The mother was flabbergasted to note that her daughter was not arguing with her over prices but was thinking very carefully of ways to stretch her allowance. That was the calmest shopping trip they both had in a long time. When the mother stepped out of the way, her daughter was able to implement many of the lessons the mother had tried to teach her through lectures and commands. This is a beautiful example of what happens when you allow your children to experience life.

A crucial aspect regarding allowance is deciding together what the allowance will be used for. As children grow older, the area covered by the allowance is expanded. With preschoolers, it could be used for random items such as a candy in the supermarket or a toy at an amusement park. With elementary school children, it could cover more expensive toys or clothing items. For middle school children, it could be used to cover outings with friends, games, clothing, etc. Teens can be expected to use their allowance to buy clothes, school lunches, entertainment, games, books, etc. Deciding how much to give and what to use the allowance for will depend on the family budget and cultural context. This may require some respectful negotiating to come to an agreement that feels respectful to everyone. For high school students, it is good practice to establish their own bank accounts in which they get automatic allowance deposits every month.

For the allowance to be an effective tool, grant children the freedom to buy what they want without interference from you. Share your concerns, but give them the space to learn from their experiences without judgment or humiliation. Instead of saying: "I told you so! You should've listened to me," ask, "What have you learned from this experience? How is this going to impact your decisions in the future?" Some parents may question, "What do I do if they want to buy candy with all their money?" We invite parents in these situations to focus on the family rules governing the items purchased. For example, if the child decides to buy candy with the allowance, the rule governing candy is invoked. A family may have a rule that candy is eaten only at a certain time of the day or week. If the child buys an item of clothing that is inappropriate, family rules governing clothing are applied. For example, inappropriate clothing items are worn only at home or with other items.

When there are siblings it is especially critical that the allowance system is clear, consistent, and understood by everyone. The age of the child must be considered when determining the amount. Explain this concept to your child as a rule for life. As they grow older their needs increase and so will their allowance. It is best to utilize an easy allowance formula. For example, my (Noha) husband gave our children a monthly allowance that was double their age until they began high school, at which point the criteria changed.

Allah has ordained that money is part of the pleasures of this life. To temper material obsessions, we invite you to train your children with Islamic financial practices. Teach children about giving *zakat* (almsgiving) and charity from their money. Some families expect their children to donate out of the allowance regularly. Others invite their children to donate when they are going through a difficult time. Some encourage children to give charity when they commit a sin such as lying or backbiting.

Lastly, to teach children living within their means, it is important that parents refrain from lending their children money. Be firm. Let them learn to stretch their dollars as far as they can. Let them struggle at the end of the month with no money. We have observed that children who learned these money lessons early on were able to spend their money wisely as adults.

Be There*

This is one of my (Noha) favorite tools. It is also one that came to me in my own parenting journey. It happened one random day. I cannot recall the specific details but I remember I was cooking dinner, having a great conversation with one of my children who approached me with a concern. The whole exchange took fifteen minutes at most. However, afterwards, I reflected on what a lost opportunity it would have been if I was not there to address that concern at that moment. And with that, "Be There" crystalized.

For parents living in the West, there is a lot of talk about spending quality time with each child. As a mother of four children, very close in age, and with the full responsibility of the household on my shoulders, I did not have much time for this idyllic special time with each one of my children. Instead, I chose to "be there" for the impromptu and spontaneous moments that would come up. I believe I made every moment count.

Being there meant the following: prioritizing time with family over other obligations, dropping everything I was doing when one of my children approached me to talk, minimizing my commitments when my children were home, turning off TV and other screens when my children were around, being in the family room or the kitchen where my children could easily approach me, exuding an inviting attitude, etc. It is amazing what happens when you become intentional about being there. Over the years, some of the best conversations serendipitously took place in my family simply because I was there.

My children are adults now. But Be There continues to be one of my mottos. Whenever they visit, I invoke Be There and change my schedule and routines accordingly. We invite you to do the same.

Closet Listening

This tool is an extension of Be There: to simply keep your ears and eyes open whenever you are in proximity of your child. As you listen and watch, keep track of questions, concerns, or reflections you may have and then share them with your child in private.

Examples of Closet Listening.

- When your children are engaged with other children during play dates.
- After a game, as team members are walking away from the field.

POSITIVE DISCIPLINE TOOLS | 79

- While shuffling kids to and from school.
- When you befriend your children on social media sites.

Closet Listening is not spying. Spying is whenever you are checking on your children behind their backs. With Closet Listening you are visibly there and the child knows that you can hear what is being said. Some parents believe they have the right to spy on their child in the name of protecting them. We disagree. Allah is very clear in forbidding spying, "...avoid spying and backbiting each other" (Quran, 49:12).

Inevitably while Closet Listening, you will come across something that is worrisome. Avoid instantly addressing your concern while friends are still around. Choose an appropriate time. Ensure it is a private and respectful conversation and use the tool I-Noticed… (p. 108).

Come Back With Your Plan

This tool is simply granting children the space to come up with a plan. It empowers children to think critically and creatively. When children practice the process of coming up with solutions, they are likely to be proactive adults who rarely see themselves as victims. It is simply asking, "What is your plan about….?"

Examples of Come Back With Your Plan.

- When siblings fight over a toy, game, front seat, etc.
- When a child has a school project requiring many trips to the store.
- When a child wants to buy something beyond allowance limits.
- When a child wants to change the schedule of chores.

Connection Before Correction

This tool invites parents to connect with their children before they attempt any correction of misbehavior. The central piece of Connection Before Correction is the parents' ability to remain calm and grounded in the face of difficult situations. When that containment of emotion is in place, parents are able to maintain their connection with children. At that point moving on to the correction piece does not elicit resistance or rebellion.

Examples of disconnection after mistakes.

- Yelling and screaming: "What have you done?!"
- Labeling children negatively (stupid, lazy, bum, etc.)
- Shaming "I cannot believe you are my child!"
- Guilt-tripping "Look how you made me behave!"
- Dismissing what the child feels "You can't be feeling this way! We don't get angry with our friends."
- Silent treatment without explaining to the child what is going on.
- Withdrawing privileges indefinitely with no clear limit. "You are grounded! No more TV for you."

Examples of Connecting Before Correcting.

Your child spilled milk on the floor. He is crying and looking apprehensively at you. Hug, soothe and say, "It's ok. Accidents happen. No harm done. Let's clean it up together."

Your son failed math. When you hear the news, begin by checking in with yourself. How are you feeling? If you are not calm, inform your son that you will talk about this issue at a later time once you have calmed down. "I am very upset right now.

Once I calm down, we will talk about this." Step away to calm down and gather your thoughts. If you are calm when you hear the news, begin by checking in with your son about how he feels. If you can read his emotional state, reflect back what you sense. After checking in, process using Curiosity Questions (p. 82), such as, "What can you do to improve your performance in this class?

Your teenage daughter admitted to smoking weed. She is anxious, apologetic and keeps saying, "I don't know what to do." Contain your emotions (acknowledge what you are feeling to yourself and avoid yelling and screaming), hug or hold your daughter, assure her that you will both work together to deal with the situation, take time to process and reflect, then sit down with her and discuss options.

Convincing Is Not Parenting*

Many parents, in an effort to be nice and kind, believe that they must convince their children of the value of a rule, system, or routine. Parents assume that if they talk enough, children will see the wisdom of what they are saying and will then be willing to collaborate. We wish it were true. The reality is that some children see the value of what parents are asking for; however, most won't. It is common that children will acknowledge the wisdom of their parents only after they have become adults or parents themselves.

Accordingly, we invite you to save your energy and time. Explain your rationale and reasons to your child. However, after doing so, focus on how you and your child can work out your different positions. Don't wait for or expect the child to exclaim: "Yes! Mom/Dad, of course, you are right!" Rather, be content with the child knowing your position or limit on a subject. That is success! It means you have sent the message correctly and your child received it accurately: "What did I say about...? What is your understanding of why I am refusing to...? What is my limit?"

At some point it may be necessary to set a limit to the discussion by saying: "I have explained my position. This conversation is not moving forward. I see how upset you are. I suggest you take some time to process what we said, and let's agree to have another discussion soon. When would it work for you to have another conversation?" Sometimes it might be necessary to simply give a Statement of Fact (p. 143) or Decide What You Will Do (p. 85).

Curiosity Questions

Many parents believe that it's their duty to tell their children what to do, how they feel, what they did wrong, etc. The list is long. Unfortunately, "telling" brings up walls of defiance, resistance, rebellion, silence, withdrawal, zoning out, etc. In many instances, the same message could be sent using Curiosity Questions. We invite you to use Curiosity Questions because you will be amazed at how much more effective the communication will be. Not only do Curiosity Questions grant you entry into your child's world, but they also empower your child to be an active participant in the conversation. More importantly, Curiosity Questions nurture critical thinking skills.

Curiosity Questions are those that begin with *what, how, when* and *who*. Sometimes it may be appropriate to use the *why* question, but avoid it as much as possible. *Why* questions are conversation enders because they put children on the defensive who then respond with, "Oh! I don't know! It just happened."

TABLE 5.1

Comparing Telling versus asking Curiosity Questions

Telling	Curiosity Questions
"Go do your homework!"	"What does your routine chart say needs to be happening right now?"
"You must wear your jacket! You are not going out without it."	What do you need to do if you don't want to feel cold?
"Ahmad is your friend! You should not be angry with him! You are a good Muslim."	"You are angry with Ahmad. What would help you calm down?"
"You will not buy this toy! It's too expensive!"	"How much money do you have? Is it enough?"
"How dare you speak to me this way! I am your father! Remember that Allah will be angry with you if you talk to me this way!"	"I can see how angry you are. I wonder what happened that you are feeling this way. What can you do to take care of yourself right now?"
"Why are your books all over the floor? Go pick them up!"	"Where do your books go?"

Deal with the Belief Behind the Behavior

Based on the Adlerian view of life, humans strive throughout their lives to belong and connect. There are four major pathways to achieve belonging and connection: attention, power, justice, and competence. However, these pathways can be traveled creatively or fruitlessly. Early in life, each individual creates (unconsciously) a theory about one's self, one's place in the world, and how one needs to go about surviving and thriving. These theories are adjusted throughout life especially through the support and love of others. If the life theory revolves around a solid and strong sense of ability and strength, the strategies used will be productive and the individual will achieve belonging and connection. However, if the individual constructed a life theory revolving around a negative sense of self and the world, strategies used will inadvertently create social and emotional problems.

calm and loving way. It is not the same as demanding that your child behave in a specific way. For example, Dad notices that Fatima is using her laptop after bedtime. Demanding would be, "Fatima, from now on, you are no longer using your computer after 10 p.m. Is this clear?" If Dad is focusing on Deciding What He Will Do, he will say instead, "Fatima, in the past I have asked you to put your computer away but it has not worked out. I have decided that at 10 p.m., I will come and get your computer from you. I will keep it in my room until after *fajr* (morning prayers). At that time, you may get it." Remember, this approach will fail if the parent does not Follow Through (p. 104).

Examples of Decide What You Will Do.

- Limiting the use of clay to the kitchen table to minimize the cleanup process.
- Removing clothing items that are inappropriate from the drawers of young children.
- Refraining from buying junk food or soda to minimize battles at home.
- Using the router's settings to restrict Internet access after curfew.
- Deciding not to take forgotten homework or lunch to school.

Distraction For Young Children

A beautiful tool to utilize for children under the age of two is simply redirecting their attention away from what they are upset about. For example, a toddler is crying because a parent just left for work. The other parent or the caregiver could say, "It's OK! Mommy/Daddy will be back later today. It's OK to be sad because you will miss them. Let's go and play with your blocks."

The window to use this tool is very short. Around the age of two, children begin to exhibit a longer lasting memory and it becomes harder to distract them. When children are no longer distractible, shift to tips on how to deal with temper tantrums (p. 162).

Effective Communication

Within every communication, there is a sender and a receiver. Many times, messages are misunderstood simply because the sender did not send the intended message or the receiver made an erroneous assumption about what was heard. An effective strategy to prevent such miscommunication is the utilization of I-Statements and Reflective Listening.

I-Statements.

Sender says:

> I feel….. (angry, sad, frustrated, etc.)
>
> When you... (ask to eat just before bedtime, throw your clothes on the floor, etc.)
>
> And I wish... (we could find a solution, you would put your clothes in the hamper, etc.)

Reflective listening.

Receiver reflects back what was heard:

> You feel... (angry, sad, frustrated, etc.)
>
> Because... (I ask to eat just before bedtime, throw my clothes on the floor, etc.)
>
> And you wish...(we could find a solution, I put the clothes in the hamper, etc.)

It is critical that family members learn how to express their feelings and thoughts without blaming or hurting one another. Accordingly, in Family Meetings (p. 96) and other exchanges, members are encouraged to own responsibility for their emotions, thoughts, and requests. Utilizing I-Statements and Reflective Listening foster an environment of respect and understanding.

In ordinary communication, assumptions are built and internalized quickly. Once assumptions are entrenched, they become the fuel for further misunderstanding. Hence, it becomes necessary to slow down communication, redirect how it's done, and insert intentional pauses to allow for check-ins.

Let's examine a typical form of communication between a mother and son, and how it can be transformed using the I-Statements and Reflective Listening formulas.

Mom [yelling and shouting]: Ahmad, I cannot believe you did it again! (full attack based on assumptions). You promised you would do the dishes right after dinner and here you are AGAIN being irresponsible (negative labeling) watching TV while I have to run around like crazy taking care of your siblings (guilt tripping, poor me, how could you?). Oh Allah, why did I have to have such a sloppy son?! (inoculating shame).

Depending on Ahmad's temperament and theory of life, he may respond in several ways. Here are two common reactions:

Ahmad [tensing up and becoming rigid]: Well, you're the one who made that stupid rule (attack back)! I never wanted to do the dishes (defensiveness). Aisha should be the one doing it not me (running away from responsibility). I will never do the dishes ever (hurt Mom back). What are you going to do about it (challenge Mom to gain control)?

Ahmad [slouching and looking down]: I am so sorry, Mom! I am such a bad son (internalizing shame). I don't know why I keep doing this (internalizing negative self-concept). I will go ahead and do it right away (shame-based motivation for action).

Compare the above scenarios to the following Effective Communication:

Mom [calmly, crouching down to Ahmad's level, after turning off the TV]: Ahmad, I feel disappointed when you promise me to do the dishes and you don't follow through. My wish is that you take care of the dishes now as you promised.

Ahmad [calmly]: Oops! I forgot. Sorry, Mom. I will do it right now.

Some parents at this point may be thinking: "Yeah, right, in your dreams! My child would never respond this way!" True, your child may or may not respond precisely in this way. But however skeptical you may be, the reality is if you don't attempt to do things differently, nothing will change. Change takes time and many attempts.

When a parent focuses on expressing what they really feel (which is not easy because it requires vulnerability and openness), there is a higher likelihood that the parent is heard, understood, collaborated with, empathized with, helped, listened to, and respected. However, using tactics like blame, attack, guilt tripping, accusation, criticism, ridicule, demeaning, denigration, making fun of, intellectualization, lecturing, belittling, and shaming will surely create distance and disrespect in the relationship.

The "wish" or request part in the conversation is important. People go through life somehow expecting that others know what they want or believe they are magically capable of reading their minds and should just know. I (Noha) make it a point to ask my clients: "Does your son/daughter/spouse/parent know?" and they very quickly respond with, "Of course they know!" Unfortunately, let me assure you of a fact: your child actually does not know what you want! Messages shrouded in blame, attack, ridicule and lecturing are messages that have been blocked by the child. Read back through the example above and see the words in brackets and the messages that are actually received by Ahmad. Nowhere in those exchanges did Ahmad receive the message that his mom is disappointed and hurt.

A common question from parents trying effective communication is "How do I get my child to talk and respond in this way?" It's simple. Change begins with you. Conversations are modeled by you. Whatever you give your child will be reflected back to you tenfold. You are the most important teacher in your child's life.

Empowering versus Enabling

Do you empower or enable your child? Jane Nelsen and Lynn Lott define enabling as "getting between young people and life experiences to minimize the consequences of their actions" (1997, p. 59). On the other hand, empowering is "turning control over to young people as soon as possible so they have power over their own lives" (1997, p. 59). In a nutshell, enabling is parents stepping in to take care of children's responsibilities. When that is the operative mode at home, children become crippled. They don't learn how to manage their lives.

Some common areas where parents struggle between empowering and enabling are homework, food, and clothes. I (Noha) was recently asked by a parent when she should start handing off the homework responsibility to her daughter. She had a six-year-old daughter, who was accustomed to her mom pulling out her homework, calling her to the table, and then sitting next to her until she completed her homework. Her story is a typical example of a parent enabling her child. What was supposed to take, at most, 10 minutes, took an hour to complete with a daily battle of wills. I invited the mom to empower her daughter through the following:

- Inform her daughter that the way they do homework is changing.
- Set the time on the Routine Chart (p. 137), of when homework will be done after school.
- Have a quiet area ready with all needed supplies.
- Expect the daughter to work alone.
- Be available to help when her daughter needs specific help.
- Avoid correcting homework or asking her to redo it.
- Inform daughter that she is responsible for putting her homework away.
- Keep the same bedtime even if her daughter has not finished her homework.
- Allow her daughter to face the consequences of not doing her homework.

- Establish a "Rule of Life," such as "fun comes after work." This means that all screen time activities come after homework is done.

There are further layers and other ways to approach the issues stated above. However, these examples serve to highlight the difference between Empowering versus Enabling your child. Refer also to the discussion on punishment and rewards (p. 59-66) to understand how punishment enables rather than empowers.

TABLE 5.3
Examples of Enabling versus Empowering

Enabling	Empowering
Doing too much for children: • Carrying their backpacks. • Preparing their breakfast & lunch when they are capable of doing it themselves. • Following children around to feed them, spoon-feeding children over 3 years, bribing children to eat, etc.	**Shift responsibility to children when they are capable:** • "You are capable of carrying your bag." • "If breakfast and lunch are important to you, please make time to prepare them before we leave for school." • "Dinner is at 5 p.m.," "Let me know when you are hungry," "You can feed yourself. When you are ready to eat, let me know," "Looks like you are done eating."
Giving children too much, even when you can afford it: • Buying the latest gadgets or expensive clothing brands. • Giving money without limits. • Buying an expensive car for a teen.	**Establish limits on giving:** • Give children allowances to cover clothes, lunch money, entertainment, etc. • Negotiate what is expected if you buy the teen a car. Some families expect teens to contribute to the price of the car or the cost of insurance, maintenance, gas, etc. • Buy a used car and involve teen in bargain hunting.
Fixing: • When you do a science project for your son because he is incapable of doing it "right."	**Accept the child's decision about how to take care of responsibilities:** • "What project can you make on your own without major help from me?" • Hold off on your comments if the project is sloppy.
Bailing them out: • You apologize on your daughter's behalf after she was rude to your friend.	**Allow children to face the ramifications of their actions:** • "Auntie Fatima was very hurt by your comment, I expect you to apologize to her in person."

Enabling	Empowering
Over protecting / Rescuing: • Running to school with a late homework assignment. • Returning to school to get a child's forgotten homework or book.	**Support without abandonment:** • "I see how upset you are because you forgot your homework. What can you do so that it does not happen again?" • "I have noticed that you are frequently forgetting your books at school. I have gone back a few times to get them for you. However, I have decided that I will no longer do that. So what does that mean to you? What would you need to do if studying for an exam is important to you?"
Lying for them: • Calling the school and saying your child is sick when they are not.	**Stating the truth, even when it will embarrass you and your child:** • "My child is not in school today because he stayed up last night." • "I have noticed that you are missing school frequently because of your irregular sleep schedule. I would like you to know that I will not be responsible for waking you up in the morning and that I will excuse your absence or tardiness only 3 times a semester. After which, you will be responsible for the consequences."
Punishing /Controlling: • You ground your child for earning a D in Math on a report card.	**Focus on the issue:** • "I noticed you got a D in Math. I would like to hear from you what is going on." • "Show me the breakdown of your grade so we can both see what area in Math you are struggling with." • "What ideas do you have for how you can work on improving your Math grade for next semester?"
Living in denial: • You strongly suspect your child is smoking weed (smell, red eyes, bong, glass pipe, etc.), but you don't do anything about it.	**Face reality:** • "I am very worried, Adam. I have noticed that you are becoming very secretive and have an irregular sleep schedule. You seem to be out of it sometimes. I am wondering if you are smoking weed." • "I hear all your reassurances but I am still worried. My gut feeling is telling me something is wrong. I think a doctor can confirm what is going on. I would like you to take a drug test so that I can be certain you are okay."

Encouragement versus Praise

During the 1980s, the "self-esteem movement" urged parents and teachers to praise children to foster their self-confidence (Crary, 2007). The goal was noble but the means (excessive empty praise) led to a generation of self-absorbed insecure young adults.

Self-esteem is critical for a successful and productive life. It is knowing and utilizing one's unique strengths. It is not something that can be fed to children through empty praise. Self-esteem is developed when individuals truly believe they are capable. This inner belief can only be inoculated through navigating challenges and learning from mistakes.

Today, educators and parents are advocating a "growth-mind set" instead of a "fixed-mind set." Growth-mind set is encouragement while fixed-mind set is tied to the empty praise of the 80s. See the following table (Nelsen, 2007) to understand the difference between encouragement and praise. You will discover that there are many more opportunities to encourage and fewer to praise.

TABLE 5.4

Encouragement versus Praise

Encouragement	Praise
Definition: • To inspire with courage. • To spur on, stimulate, motivate.	Definition: • To express favorable judgment of… • To glorify, especially by attribution of perfection. • An expression of approval.
Teaches self-confidence and self-reliance in the long run.	Teaches dependence on others for ideas, thinking and self-worth in the long run.
Specific. • "You did such a great job cleaning the car."	General. • "You are such a good boy."
Recognizes the deed: goal centered. • "You prayed all five prayers on time today."	Recognizes the doer: ego centered. • "You are such a good Muslim."

Encouragement	Praise
Given in all situations: whether a person is succeeding or failing. • "You are working very hard; it's very clear. This semester you raised your GPA by 0.2 points. Look at that! The new changes you implemented in your study schedule are working for you."	**Given only in situations where a person has succeed or completed a task.** • "I am so proud of you! You've done it again. Your GPA is the highest in the class. No one else is like you."
Given at all times: before, during, and after a task is complete. • "You are working hard every day to memorize Quran. You have been able to maintain your schedule of memorization for a week now *masha Allah* (May God protect you)!"	**Given only after an activity is finished.** • "Well done! You have memorized *Juz Amma* (last section of the Quran)."
Value and worth of person remains constant regardless of approval of others. • "You are proud of your effort."	**Self-worth is tied to approval and standards of others.** • "I am so proud of you."
Stresses that the person is part of a group. • "You helped the team by pitching the ball to Ahmad."	**Stresses competition and perfection; all else is failure.** • "You are the best player. The team would be nothing without you."
Empowers a person to feel good no matter what the situation is. • "You put a lot of effort into your science project."	**Person feels good only after a success.** • "You got First prize. I am so proud of you."
Promotes an internal locus of control. • "You figured it out for yourself."	**Promotes an external locus of control.** • "You did it exactly like I told you."
Doing one's best brings it out. • "I noticed how your ball handling has really improved in just a few months."	**Being the best brings it out.** • "You are the best dribbler."
Puts the responsibility on the child. • "This A reflects your hard work and perseverance."	**Puts the responsibility on the one who praises.** • "I am proud of you for getting an A."
Invites the child to change for themselves. • "What do I think?"	**Invites the child to change for others.** • "What does mom/dad/friend/teacher think?"

Eye to Eye

One of the cardinal rules of communication is making eye contact. This begins from the moment your child is born. Ensure that when you are speaking or asking your child to do something, you are both at the same level and making eye contact. This means that when your child is younger, you crouch down to their eye level.

When they become teens and they become taller than you, you sit facing each other on a couch or at the dining table.

This tool, Eye to Eye, unconsciously mitigates some of the power differential that physically exists between parent and child. Try it yourself. Next time you want to share something, get down (or up) to the child's eye level. You will discover that it is very difficult in that position to be excessively angry or upset.

Family Meetings

Family Meetings are regularly scheduled meetings that include all members of the family. The goal is to share appreciation, discuss ideas and future plans, and to solve problems. They are the cornerstone of Positive Discipline. When done consistently they color the family culture with a positive effect.

Family Meetings provide the following opportunities.

- Sense of belonging.
- Being heard no matter how young the child is.
- Catching and sharing positive interactions.
- Expressing feelings and concerns.
- Finding solutions for challenges and recurrent issues.
- Planning family activities.
- Assigning responsibilities depending on age and capability.

Family Meetings format.

1. Compliment circle. This is the opening of every meeting. Family members extend compliments to each other. Everyone has to participate. Compliments foster a positive focus in the family and shift attention away from problems. For example, "I would like to appreciate Ahmad for allowing me to go first playing video games today;" or "Dad, thank you so much for cooking my favorite dish yesterday!" and *"Jazaka Allahu khair* (May God reward you with goodness) Samir for picking up milk on your way home."

2. *Agenda items.* During the second part of the meeting, agenda items are discussed, beginning with the earliest entry. Agenda items are challenges written during the week in a designated notebook. The family member with the concern is invited to bring up the issue respectfully using I-Statements (p. 87) while choosing how to deal with the issue:

- Share the issue.
- Share the issue and ask for others' perception of the problem.
- Share, ask for perceptions, and ask for solutions.

   Examples of agenda items.

- Maher and Fatima disagree on who can ride in the front seat.
- Ahmad does not have enough time to finish his homework before bedtime.
- Mom is having a difficult time doing all the laundry by herself.
- Dad would like help with the garden.

3. *Discuss future plans.* During this part of the meeting, the family discusses any future plans (vacations, parties, visits, etc.) or weekly plans (dinner menus, pick up and drop off, practice schedules, etc.).

Tips for productive Family Meetings.

- Have short meetings—no more than 20 minutes is suggested.
- Hold the meeting on the same day and time every week.
- Designate a notebook as an agenda book. Avoid using loose papers as agenda sheets because they can be easily misplaced.
- Family members take turns being chairperson and secretary of the meeting.
- Have the agenda in an easily accessible location.
- Agenda items are addressed in the order they were written. Parents' concerns do not take precedence over the children's.
- Parents model the use of I-Statement and Reflective Listening (p. 87).
- Be firm about respecting one another. When a member is disrespectful, train in the use of I-Statements and Reflective Listening. Some families have the formulas on a piece of paper in the center of the circle as a reminder.
- Avoid being stuck on one issue. If no solution is in sight, postpone the conversation to discuss further at the next meeting.
- If the family is discussing an issue and the 20-minute limit is reached, then the meeting is adjourned for that day. The issue will be further discussed in the next meeting. Sometimes new solutions and angles can be recognized between meetings.
- Respect all solutions shared. The member who raised the concern gets to choose which solution to try. Allow children

to discover the ineffectiveness of some solutions on their own.

• All members participate equally. Parents avoid monopolizing the session.

• **The problem is the problem, not the family member.** Avoid labeling any family member. Rather, describe the problem. ("Khaled is having difficulty waking up in the morning" instead of "Khaled is irresponsible and lazy").

• Follow through on agreements made.

• Involve children as young as four years old.

• When teens begin to resist attending meetings, acknowledge their feelings while calmly stating they are expected to participate.

Be aware that, in the beginning, Family Meetings will seem artificial and awkward. Issues may take longer to resolve. However, as more and more issues get resolved, and as family members become acquainted with the problem-solving process, meetings will become shorter, smoother, and a natural part of your family life.

Focus on Solutions

Jane Nelsen was the first to shift the parenting narrative toward solutions instead of wasting energy on creating consequences and punishments. Focusing on Solutions is a major paradigm shift for most parents. When children are young (infants, toddlers, younger preschoolers), solutions are mainly Structuring the Environment (p. 145), Routines (p. 137), and Decide What you Will Do (p. 85). With older children, parent and child engage in conversations and discussions to Problem Solve (p. 134).

For example, Sara is a second grader who has forgotten her homework at home. As Mom is pulling into the school, Sara informs mom that she forgot her homework yet again. Mom, in her endless love for Sara, does not want her to face humiliation or be reprimanded by the teacher. So, she rushes back home, gets the homework and brings it to school. Mom is feeling upset and frustrated. Let's look at how a Focus on Solution discussion might play out for this example.

Sara has forgotten her homework again. Mom brings it to school, saying: "This is the last time I will bring your forgotten homework to school. Tonight you and I need to come up with a solution for this issue." Later that day, when both are calm, they begin their discussion:

Mom: Sara, I have noticed that you forgot your homework three times last week. What is going on?

Sara: Oh, I don't know. I just forget it on the table. I don't know what's going on.

Mom: So you see the problem is forgetting your homework on the table after you are done with it. Is this how you see it?

Sara: Yes, exactly.

Mom: Hmm. I wonder what you can do so you don't forget your homework at home. I know you care about submitting your homework on time. I also know that I feel irritated and frustrated when I have to rush back home to get it for you. What am I saying?

Sara: You are saying that I care about my homework and you are getting upset because you are bringing my homework to school.

Mom: Yes. That is exactly right. I also would like us to brainstorm some solutions. What do you think will help you remember your homework?

Sara: Hmm. I don't know. You tell me what to do.

Mom: I believe it's more important for you to come up with the solution than me telling you what to do. How about if you take some time to think about what you can do?

Sara: [Frustrated] But I cannot think of anything!

Mom: Right now you are having a hard time thinking of something. Give it time. I am certain you will have a great idea for this problem. How about we meet again tomorrow so you can tell me what you have thought of?

Sara: [Sighing deeply] I guess.

Mom: You seem to be feeling discouraged right now because you don't have a ready solution. I guess you are also worried about what you will do if you forget your homework again and I don't bring it to school.

Sara: [Agitated] Yes that, too. What am I going to do?

Mom: [Calmly] So what happens if you don't bring your homework?

Sara: I lose my grade for that assignment.

Mom: Hmm. I see. It seems you won't like that.

Sara: No. I won't. I will feel embarrassed.

Mom: Yes. I see that. Well, I am sure once you come up with a solution, you won't lose your points nor feel embarrassed anymore. Let's talk tomorrow *insha Allah* (God willing).

Typically in our experience, children do come up with solutions when asked for input. However, we wanted to demonstrate to you how to handle the situation if your child is resisting the collaborative process of Focusing on Solutions. Whenever there is resistance, give them time to think and reflect with an Agreed Upon Deadline (p. 73) for meeting again. Let's look at another way of responding to Sara after she asks her mom to tell her what to do:

Mom: I believe it's more important for you to come up with the solution than it is for me to tell you what to do. Hmm. Let us try to figure out what is happening. (The discussion may generate ideas for you.) So tell me, where do you leave your homework on the days you forget it? And where is it on the days you don't forget it? (Curiosity Questions, p. 82).

Sara: When I have it with me it's usually when you remind me in the morning to check and see if my homework is with me. When I forget it it's usually because you did not remind me. (When parents are transitioning from doing everything for their children to training them in independence and accountability, this parent-blame is common).

Mom: [Calmly] Hmm. I see. So you only remember to take it when I remind you in the morning.

Sara: Yes! Exactly. Mom! You have to remind me.

Mom: [Calmly] I can see how you are used to me reminding you. That is my mistake. I can see how I am contributing to the problem. Hmm. Let me think for a minute. [Pauses]. I am looking into the future and I cannot see myself reminding you of everything important in your life. Can you imagine how funny it would be if you were to wait for me to remind you to take your report to work when you are an adult? That won't work. We need to train you in reminding yourself. So what can you do to remind yourself?

Sara: Hmm. I don't know. I always forget things.

Mom: I see. Right now you are relying on me to remind you. It will be tough in the beginning for you to remember yourself, but you need to learn to do it on your own. What would be helpful for you?

Sara: Maybe some kind of note or something! I don't know!

Mom: A note is a great idea actually! Well done. Where would you like to tape this note? What place would be best for you?

Sara: Hmm. Maybe my bedroom door? Or how about the garage door so I can see it on my way out?

Mom: Either one is fine with me. You choose which one you want to try. What would it say?

Sara: Take homework.

Mom: Sounds great!

Mom: So we are agreeing on the following: You are going to write a note that says, "Take Homework." You will post it on... Where do you want to post it, Sara?

Sara: The garage door.

Mom: Ok so you will post it on the garage door. And you understand that I won't be bringing your homework to school anymore. Right?

Sara: Yes. Right.

Mom: And Sara, if this does not work out, we will work together to find another solution.

Sara: OK, Mom.

Mom: Thank you, Sara. I really enjoyed solving this challenge with you.

Certainly this is not the only way to solve the forgotten homework challenge. There are as many solutions as there are creative children. Some parents may be wondering why mom doesn't come up with ways where she "helps" Sara with this challenge. For example, why can't Mom put the homework in her backpack every night? If you noticed in the discussion, the focus was on Sara coming up with and implementing the solution herself. Remember that the ultimate goal is to raise Sara to become responsible and independent, and this lesson needs to be taught early on. She needs to do it herself. No doubt, she will make mistakes along the way, but mistakes committed while young are not as grave as when one is older.

So how is Mom going to support Sara in this process of learning independence and responsibility? She will step aside, allowing Sara to think, and will continue to have problem-solving discussions until the issue is resolved. Someone may ask, "Where is the kindness?" The kindness is in being calm, matter of fact, without yelling, screaming, denigrating, or ridiculing. Where is the firmness? In following through even when the forgotten homework is very important for her grade.

Follow Through

If you say it, mean it. If you mean it, do it. Follow Through builds trust and confidence in the parent's words. I (Munira) had decided early on that if I made an agreement with my children, I would Follow Through. For example, when I said we would go shopping after school for project supplies, we would do it, even if I was tired. When I said, we would not go to a birthday party if homework wasn't completed, we would not go, even if the children begged. My children learned that I did not offer empty promises or proclamations. If you get into the habit of not following through, your child learns to tune you out, ignore your requests, and sometimes resist everything you say. When you Follow Through, you send the following messages:

- I mean what I say.
- I respect myself and my child.
- I am responsible for what I say.
- It's fine to be frustrated. We cannot have our way all the time.

When my (Noha) children were young, I would make a proclamation, only to doubt the wisdom of my decision. I wondered at the time if I should keep my word or admit to my children that I made a mistake and renege on my word. It was not easy. Most of the time, I Followed Through even when I knew I made a mistake. I wanted to ensure that my children knew that my word was solid. However, after following through a time or two in an area where I felt I had made the wrong decision, I would tell my children that I had thought about it some more and had changed my mind. More importantly, I worked hard to avoid making proclamations on the spur of the moment. I would tell my children, "I need to think about it and will get back to you." Now, as a therapist, every time I see a parent in my office whose child is not listening, I know immediately that the parent probably does not Follow Through, and we begin working on that.

Get a Life

Who are you? Is your identity limited to being a parent? Do you see yourself beyond your role as a parent? If your life revolves around being a parent primarily, then your sense of self will be closely tied to the successes and failures of your children. This is not a good formula by which to live. Simply put, your children have their own agendas for their lives. Your sense of self needs to be separate from your children's lives. Otherwise, as they enter adulthood, you will set yourself up for disappointment and heartache.

Some parents may be thinking, "But I want to stay home with my children! Of course my life is going to revolve around them! Of course I won't be able to see myself beyond my parenting role." Cherishing your position as a parent and valuing your role as a stay-at-home parent is a wonderful gift to bestow upon yourself and your children. However, when your life revolves solely around your children and you let go of personal interests and hobbies, you inevitably become over-involved in their lives and lose your sense of self. If you are a stay-at-home parent, we invite you to find interests and activities that go beyond your parenting role.

I (Noha) was blessed to be a stay-at-home mom. I am aware that this is not feasible for all parents, and I am grateful to Allah for blessing me with this gift. I cherished my time with my children. At the same time, I volunteered at my children's school, the mosque, and local organizations. I was also involved with my friends, took computer classes, and pursued various hobbies. My central role during those early years was my parenting role, but it was not my only identity. I invite you to find ways to express yourself outside of the box of parenting. The parenting role will eventually wind down. Model for your children a life of personal pursuit along with your commitments to your family. (See Attitudes of Gratitude, p. 307)

Grab All Box

This tool is a combination of Structure the Environment (p. 145) and Decide What You Will Do (p. 85). There will be situations when, in your struggle to maintain an organized household, your children will not follow through with house rules pertaining to picking up belongings and putting them away. So, instead of becoming frustrated, angry, and then yelling and screaming, establish the Grab All Box system. Simply agree on a cut-off time by which items must be put away. Any item that belongs to the child and is not put away before the cut-off time will be collected by the parent and put in the Grab All Box.

For the tool to be effective, the parent needs to be clear about what will happen to those items. Will the child be allowed to retrieve the items? Will the parent put the items away for a set time and then allow the child access? Will the items be donated after a certain time? There are many possibilities. What is important is that the family establishes a simple system that can be enforced and followed through.

Hugs When Upset or Not

What could be simpler than giving a child a hug? Even better, let your child know you need a hug. Asking for a hug may evoke a child's inborn desire to contribute. Sometimes a hug is all that is needed when a child is having a tantrum (toddler), feeling dejected when struggling with homework (elementary and older), or feeling upset because a friend is no longer a friend (high school and college).

A hug will not necessarily solve a problem except, possibly, with toddlers in the throes of a temper tantrum; and sometimes a child may not be ready to give or receive a hug. When both are ready to give and receive, a hug is a very powerful, immediate, non-verbal assertion of love and connection. Hugs, however, are not to be forced—even by parents. A simple, "Would a hug help you right now?" or simply opening your arms silently will indicate if your child is open to receiving a hug. This is especially important for teens whose view of the world is shifting. When children refuse to be hugged, allow them their space. Validate their feelings "I can see how upset you are" and invite them to find you if they change their mind and want that hug after all: "I will be in the kitchen if you change your mind."

When a child refuses to be hugged, it is easy for a parent to feel hurt. Parents may resort to thinking, "My son does not love me anymore!" or "How could she do this to me; doesn't she know how much I have sacrificed for her?" However, this kind of thinking could lead to further disconnection. Rather, understand that it's not about you. Respect that your child is upset at the moment and needs time to figure it out. Focus on remaining present and available for when you are needed, and this will depersonalize the rejection of a hug. More importantly, understanding this dynamic allows children to have the personal emotional space needed to deal with their feelings. This life skill is the seed of emotionally healthy adult relationships.

I Notice_____ Instead of Did You_____?

Nothing triggers a defensive response as much as attack and blame statements. Many times the choice of words evoke misperceptions and, in turn, generate negative reactions. A simple change of words can have a dramatic impact by creating an emotionally safe space to dialogue and focus on solutions. Using "I Notice…." mitigates unintentional attack and blame. Table 5.5 has examples of common phrases parents use and alternative ways using "I Notice:"

TABLE 5.5
Common phrases parents use and alternative ways using "I Notice"

Common Phrases	I Notice...
"Did you take out the trash as you promised?"	"I noticed that the trash bin is not at the curb."
"Did you stay up late last night as usual? Did you play video games again till 2 am?"	"I noticed when I woke up at 1 am last night that your light was on."
"Did you brush your teeth?"	"I noticed that you have not been to the bathroom yet."
"Is this the report card of someone who studies hard?"	"I noticed that this semester, you were spending more time on your computer playing games than studying."

Jobs

When children see their family as a "team," they realize that each team member plays an important role. Everyone has responsibilities; parents go to work, and children go to school. Jobs are an opportunity for each family member to contribute and feel a sense of belonging to the "team." The responsibility that goes with performing jobs also teaches children that their contribution matters, and they learn how to give rather than just take. Jobs begin with children as young as four years old with activities like setting the table for dinner and getting the mail. As children get older the jobs become more complex, like throwing out the trash, helping with laundry, washing dishes, etc.

My sons (Munira) have had jobs since they were four years old and the process of determining their jobs has continuously evolved. When they were seven and eight years old, they brainstormed the jobs they could do. They posted the list on a sheet of paper and checked them off daily as they completed them. When they were 12 & 13 years old, they negotiated which jobs they would each take and how often they would rotate duties. Needless to say, there were many complaints over the years about the chores and they sought ways of delaying or shirking their responsibilities. In those instances, we would have a Family Meeting (p. 96) to discuss the problem and come up with new solutions. Do not despair when children shy away from mundane housework. Remember that the responsibility of doing jobs is more important than the actual task being accomplished. My husband even renamed Jobs in our home to Contributions because it was a better descriptor of what they were doing. Revisiting the significance of Jobs with your children will keep the focus on the long-term values you are seeking to teach — responsibility and contribution. For each age group in Part III, you will find suggestions for jobs that are appropriate for that stage.

Know Who They Are, Not Where They Are

In the 1980s, a particular TV ad asked viewers the question, "It's 10 p.m.. Do you know where your children are?" At that time, my children (Noha) were still infants and toddlers, and I used to wonder, how do parents not know where their children are? I promised myself at that moment that I would always know where my children were. Time passed and my children grew into teenagers. Throughout those years, I began to realize how futile it was for me to assume that I would know what they were doing all the time. They tested me in many different ways, and I realized the hard truth: No matter how good a mom I was, I would not know everything about them. I was humbled. I am grateful to Allah that I learned that lesson early. Otherwise, my children and I would have suffered tremendously and hurt our relationship with one another.

This is why it is important that you know who your children are. This knowledge base is what will help you discern the early signs of trouble if it were to happen. Direct your energy and effort to know who your children are rather than just keeping tabs on their activities (physical and virtual). What you need is to Be There (p. 77), involved, engaged, listening, observing their patterns, making connections, and taking mental notes about all that you learn.

Letting Go

Letting Go is one of the most difficult tools to adopt. Paradoxically, Letting Go is necessary for your child. Letting Go is recognizing the limits of your control and choosing to hand over the reins of responsibility to the child. Since children vary in their temperaments, some children will force the Letting Go by fighting and rebelling. Others, who are by nature averse to confrontation and whose parents do not let go when the time is right, become passively dependent adults who have no voice.

Parents who understand that their job is to train and guide will also plan for the inevitable Letting Go by empowering their children, training them to be responsible and accountable, and being genuinely joyous when their children leave the nest. Children of such parents believe in their abilities to handle what comes their way. They also experience life without the burden of guilt and judgment.

Letting Go occurs in stages. It does not suddenly occur at the age of 18 when your child is legally an adult. Letting Go happens every time a parent provides the space for the child to be in charge of an area in life.

Examples of Letting Go.

- Allowing children to eat on their own even when they take a long time or make a mess.
- Expecting children to prepare their breakfast and lunch.
- Respecting how children want to do their science projects.
- Children doing their own laundry and ruining clothes in the process.
- High schoolers choosing their classes.
- Young adults deciding their college majors.
- Allowing children to make mistakes (and even to fail) and having faith in them to learn from these experiences with your loving support.

Limited Choices

This tool is used primarily with younger children. When toddlers begin to express their independence, their voice, their wishes, and say the word "NO," parents diffuse many situations through Limited Choices. Young children get overwhelmed quickly. In emotionally laden situations, offering them a couple of options directs their energy to make a decision which helps them contain their emotions. Typically as children grow older, Limited Choices loses its effectiveness as a daily tool. However, it remains an effective tool to be used infrequently with older children.

Tips for Limited Choices.

- Offer only what works for you.
- Be firm. If the child whines, simply say, "These are the options available. Which one works for you?"
- If the child suggests something else, respond calmly, "That is

not one of the options for today. Maybe another day."

Examples.

- "Would you like to have cereal or muffins?"
- "Would you like to wear the red or the blue shirt?"
- "Would you like to sit next to Ahmad or Zaid?"
- "Would you like to put on your shirt or your pants first?"
- "I can take you to the library on Tuesday at 3 p.m. or Wednesday at 5 p.m. Which time works best for you?"
- "We can have your friends over Friday after school for 2 hours or Saturday at 12 noon for 4 hours. What would you like to do?"

Listen

"Children are more likely to listen to you *after* they feel listened to" (Nelsen, 2006, p. 29). This is one of the cardinal principles of Positive Discipline. Life in the 21st Century is hectic. Parents are constantly on the go and sometimes it is a major effort to slow down and listen.

To use the Listening tool effectively, parents must pause and be present (pay full attention). Many times the parent does not need to respond. The child may simply need to share an idea that is important at that moment. However, repeating back to the child what was heard is an empowering experience. When parents listen, they send the message that what the child has to say is important, which in turns mean *the child* is important in their life. This is the seed of connection.

Listening without the need to respond becomes pivotal during the teen years. Practice listening to your teens without lecturing, moralizing, judging, condemning, or dismissing their ideas. Teens are extra sensitive to what their parents say. They sometimes misperceive a well-intentioned suggestion as suffocating control. Many times, parents will not like what teens share; but, in situations where there are no specific concerns, the parents are invited to refrain from sharing their moralizing thoughts. When teens feel safe sharing, they will feel connected to their parents and will continue to be transparent. When serious concerns arise, parents share their worries with as few words as possible and only after having listened and repeated back what they heard. Listening is not being passive. In some situations, after listening, a parent will need to establish a boundary or a limit with the teen using the Problem Solving tool (p. 134)

Logical Consequences

There is a very fine line between logical consequences and punishment. Many parents use punishments declaring that they are utilizing logical consequences. According to Jane Nelsen (2006), logical consequences are characterized by four criteria: related, respectful, reasonable, and helpful.

Any response by a parent that does not meet all four criteria is most likely a punishment. For example, Maryam has a difficult time controlling her anger. She has frequent intense meltdowns to the extent that she throws things around the house. Her parents, guided by a long-term parenting lens, established a logical consequence: when she is done with her meltdown, she has to go around the house and clean up whatever havoc has occurred. This is an example of a logical consequence. What transforms this consequence into a punishment would be any (or a combination) of the following:

- "I cannot believe you have done this again! What kind of a monster are you? You never learn!" Yelling, screaming, and labeling are disrespectful to you and your child.
- "Not only do you have to clean up your mess, but you will also be grounded from watching TV for this whole week." Grounding is not related to the situation.
- "You will clean up this mess, and you will clean up the messes of all of your siblings for the entire week." Cleaning up the messes of other siblings is unreasonable and unrelated.

One of my teens (Noha) struggled with waking up on time for school. For every tardy arrival or absence, I had the authority to excuse my teen. I noticed that over the span of a few weeks, I was excusing my teen frequently for what I believed was irresponsible time management. At first I was uncertain how to respond. I contemplated many options. Do I go into control mode (which is my default when I want things to change)? Do I fight with my teen every night about bedtime? Do I take on the responsibility of waking up my teen every day? Do I just continue excusing the child with no limits? What do I do? I was conflicted.

I had to calm down first, think about what is important, reflect on my limits, recognize the long-term goal, and then come up with a plan. After doing all this soul searching, I came up with the following conclusions:

First, from a long-term parenting point of view, my teen needed to be in charge of going to bed on time and waking up on time. In a couple of years, this child would be in college and will face the same problem. So there was no point charging in and forcing bedtime routines. By the time this challenge surfaced, my teen had gone through many years of following through with a bedtime routine. So the challenge was not related to lack of awareness or training. It was a challenge of a different sort. My teen was navigating adolescence, and for some reason bedtime routines became one of the areas where she used to assert independence. Understanding the developmental stage and knowing I had fulfilled my duty of early training, I realized it was time to let go of this challenge. I chose not to fight this battle.

Second, letting go of the battle is not the same as doing nothing. I have control over my actions. I can choose to set limits around the issue without the need to control what my teen is doing. Accordingly, I decided to limit the number of times I would excuse my teen due to tardiness or absence. We had a meeting and I used the Positive Discipline tool of I Notice…Instead of Did You (p. 108): "I have noticed that you are frequently late to school. In the last month, you were tardy three times and I excused you all 3 times." Then I said, "I have decided that I will excuse you three times per semester for tardiness or absence. Anything after the third excuse is your responsibility." I asked, "What are the consequences of unexcused tardiness or absences at your school?" My teen informed me it would be detention. I asked: "What is your understanding of what is going to happen with regard to your tardiness and absences from now on?" My teen was able to state back my limit, and we ended the conversation there.

What was critical following this conversation was Follow Through (p. 104). I made certain I would keep track of how many times I excused her, and I did not cave in and try to bail her out when detention became a reality. I maintained my limit.

Logical Consequences require the intervention of an adult while Natural Consequences are those that occur when an adult does not intervene. We invite you to use Logical Consequences infrequently because they don't necessarily solve the problem. The power lies in giving parents a plan for what to do when the challenge occurs again. Natural Consequences and Focusing on Solutions are more effective tools. For further understanding of the difference between Logical and Natural Consequences, refer to p. 125.

Message of Love

How do you express love? More importantly, do your children know that you love them? For American Muslims, the phrase "I love you," is a hallmark of our narrative and culture. I (Munira) heard messages of love from my parents daily. In our small rituals of saying, "I love you," hugging, and kissing when we left, arrived home, or when we went to bed.

Expressing the Message of Love is cultural. I (Noha) grew up in the Middle East. My family was not the verbal "I love you" type of family. However, I never doubted my parents' unfailing love for me and my siblings. Their love was clear in all they did for us: unwavering support, listening, encouragement, being there, etc. I knew that I was loved, and I did not need the words, "I love you," to experience it. However, raising my children in the U.S., I definitely used, "I love you," in addition to all the loving ways I absorbed from my parents.

Reflect on how you send the message of love to your children. There is no one specific way since love is expressed in words and actions. For further insights into the different ways of expressing love, check out Gary Chapman's book, *The Five Love Languages*.

Mirroring

Adults are mirrors for children. Whether parents or teachers, children see themselves through the eyes of the adults in their lives (Glasser, 1999). Mirroring is simply reflecting back to your children their emotions and behaviors. It is accomplished in every parent-child interaction. Two major areas where Mirroring is critical are:

> *1. Emotions.*
>
> "Belal, you seem to be sad. What happened?"
>
> "Zainab, you look so excited. I would love to know what you're excited about!"
>
> "Khaled, you look so upset. Anything I can do to help you feel better?"
>
> *2. Gifts & Strengths.*
>
> "Wow! *Masha Allah* (May God protect you) Adam, you finished the science project all by yourself and two days before the due date! This shows your organizational and planning skills."
>
> "*Jazaka Allahu khair* (May God reward you with goodness), Yusuf, for helping your aunt with her bags. That was very responsible and thoughtful of you."
>
> "Sara, I have noticed that when someone is feeling down or is alone, you make it a point to sit with them and talk to them. You are a natural at sensing the emotions of other people and at being empathic. Such an ability will carry you far in life."

Mirroring is critical because it draws the children's attention to what they don't see about themselves. This is one of the many gifts parents bestow upon their children. The more children know about themselves, the better equipped they are to deal with life. For example, when children are cognizant of their emotional reactions, they are empowered to make better decisions about how to contain their emotions. As the Chinese saying goes, "Control your emotions before they control you."

Mistakes are Opportunities for Learning

This tool is a mental reframing of the concept of mistakes. Ask yourself: How do you view mistakes? What messages did you receive as a child about mistakes? What types of messages are you sending your child? Children may construe the messages parents send to mean that they themselves are "bad" or "something is wrong with them." Such erroneous interpretations may lead to adults whose sense of self is entangled in shame and worthlessness. We invite you to become aware of the words and actions you use when responding to mistakes.

Take for example, the prophetic legacy in the story of the Bedouin who urinated in the Holy Mosque of Madina (p. 26). This story was an example of a mistake. Yet, how did the Prophet (pbuh), deal with it? Did he punish? Did he scold? Did he say, "How could you make such a stupid mistake in our holiest of places?" Did he say, "You are ignorant! You need to learn more about this religion." No. He did not react in any of these ways. Instead, he focused on solutions. He instructed his companions to pour water over the area to purify it and to teach the etiquette of the mosque. The mistake was an opportunity to teach, not an opportunity to shame and humiliate.

Children learn from mistakes when they are held accountable while their self-respect remains intact. I (Munira) shared this message with my children when they were three years old. When they made mistakes as toddlers, I would invite them to think of ways to fix the problem and afterward had them share what they learned from their mistakes. As my children got older, they shared with me their mistakes without fear and focused on solutions immediately. I avoided responding with anger or shame while actively listening to them and would offer suggestions when they struggled with finding solutions. Many times there was nothing they could do to repair a situation. In those instances, I mirrored their feelings of frustration, allowed Natural Consequences to take their course, and focused on what they learned from the experience.

For example, my 11-year-old was taking an online course and one evening completely forgot to attend his class. He was upset because he had prepared for the class but got distracted with a television program. Class rules mandated that he would lose the participation grade for that session, which could affect his overall grade. He was upset for forgetting the class as he disliked being irresponsible. I mirrored his feelings and invited him to think of what he could do differently to prevent this problem in the future. He thought of setting an alarm on his computer as a reminder. He also decided to create a print-out above his desk with the times of the class. I also suggested that he email his teacher apologizing for missing the class as a display of taking personal responsibility for his mistake. Even though he lost points toward his grade, he learned multiple life lessons in just that one experience: time management, follow-through on commitments, containing disappointment, and owning personal responsibility. Figure 5.1 illustrates the relationship between the three major parenting styles and the messages sent about mistakes

TABLE 5.6
Responding to Mistakes

Responses to mistakes that inoculate perfectionism, helplessness, or shame, and paralyzing guilt	Responses to mistakes that inoculate accountability, responsibility, critical thinking, and problem-solving skills
"I cannot believe you broke the vase! You are so clumsy!"	"Khair insha Allah (May God Send you what is good). It was meant to be. Please clean it up."
"What is wrong with you? How can you make such a stupid mistake on your test?"	"Hmmm. You know the material well, I am certain of that. I wonder what happened for you to make this mistake."
"You forgot your wallet at the park! I cannot believe how irresponsible you are!"	"Khair insha Allah (May God Send you what is good). You will need to contact the bank to stop all your cards. I suggest you do this immediately."
"You are not allowed to make any mistakes on your tests/homework!"	"Simply focus on studying and doing your best."
"You shamed me in front of your uncle. How could you do this to me!"	"I was embarrassed by what you did. What could you do to make amends?"

Mutual Respect

Respect is reciprocal. The foundation for respect between the parent and child is built from infancy. Let's step into the shoes of your toddler and experience what a typical day may feel like. Aliya is two years old and she is unexpectedly awoken in the morning by Mom with a shirt suddenly pulled over her head to get her dressed. Aliya is ushered into the kitchen where Dad has made her a bowl of cereal and placed into her high chair. While Aliya is eating, Mom and Dad are discussing how her toilet training is going. Aliya is focused on her cereal floating in the milk. She notices how they keep floating to the top when she pushes them down. Mom interrupts her by cleaning her mouth with a wet washcloth. Aliya starts to whine. Mom says, "You are

FIGURE 5.1

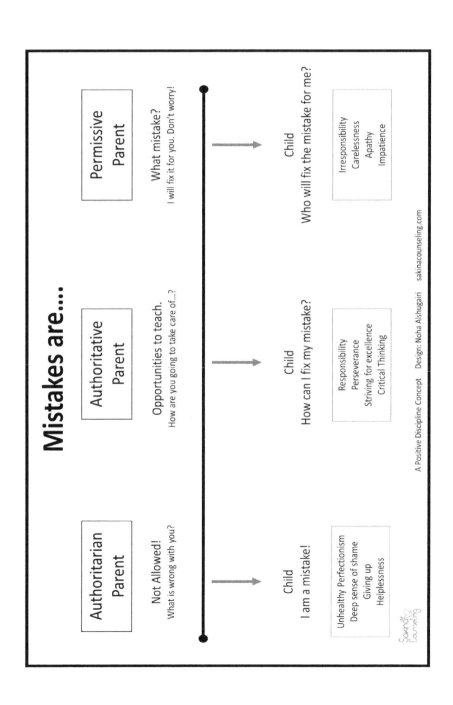

Mistakes are...

Authoritarian Parent

Authoritative Parent

Permissive Parent

Not Allowed!
What is wrong with you?

Opportunities to teach.
How are you going to take care of...?

What mistake?
I will fix it for you. Don't worry!

Child
I am a mistake!

Child
How can I fix my mistake?

Child
Who will fix the mistake for me?

Unhealthy Perfectionism
Deep sense of shame
Giving up
Helplessness

Responsibility
Perseverance
Striving for excellence
Critical Thinking

Irresponsibility
Carelessness
Apathy
Impatience

A Positive Discipline Concept   Design: Noha Alshugairi   sakinacounseling.com

Sakina Counseling

only playing with your food. You must be done." She removes her from the high chair. Dad swoops Aliya up and takes her to the car. They are running late for daycare. They arrive at daycare, and the caregivers start kissing and tickling her. They are so excited to see her. She joins the other kids but starts crying because another toddler in the class bumps into her by accident. The caregivers tell her, "You are okay. It doesn't hurt." Aliya finds a set of blocks and starts intently building with them. The caregiver comes over and quickly cleans up the blocks, tells her it is time for "circle time," and ushers her to the carpet. This is Aliya's day, and it is only 9:00 a.m.

Now imagine a similar scenario, but as an adult. You are awoken by your spouse abruptly and handed an outfit to wear for the day. You arrive in the kitchen to a plate of pancakes prepared for you. You weren't really feeling like pancakes this morning, but you go ahead and eat them. Your spouse is on the phone with a friend telling them all about the difficult day you had at work yesterday. While you are eating, you think some fresh strawberries on the pancakes would be a delicious topping. As you eat, your spouse tells you that you just spilled some syrup on your shirt and dabs a washcloth on you. You get up to find the strawberries. You spend five minutes looking for them but can't seem to find them. When you go back to sit down, your plate is gone because your spouse thought you were done. You are running late for work, so your spouse gathers your belongings and ushers you out the door. You are handed your lunch bag and a cup of coffee. You get to work and your colleagues bombard you with work requests. You sit at your desk and find someone left crumbs on your desk. Your boss tells you, "It's okay, get over it."

You start focusing on your work when your boss suddenly comes over and drops a new project on your desk. You have a meeting in the conference room and you need to be there now. This is the start of your day.

Experiencing this type of day would probably make you feel upset, frustrated, mad, startled, misunderstood, and confused. Yet, it may be the experience that your infant/toddler has every morning. What is missing throughout both of the above vignettes is respect. Adults tend to expect and demand respect from others, but they forget to show respect to their children. That is unfortunate, as parenting grounded in respect from the start leads to respectful relationships.

Replaying the vignette above looks as follows: Before putting a shirt on Aliya, mom lets her know she is helping her get dressed. Dad offers Aliya Limited Choices (p. 112), "Would you like cereal or eggs?" Both parents include Aliya in the conversation. They speak with her—not about her. Mom asks, "How is the toilet training going? Are we going to give it a try again today?" When Mom and Dad observe Aliya concentrating on something, they keep interruptions to a minimum. Mom inquires if Aliya is done eating and respects her response. When Aliya is done eating, Mom hands her a napkin. When Aliya struggles with transitions, both parents Mirror (p. 118) her feelings: "You are frustrated, hurt, in pain, etc." Mom and Dad also help Aliya transition from activities by following the posted Routine (p. 137) chart and reminding her of how much time remains before the next activity. Imagine how differently Aliya feels by the time she gets to school. When you show your children respect, they feel capable, content, and learn to treat you with respect.

Natural Consequences

Natural Consequences are consequences that take place when adults do not interfere. It is unfortunate that parents withhold this wonderful teaching tool in the name of love. Children learn best (just as adults do) from going through life experiences, both good and bad. My father (Noha) used to share an Arabic proverb whenever someone learned from experience: "Everyone learns best from their own pockets." As a parent, my father's voice would reverberate in my head with this simple proverb whenever my children chose to dismiss my warnings and learned the hard way from their own experiences. With time they came to respect and heed my concerns. Needless to say, I felt relief and validation whenever it happened.

TABLE 5.8
Examples of Natural Consequences

Situation	Natural Consequence
It's cold outside. A child leave the house without a jacket.	The child feels cold.
A child forgets lunch at home.	The child feels hungry.
A child forgets water bottle at home.	The child feels thirsty after a game.

Natural Consequences are simply parents stepping out of the way and allowing children to face the ramifications of their actions. Many parents have a difficult time with this tool because they love their children so much. They feel that if "something bad happens," the parent is abdicating responsibility. If a parent's focus is on the short-term, it would appear to be a foregoing of responsibility. However, with a long-term parenting lens, giving children space to experience life is a stepping stone toward becoming a responsible adult.

The ramifications of suppressing Natural Consequences become clear when children become adults. Unfortunately, when children are repeatedly told how to feel—dismissing their own body signals (hunger, thirst, cold, anxiety, fear, etc.), they look for others to fix their emotions for them. This is the core dynamic in addictions. When children learn to rely on their parents to bail them out every time there is a need, they do not develop the capacity of facing life's problems with critical thinking and responsibility. When will they learn that it's up to them to fix their problems? The lessons learned early in life are easier to deal with than the lessons learned later in life. Allow your child to deal with the consequences of a forgotten homework assignment in preparation for the larger responsibilities of life: work deadlines, carrying a passport to travel, paying bills on time, praying on time, etc.

What follows is a demonstration of how to utilize Natural Consequences with a common complaint by parents: cold weather and jackets. In a similar fashion, Natural Consequences can be applied with other issues. Notice as well the other Positive Discipline tools utilized: Take Time for Training (p. 147), Curiosity Questions (p. 82), and Decide What You Will Do (p. 85).

- When children are very young (under three years of age), the parent will be responsible for getting their jackets.
- At 3 & 4 years of age: Train the child to get the jacket. Hang the jacket at the child's level so it can be easily reached. As you are leaving the house, ask your child to get the jacket.
- Over 4 years old: A parent simply says, "It's cold outside. I am taking my jacket. Would you like to take your jacket with

you?" If the child says yes—great! If the child says no, the parent can ask, "What would happen if you don't have your jacket with you and you feel cold?" If the child insists on not taking the jacket, the parent says: "You have decided not to take your jacket. So, if you feel cold because you don't have your jacket, I will expect you to refrain from complaining since this is your choice. I will have no solution to help you at that point. Is this clear? What did I say?"

• In the event that the child leaves without the jacket and the parent notices the child is feeling cold, the parent must refrain from saying: "I told you so." Instead, show empathy by saying: "It seems you were not expecting it to be this cold. I have a hunch you have learned a lot from this experience."

• As the child grows older, the parent makes the statement that the responsibility of deciding whether to take a jacket or not is the child's and that the parent will no longer be reminding the child. The parent may choose to say instead, "It's cold outside and I am going to take a jacket."

Many parents object when invited to shift the jacket responsibility to their children, "But my child will get sick! And I end up having to take care of them. So this is why I have to continue reminding them." We invite you to think long-term. Ask yourself: "When will my children learn if I don't hand over the responsibility to them?" Whatever age you have in mind, remember that, ultimately, things learned at a young age are internalized more deeply than those learned later in life. Keep in mind that if your children don't make the connection between feeling cold and choosing to bring their jackets, they are not learning cause and effect. They are rather internalizing the expectation for their parents to tell them what to do. More worrisome is when children blame parents for what is occurring in their own lives because of such dependency.

One clarification is necessary here. Natural Consequences are not to be used in situations where there is real danger. The safety of children must be ensured. For example, allowing toddlers to run into the street so they can learn via Natural Consequences is ludicrous. Having no limits on junk food to teach through Natural Consequences is also not wise. Someone may say, "How about not wearing a jacket and getting a cold? This is a safety threat." The difference between getting a cold and being hit by a car is that one may or may not occur, while the other is a certainty. In addition, getting a cold is not life threatening even if it occurs. Accordingly, brace yourself to watch your children struggle and grant them the gift of learning from their life experiences. Natural Consequences are an effective and empowering strategy as long as they are framed in safety. Charge on!

One Word /Ten Words or Less

If the onslaught of lectures utilized by parents were recorded, parents would be shocked by how frequent and ineffective these lectures are. Children tune parents out very quickly when parents do all the talking. A more effective approach is the tool One Word/Ten Words or Less. Basically it's shifting to less verbiage.

One Word is used when a situation was discussed beforehand, and the One Word is a clear indication of the request. For example, during a Family Meeting (p. 96) in which jobs were discussed, a child chose to do the dishes after dinner. If the parent comes into the kitchen, and notices that the child has still not done the dishes, the parent may simply say, "Dishes," in this situation. This should be enough to give the child the message. There is no need to repeat the agreement or to lament the irresponsible behavior.

Examples of One Word.

- "Backpack." When it's thrown in the middle of the hallway.
- "Plate." When child leaves plate on the table after eating.
- "Lunch." When child has forgotten lunch in the kitchen.
- "Story." When parent is heading to child's room for story time.

Ten Words or Less is used in situations when parents need to discuss an issue. The parent makes a statement of ten words or less and then waits for a response or reaction from the child. This way, the parent breaks down the discussion into small bits, which keeps the child engaged and tuned into the discussion; this is a much more effective strategy for getting children to talk and express themselves.

Examples of Ten Words or Less.

- "You're upset because Malak doesn't want to play with you."
- "After you pick up your toys, we will read the story."
- "I noticed last week that you struggled to wake up."
- "The school left a message saying you were tardy today."
- "My credit card statement shows a charge for a download."
- "Where did you spend all of your allowance this month?"

Pay Attention

Life nowadays is certainly complex. While valiantly trying to get through their responsibilities, parents may tune out their children in order to get things done. This is the story of every parent at one time or another. Many times, it happens unconsciously, especially if the parent believes that the child is talking about something "irrelevant."

I (Noha) really struggled with Paying Attention. I thought that as long as my children were not saying something "important," I could just continue doing what I was doing and simply listen (i.e. tune them out) until they were done. However, children are smart. My children knew when I was really listening or distracted by my tasks. I invite you to Pay Attention the next time your child speaks about something "irrelevant." Take a few minutes to actively stop what you are doing, look your child in the eye, and simply listen. I guarantee that your child's need for your attention won't last for more than ten minutes at a time. However, the benefit of such dedicated attention is immeasurable. It carries over in your children's beliefs about their place in your life.

Finally, in a world where everyone has a tablet or smartphone, parents need to be conscious about how they are spending time at home. Are you distracted by your devices from really being present with your children? Are your children speaking to your back because you are focusing on your screen? Paying Attention is about being present with your children without the distractions of electronics, tasks, or friends. It's about recognizing that their presence in your life is actually short. So, cherish the moments when they seek you.

Positive Time-Out

Time-out as a discipline tool has been used extensively by parents and teachers for years. Generally, it is used as a punitive strategy to manipulate behavior. When it was introduced as an alternative to spanking and other physical punishments, it was hailed as a step forward. Certainly, compared to earlier harsh discipline methods, it was indeed progress. Positive Time-out is another step forward from the traditional "time-out."

In traditional "time-out," the child is sent to a spot for isolation and is told not to leave that spot until granted permission. Some adults call it the "thinking place" where children are supposed to think about what they did and the consequences of their actions. The problem with this traditional time-out is that it is a fully authoritarian discipline style (p. 31). There is no focus on solving the actual problem; rather, the time-out serves as a way for the adult to control the child's behavior. In many situations, the child rebels against the time-out by crying, yelling, screaming, and refusing to go. Sometimes, parents, in their frustration and helplessness, drag their children to their rooms and close the door. I (Noha) was one of those parents. I wish I knew about Positive Discipline at that time.

Positive Time-out is a dynamically different approach. Parent and child design a spot in the home that will be used as a self-soothing place. This is key. The Positive Time-out spot is not a punitive place. It's a place of calm and serenity for anyone that is having a difficult time with their emotions (sadness, irritation, anger, helplessness, confusion, etc.). Parent and child collaboratively brainstorm ideas for what to call the spot and what items to include to create a space of peace.

Recommendations for Positive Time-out space.

• Soft blanket.

• Teddy bears.

• Pillows.

• Books.

• Squishy ball.

• Puzzles.

• Board games.

• Blocks.

• Prayer beads.

• Prayer rug.

• Picture books.

• Coloring books.

After designing the area together, the parent explains to the child that this spot will be used by anyone feeling emotionally agitated. In some families, each family member creates his or her own personal time-out space. No one will be forced to go to the Positive Time-out. Family members are invited to go there "Would it help you to go to the Positive Time-out?" or they can choose to go there on their own. Also, the decision to leave the area lies with the person who is agitated and engaged in self-soothing. No parental permission is required to go or to leave.

Here is an example of how to use a Positive Time-out with Khaled who is four years old. In the last family meeting, the idea of Positive Time-out was introduced. Family members worked together deciding where and what to have in the space. Khaled was excited about the idea. However, one afternoon he throws a tantrum in response to Mom saying, "It's not time to play outside." Mom calmly crouches down to Khaled's level and says, "I can see how upset you are because we are not going outside right now. Would it help you to go to the feel-good place right now?" Khaled may say, "Yes," and goes there to calm down. In this situation, Khaled is beginning to depend on himself for self-regulation. He may conversely say, "NO! I don't want to!" At this point, Mom gently pats him and asks, "Would it help if I went with you?" If Khaled says, "Yes," they go together to the feel-good place until he calms down. Mom does not engage in lecturing, explaining, or defending. Instead, she simply focuses on Mirroring (p. 118) how Khaled is feeling and directing his attention to how he is going to calm down. If Khaled says, "No! I don't want to go to the stupid…" Mom simply follows the steps for dealing with tantrums (p. 162).

The Positive Time-out is used at an age when a child is able to make and verbalize decisions—usually between the age of two and three years old. Some parents begin using a Positive Time-out earlier by modeling the tool for their children. A parent can hold the non-verbal child's hand as the child is crying and guide the child to the Positive Time-out place while saying, "I can see how upset you are. Let's go to… so you can calm down." Once the child has calmed down, the parent reflects that and then directs the child's attention to what needs to happen next. Parents can also choose to take a Positive Time-out themselves when they need to calm down so that a situation does not escalate. In these situations, the parent models to the child how to take responsibility for one's own emotions by calming down before engaging further with others.

The goal is to create a place to self-soothe. Therefore, it is critical to avoid items that can fuel emotional agitation and are not conducive to establishing healthy self-soothing habits. Avoid placing electronics such as devices for watching TV or playing video games. If children do not learn early in life to sit with their negative emotions and self-soothe effectively, these children may be prone to addictive behavior as adults. In my office (Noha), I have observed clients who engage in destructive addictive behaviors (drugs, pornography, unhealthy relationships, etc.). They are clients who, as children, did not learn how to self-soothe effectively. These clients learned to suppress their negative emotions. They learned to distract from overwhelming emotional distress via unhealthy habits. When these unhealthy habits became their way of dealing with emotional pain, these clients lost the opportunity to learn emotional resiliency. Give your children the gift of self-soothing.

Problem Solving

This tool is used when the parent wishes to find a solution for a noticeable pattern of disruptive behavior. First, it is important that parents pick their battles. Choosing which battle to tackle will depend on the child, what other issues are coinciding, the family situation, and the parent's ability to enforce and follow through. Only when parents feel they are ready to improve a situation should they use the following procedure to solve problems:

- Let the child know in advance that you both are going to have a meeting, and agree on the day and time.
- Begin the meeting by stating, "I have noticed…" (p. 108) and "I feel…" (p. 87).

- Invite the child to repeat what you have said.

- Allow the child to respond and acknowledge the child's feelings.

- After all points about the issue have been voiced, the parent states, "We are going to brainstorm solutions to this problem. What solutions would you suggest for this issue?"

- Write down all the solutions you and your child can think of.

- Avoid explaining why any one solution may not work.

- After all solutions have been listed, begin eliminating solutions that are totally unacceptable by either one of you.

- Avoid the trap of attempting to coerce or convince your child of one of your solutions.

- Continue brainstorming ideas about how to solve the problem until you come to a solution that works for both of you.

Here is an example: Mom observed that her 13-year-old son, Bilal, is refusing to have dinner with them, and when he does come to the table, he is sulking and irritable. She does not know what has changed. She asks Bilal for a time to sit and discuss the dinner problem. Here is how she facilitated the Problem Solving:

Mom: I am not sure what is going on. Here is what I have noticed: when I have called you to dinner, over the last couple of weeks, you either refused to come or you are upset when you do come. So what is going on?

Bilal: Oh, Mom, dinner time always interrupts my video game. So when you call me and I am in the middle of my game, I don't want to come.

Mom: So the main reason we're having a problem is because I interrupt your video game?

Bilal: Yes. I have to finish my game before I am interrupted.

Mom: So help me understand. Why can't you simply pause the game, eat dinner, and then resume playing?

Bilal: Mom! I can't pause the game!

Mom: What do you mean you cannot pause the game?

Bilal: Basically, in strategy games, one has to reach a certain point in the game before you can exit or pause. Otherwise, you lose what you have gained.

Mom: Hmm. I did not know that. So what are we going to do? It's really important for us to have dinner together. I also understand that you need to have your uninterrupted video game time. So how are we going to reconcile this issue? Let's brainstorm solutions.

Bilal: Well, we can just delay dinner till I finish my video game.

Mom: Ok that is one solution for now. I suggest that you do your video game time after dinner. What else can we do?

Bilal: If I know when dinner is going to be, I can plan my schedule so I am done with my game before you call me to dinner.

Mom: Oh wow! I can see how our unpredictable dinner time is contributing to this problem. OK. So far we have three solutions: delay dinner, play after dinner, or let you know when dinner will be. Delaying dinner doesn't work for me. I can let you know when dinner is going to be or you can delay playing till after dinner. What do you think?

Bilal: Delaying my game till after dinner doesn't work for me because I like to focus on my work after dinner. But I like the idea of you letting me know when dinner will be.

Mom: Great! I will do that.

Sometimes, a Problem Solving session does not lead to a suitable solution. When that is the case, it's helpful to postpone further discussion to another time, or agree to try one of the discussed solutions for a week and reevaluate the situation in the next Family Meeting (p. 96). As a last resort, sometimes parents will need to Decide What They Will Do (p. 85). Some parents wonder why bother with the long process of Problem Solving and why not just use the Decide What You Will Do tool from the beginning. While parents will use various parenting tools, it is critical to practice using the Problem Solving tool early to train both the child and the parent in its effectiveness. Eventually it will become the primary tool used with teens. When the Problem Solving tool is used frequently, it cultivates the following:

- Mutual respect.
- Critical thinking skills.
- Insight into what is going on with the child.
- Better communication and connection.
- The sense that "we are one team, working together."
- A process of give and take.
- Understanding that others have different priorities or understandings.

Routines

Routines are an undervalued parenting tool because of today's "24/7 always-on" lifestyle. Life routines that were necessary at one point in human history due to the limitations of daylight are no longer in place. Electricity extends every day to the next dawn. The Internet keeps people connected to one another, work, and seamless online markets. Technology's instant connection allows many parents to live their lives minute by minute, deciding what to do next at the spur of the moment.

For some parents, Routines are a natural part of their day because this is how they live their lives. Such parents automatically create and maintain Routines with their children. For other parents, Routines destroy the novelty of life and the thrill of spontaneity. This group of parents typically rejects the concept of Routines until they understand their value. Establishing a Routine is typically a challenge for first-time parents, because life no longer revolves around the parents' plans but, rather, around the newborn.

Routines are an excellent way to Structure the Environment (p. 145), empowering parents to control situations in a respectful manner. They are most critical at transition times during the day: morning, bedtime, after school, and mealtime. Routines are crucial to the healthy development of children because they carry inherent messages. They ingrain in children a sense of safety and security. They internalize the beliefs that "the world is a safe and predictable place" and "adults are dependable and trustworthy." The power of Routines lies in planning ahead, appreciating the time spent on mundane activities, reducing arguments, and anticipating what comes next. Certainly none of these values will be achieved without Follow Through (p. 104).

Tips for daily Routines.

- Have a consistent wake-up time Monday through Friday.
- Pick out clothes the night before.
- Prepare lunch the night before.
- Have backpack by the door or in the car the night before.
- Be clear on what options are available for breakfast.
- Get into the habit of having children prepare their own

breakfast when they are old enough (4 years and above).

- Establish a rule of no TV in the morning.
- Establish limits on TV, video games and phones after school.
- Have dinner at a regular time every day.
- Establish a quiet time (for the whole family, including yourself) in the afternoon when homework is done.
- If dinner is late, establish a time for snack. Be clear about what is allowed as a snack.
- Have a quiet activity (so children can wind down) just before bedtime. Some families do baths followed by story time and lights off.
- Avoid associating any rewards or punishments with Routines.

TABLE 5.9
Example of Routine chart for elementary-aged child

Time	Activity
6:00 A.M.	Wake up, make *wudu* (ablution), pray *fajr* (early morning prayers)
6:20 A.M.	Wash face, brush teeth and hair, get dressed
6:45 A.M.	Have breakfast
7:10 A.M.	Grab backpack, lunch, and get into the car
7:20 A.M.	Leave for school
3:00 P.M.	Come home from school, make *wudu* (ablution) and pray
3:20 P.M.	Have a snack
3:45 P.M.	Begin homework—when done, go play
6:00 P.M.	Dinner with family: Eat, help with clean up
7:00 P.M.	TV or video game time (if homework is all finished)
7:30 P.M.	Take a shower and brush teeth
7:45 P.M.	Reading time
8:15 P.M.	Snuggle time with Mom or Dad
8:30 P.M.	Lights out

In the beginning, following through with Routines means the parent will follow the Routine without expecting children to follow it independently. For example, Mom and Rana created the Routine chart above. The agreed upon Routine is on a chart hanging in Rana's room. In the morning Rana prayed *fajr* (morning prayer) and Mom observes Rana playing with blocks. As a Follow Through Mom approaches Rana and asks, "What does your Routine chart say you need to be doing right now?" If Rana responds with, "I don't know. I forgot," Mom responds, "I will wait for you to go check the chart and tell me." At this point, Mom actually stands at the door quietly waiting until Rana gets up and checks the chart. The Routine chart becomes "the boss," and Mom avoids commanding and demanding.

The earlier parents use Routines, the less resistance they will encounter. For older children who have not yet incorporated Routines, parents are encouraged to establish consistent Routines in areas directly under parental control (e.g. dinner time and Wi-Fi cut off times). Implementing Routines is not a battle to be fought during teen years. Start early!

Say NO, Use Sparingly

In Islam, everything is *halal* (acceptable) except for what is clearly and distinctly *haram* (forbidden). Islam in fact, is a religion of "Yes," despite the common misperception that it's not. We invite you to write down all the *haram* rulings in Islam, and you will be pleasantly surprised to see that the list is very short indeed. Unfortunately, the cultural interpretations of Islam expand the forbidden circle to the point where many children automatically associate Allah with Hell instead of Heaven. Many young American Muslims bemoan the fact that the Muslim community focuses on the *No* of Islam rather than the Love of Allah. Regrettably, many Muslims are so turned off by this restrictive and suffocating view of the faith that they struggle in their relationship with Allah. While some undergo a major reevaluation of Islam before they connect well with Allah, others don't find their way back to Islam. We invite you to turn the tide. Let's teach Islam of the Loving Allah rather than Islam of the Wrathful Allah.

When parents approach discipline, they can apply the same rule that Allah has utilized. Use "No" sparingly and only when necessary. "No" is an important word that is communicated through words and actions. Since we live together in a community, limits are necessary in life. There is nothing such as limitless freedom. However, when children constantly hear "No" from parents, the word loses its effectiveness. Children won't know when something is actually critical and must be avoided. They will begin to question and resist every time parents say, "No." Conversely, parents who never say "No," send the message, "Life will go according to what you (child) want." Children who have not learned to respect reasonable limits may become entitled, disrespectful, contemptuous, selfish, and demanding.

Examples of using "No."

- "Can I just have one piece of candy? Only today!" "No."
- "No. Sorry, honey. I can't buy this toy because it is more than $20 and we can't afford it."
- "I know you would like to have fast food every day. However, we can't do that for two reasons: We can't afford it and it's not healthy."

In situations where the child is aware of the rules, a simple "No" without any other add-on statements is best. Even when the child questions or whines, simply repeating "No" calmly is most effective.

Special Time

This tool is about carving out one-on-one time on a weekly basis with each of your children. Special Time does not need to be long. A good suggestion is 20 minutes per week per child.

Criteria for Special Time.

- Consistent: same day and time.
- Parent establishes a monetary limit.
- Child decides how to spend that time within the framework established by parent.
- The time is not used for lecturing, nagging, or interrogating the child.
- Parent focuses on listening and enjoying their time together.

In times of crisis and difficult challenges, Special Time becomes paramount in repairing the parent-child relationship. Some families have difficulty carving out time for each child in the family on a weekly basis, and they opt instead to do monthly or bimonthly Special Time. Some parents get creative and use "late-start school days," as an opportunity to connect one-on-one with the child attending school that day.

I (Noha) personally could not implement this tool. *Alhamdu Lillah* (all praise to God) with four children and a tendency to be involved in many things at the same time, I did not prioritize this tool. However, my unique way of doing Special Time was to drop everything, Be There (p. 77), and listen when my children approached me. Special Time in my home occurred spontaneously depending on the unique needs of each child. Sometimes it was working with my child on a project for school. Sometimes it was attending a school function where my child was performing or going on a field trip as a chaperone. Sometimes it was nurturing my child's own unique personal interests. If a parent is present with open eyes and ears, Special Time opportunities will happen.

Statement of Fact*

Many parents, in their efforts to be nice and kind, use questions like, "Would you like to go home now? Don't you think you've played enough?" What is needed is a Statement of Fact, "We will leave in 5 minutes. Get ready, please." Other parents, hoping to be kind and nice, may state what is going to happen, but do it timidly and hesitantly and then follow it up with a question about how the child feels or thinks. "I know you want to play more but Dad called, and we need to leave. What do you think?" The problem with these types of exchanges is that they are begging for a "No" response. Typically, parents are caught off guard because they were simply attempting to avoid commands. Using questions when communicating with children about the areas that are under their control is useful. However, when the child has no say in a situation, a Statement of Fact is necessary.

For example, Mom needs to stop by the store after picking up Ibrahim. Mom knows that Ibrahim does not like going to the store, and she usually accommodates that. However, today the schedule is tight. A parent that asks questions would say: "Is it OK if we go to the store because I need to pick up some milk?" The question opens the door for Ibrahim to say, "No." A parent using Statement of Fact would say, "Just to give you a heads up, I need to pick up milk from the store. It won't take long *insha Allah*

(God willing)." If Ibrahim whines and nags, Mom stays firm, acknowledges his feelings, and directs his energy toward a solution, "Yes, I know you don't like that. Unfortunately I need to go today. What would be helpful for you while you are waiting? Would you like to come in with me or stay in the car?" (This is assuming Ibrahim is old enough to be left alone in the car.)

Be aware of the guilt trap. Some parents erroneously believe that they are responsible for their children's happiness. In situations where children have no choice, these parents compensate by apologizing and placating. For example, Mom may offer Ibrahim a treat to alleviate his "suffering." Children raised believing that their parents are responsible for their happiness develop a strong sense of entitlement. They believe that others owe them happiness. Tragically, such children lack the ability to own personal responsibility for their lives. In adulthood they fail to become independent financially, emotionally, and physically.

The Statement of Fact tool is especially powerful with children who have strong personalities. These children are vocal in expressing their likes and dislikes and are in a constant tug of war with their parents. There are frequently tense conversations about what is going to happen. I (Noha) remember the first time I used this tool with one of my children. I distinctly remember feeling apprehensive, expecting the usual antagonism and questioning from my child. Imagine my shock when my child did not react as usual. I was flabbergasted! I could not believe my ears nor my eyes when my child simply listened and walked away.

Tips for using Statement of Fact.

- Use it in areas that are under your direct control.
- Avoid sounding timid or hesitant. Use a calm firm voice.
- Avoid asking how the child feels about it.
- If the child whines or nags, acknowledge feelings and ask what you can do to help ease the situation.
- Avoid falling into the guilt trap. It's fine if your child is unhappy or frustrated over the situation.

Structuring the Environment*

Modifying the environment, physical and virtual, is a powerful parental tool that reduces family battles with minimal fuss.

Examples of Structuring the Environment.

- Storing tempting food items (candy, chocolate, etc.) out of sight and out of reach.
- Securing cupboards or potentially dangerous (toxic substance, stairs, toilets, etc.) areas via child safety gadgets.
- Establishing quiet and organized home zones for studying.
- Limiting electronics to the family room.
- Regulating Internet time (via router controls).
- Blocking access to inappropriate online material.

While this tool is mainly used to mitigate challenges, it is also used to empower. For example, toddlers who gain a sense of autonomy and confidence when allowed to explore their environment can be allowed easy access to plastic containers at the bottom of a kitchen cabinet. For preschoolers who need to feel independent and capable, cereal boxes and small milk containers can be placed at their level. With children in elementary school, install hooks and shelves for organizing their belongings. Allow teens to have an electric grill on hand to cook their own food.

Supervision

This tool takes on different forms as the child goes through the various stages of childhood. When the child is an infant, parental supervision is responding to cues indicating hunger, tiredness, diaper change, etc. As the child becomes mobile, supervision expands to include preventing harm and danger by Structuring the Environment (see above).

As the child becomes more independent, the supervisory role of the parent becomes one of monitoring and less contingent on physical presence. The parent begins transferring some of the responsibility to the child while remaining close at hand to help as needed. For example, establishing the rule that all electronic devices are to be used in the family room (and not in the bedrooms) is a powerful way to allow the parent to monitor the use of the Internet. Another example of supervision is knowing the child's schedule ahead of time and expecting the child to inform the parent when that schedule changes for any reason.

Supervision and monitoring are not the same as spying on children behind their backs. Parents do not need to know everything that goes on in their children's lives. There will be things that children will hide from their parents, and this is normal. Don't panic. Focus on having a trusting relationship with your children, and they will approach you if they need you. Spying and demanding to know everything will backfire and send your children running away from you. Focus instead on saying to your children, "I love you. I want you to know that if you are ever in trouble, please contact me. I promise to help you without getting very angry."

Take Time for Training

Establishing new habits takes time. When you are teaching your child a new skill, establishing a new rule, or following a new routine, give yourself and your child enough time for the "new" to be incorporated into your lives. Giving it time also means knowing that you need to be there alongside your child as the "new" is learned. Sometimes parents expect that once they establish a new rule, a child will obey it immediately and the parent's job is done. If only it were that simple!

Few parents think about parenting as being a methodical process—one that involves teaching children a skill or a habit. Most parents simply expect children to implement what they are taught immediately. Learning something new is a process.

Phases to learning something new.

1. Parent demonstrates how it's done.
2. Parent and child practice it together with the adult taking the lead.
3. Parent and child practice it together with the child taking the lead.
4. Child practices it alone.

Tips to effectively train a child.

• Model what you are teaching in your own life.
• Break the task into small pieces.
• Move on to the next small piece once you see the child has

gained some mastery.

- Focus on teaching one new thing at a time. Avoid being excited about teaching a child everything at once.

- Avoid focusing on perfection. Your child may end up being more meticulous or less attentive to detail than you. Teach the skill while granting the child flexibility in how it's done. It's more important that it's done than done perfectly.

For example, my husband (Munira) taught our children how to bathe independently by breaking down the tasks into smaller parts. The first small step was pouring water on their head. The second step was rubbing the shampoo into their own hair. The third step was them pouring just the right amount of shampoo into their own hands so they could do the task by themselves. Eventually all the steps of taking a bath (turning on the water, drying, getting dressed, etc.) were learned over the course of several daily lessons. All of these lessons put together created the ability for our children to take baths independently.

Timers for Young Children

Young children have a difficult time conceptualizing time. Our current lifestyle of utilizing smartphones in our daily lives has minimized the reliance on actual clocks and watches. Thus, many modern homes lack visible time-tracking devices. From a child's point of view, time flows from one day to another with no end or beginning. In such homes, a young child is engaged in an activity only to be told to hurry up because the family needs to leave the house, go home after having fun at the park, or go for a car ride with no end in sight. When children can't track the intervals of time, they usually begin to nag and whine because the passage of time is seamless or forever. Hence, the utilization of clocks and timers becomes a regulation tool for time and, by extension, for emotions. Being able to monitor the passage of time is empowering for children since it gives them a sense of control over what is going on. They feel secure and safe knowing what to expect and they begin to perceive themselves as team members.

Put a clock in the child's room. As the child begins to recognize numbers, tracking time becomes easier. Begin by using a clock the child can hear and read. Show the child how to read the time. In the beginning it may seem as if the child does not understand the concept, but, with practice and follow through, the child eventually gets it. Ensure that Routine charts include time intervals. (Example: 12:00 - 12:30 pm: Lunch).

Utilize a timer to let your children know when you will be available to spend time with them or to define how much time you will spend with them. For example, you are working on a task and your son wants to play with you. You need 30 minutes to finish your task. You can respond to your son with, "I will be done in 30 minutes *insha Allah* (God willing). When the timer goes off, I will be with you." Empower your son even further by giving him the timer to hold while you finish your task. You can also set the timer for the amount of time you will spend with him. For example, "Daddy will spend 10 minutes playing with you, and then I need to go finish my work." When the timer goes off, simply say, "That was so much fun. I look forward to doing this again tomorrow *insha Allah* (God willing)." If your son whines and nags about it, stay firm, hug your son, and acknowledge his feelings. "I know you would like me to spend more time with you. *Insha Allah* we will do this again tomorrow. Now I need to go finish my work. It's OK for you to be sad because you want me to spend more time with you. What can you do on your own right now while I finish my work?" Then return to your work even if your son is pouting. Let him sit with his feelings to learn how to self-soothe.

Some children need help tracking time while doing homework. They feel overwhelmed by homework and their anxiety inhibits their work. These children prone to anxiety will benefit greatly from breaking down their study time into short intervals spaced by breaks. For example, a parent invites her daughter to set the timer for 30 minutes. During that time, the daughter is expected to work on her homework. When the timer goes off, she takes a 15-minute break and then returns to work for another 30 minutes.

Understand the Stage of Development

Knowledge is power. Ask any parent the difference between parenting the firstborn and the second-born and most will say, "Oh! I knew what to expect with the second, so it's not as stressful." A lot of anxiety, battles, and chaos is mitigated, when parents know what to expect. Knowing that a specific challenging behavior is characteristic of a childhood stage provides relief for parents—especially if coupled with knowing how to respond. We invite you to review the phase of development your child is going through in Erikson's Psychosocial Stages (p. 52).

Winning Cooperation

The secret ingredient to gaining cooperation is expressing empathy for the child. Once the child's perception is clearly understood by the parent, the child will be more willing to hear the point of view of the parent. Many times parents want children to listen to them first and, once they have expressed their opinion, they are then ready to listen to their children. However, consider what would happen if this paradigm were reversed and the parent began by listening. The child would instantly feel a connection to the parent which mitigates defensiveness and resistance. Disengaging from emotional battles with children is a prerequisite for Winning Cooperation. Take, for example, Dad working with Rhonda over her excessive TV watching:

Dad: I have noticed that you are watching TV for more than 2 hours a day. I am concerned about this habit because it interferes with your schoolwork and other responsibilities. What would be an acceptable TV limit that we both can work with? What am I saying?

Rhonda: [Exasperated] You are saying that I am watching too much TV and you want me to have no life!

Dad: [Calmly] Yes, I am saying you are watching too much TV. I can see you are becoming frustrated already. I do want you to have fun, but I also would like to see you living life productively. So, I am not saying no more TV. I am simply asking you for a TV time limit that would be reasonable. So what do you suggest?

Rhonda: This is crazy! All my friends watch TV as much as they want and their parents don't interfere! You are the only father who is this strict! Why me?

Dad: [Calmly] You believe I am unnecessarily strict and you wish I would allow you to watch TV as much as you want.

Rhonda: Yes! Exactly. Everyone in my school does that. Please Dad! Please.

Dad: It's difficult for you to be different than your friends. You wish I would just allow you to watch as much as you want.

Rhonda: Yes, exactly, Dad! Please.

Dad: Unfortunately, I won't. This is an area that I believe is important for life. So what time limits are you willing to accept?

Rhonda: Oh, I don't know! So, you don't like the 2-hour limit. How about 1.5-hours every day?

Dad: Hmm. How about I meet you in the middle and we say 1-hour a day and 2-hours on the weekends?

Rhonda: FINE! I guess. Okay, then.

As is clear from the above example, Dad avoided getting pulled into Rhonda's emotional agitation. Instead, he validated her feelings and focused on the issue (the hallmark of Winning Cooperation). Dad continued to listen and empathize while firmly maintaining his limits.

Wheel of Choice

This simple concrete tool is very handy with young children. It can be used in different ways. The Wheel of Choice is a circle divided into wedges containing various options for responding to a specific situation. When that situation arises, the child is handed the Wheel of Choice and asked to choose an option. Figure 5.2 is a Wheel of Choice created by Sumaya Abdul-Quadir, a parent in one of my (Noha) parenting classes. She was struggling with her daughter's angry outbursts, and she decided to create this lovely chart incorporating some of the Islamic guidelines about anger.

This is what Sumaya said about using the Wheel of Choice, "My daughter Anisa and I made the Anger Wheel of Choice. I realized that I needed the wheel more than my daughter so that I could be an example of how to deal with frustration and to also avoid being the mom who 'yells all the time.' I told my daughter that I was going to make it and we would BOTH use it. I also asked her to remind me to use the wheel if I forgot. *Subhan Allah* (glory be to God), I saw a huge difference, not only in myself and my behavior when I'm angry, but also an immediate change in how my daughter manages her own anger. It was gratifying to watch my five-year-old take ownership and responsibility for her emotions, and then communicate them peacefully to me. *Alhamdu Lillah* (all praise to God)."

Figure 5.2
Anger Wheel of Choice

The Wheel of Choice can be created through a collaborative process with the child. Set aside a time when both the parent and child are calm and not rushed. Explain to the child the goal of the chart. Have a blank wedged circle available. Brainstorm ideas that address the concern.

We hope you have gained a deeper understanding of the various Positive Discipline tools. In the next section we apply these tools in addressing challenges specific to different stages of the parenting journey: early & middle childhood, teen years, and young adulthood.

PART III

THE
PARENTING
JOURNEY

CHAPTER 6

THE EARLY YEARS (0-5)

In these early stages of life, babies, toddlers and young children go through enormous physical and emotional development. They are learning about themselves and their environment—what they can expect from their caretakers, their capability to do things and how their actions impact their environment. These primary years are the foundation for personality development. How parents respond during these years imprints children for life. It's unfortunate that many do not recognize the critical role of these early years. In this section, we will detail the common challenges parents face, which typically revolve around daily life activities.

Sleep

Two years and under.

Talk to parents of newborns, and the one complaint they all share is their lack of sleep. When dealing with an infant's sleep schedule, there are two current big ideas. The first advocates following the child's rhythm without modification or interference from the parent (Granju & Kennedy, 1999). Usually these parents worry about their infants' growth and, hence, they feed their children on demand which includes night feedings. Dr. William

Sears is a leading expert in attachment parenting and he encourages parents to sleep in the same room as the baby or even the same bed to promote attachment.

The second big idea advocates gradually eliminating the night feedings which, when done consistently, results in the child sleeping through the night. Dr. Richard Ferber is the leading proponent of this idea. His method for getting infants to sleep through the night involves minimizing interactions with the baby during the night while gradually extending the intervals so that the baby is allowed to self-soothe.

Deciding which method to follow is a personal choice that reflects the parent's beliefs about what a child needs. Be intentional about what you choose. Avoid doing the dance: some nights pushing for no feedings while other times deciding to allow feedings. Be intentional, consistent, and choose what works best for your family.

A recent study (cited in Cowden, 2016) highlighted that using sleep training strategies with infants did not cause stress nor emotional problems. The study is significant as many parents in recent years have been hesitant to implement sleep training methods, worrying about traumatizing their children if they do not respond to their needs during the night. The study focused on delaying parental response during the night and delaying infant's bedtime. Stress hormone levels in infants were measured throughout the study while behavior, emotional, and attachment markers were assessed at the age of 12 months.

General tips for sleep training (Spock, & Parker, 1998).

- Play with your baby a lot during the day.
- Wake your baby up during the day if the usual time has elapsed since the last feeding.
- Keep interactions to a minimum after night feedings.
- Never wake your baby up for a night feeding unless there is a medical reason.
- Get baby used to falling asleep in the crib, not your arms.
- Babies get used to regular household noises. No need to enforce a silence curfew.
- Avoid picking up the baby immediately during the night. Allow time for the baby to go back to sleep on its own.
- Establish winding down bedtime rituals (For example: consistent bedtime hour, bath, feeding, reciting Quran, put to bed, turn off lights).
- Remember that what babies associate with falling asleep will be expected during the night when they wake up. The more you allow them to fall asleep on their own, the better they will be able to go back to sleep during the night.
- Place the crib in such a way, that the baby won't see the parents when waking up at night.

Two and three years old.

Usually children over the age of two are able to sleep through the night on their own. Not every child will, though. Sleep battles that occur after the age of two are typically a result of an inconsistent bedtime routine reflecting a laid back parental daily structure. While adults are capable of handling a fluid sleep structure, children get irritable and are more prone to tantrums. It is highly recommended that a child has a consistent bedtime routine. Also at this time, some children who have been great sleepers may begin to experience difficulties due to fear of the dark, monsters, or bad dreams. Staying consistent with routines while reassuring the child is necessary. Training the child in self-soothing practices such as reciting Quran, making *wudu* (ablution), cuddling with a stuffed animal, and breathing exercises is empowering.

Visual routine charts are the most effective with children as young as one year old. Parents paste pictures of the child engaged in the various aspects of the bedtime routine. While the parent and child go through the routine, the parent points to the picture and states what they will be doing. With repetition, the child will anticipate and expect what comes next as long as the parent consistently Follows Through. The earlier the routine chart is established with a child, the easier it is for the child to follow routines without resistance.

Bedtime routines have a long lasting impact on children, more than parents perceive. Researchers (cited in Whiteman, 2013) found that inconsistent bedtimes in early childhood had a negative impact on children's cognitive development as they got older. These children also were more prone to have behavioral and emotional difficulties. However, parents who eventually implemented routines were able to reverse these damaging effects. It is never too late for parents to create a routine with their young children, especially regarding their bedtime.

According to the National Sleep Foundation (Hirshkowitz, 2015), getting enough sleep is critical for humans to function well.

Their newly delineated recommendations for children are:

- Newborns (0 to 3 months): 14 to 17 hours each day.
- Infants (4 to 11 months): 12 to 15 hours each day.
- Toddlers (1 to 2 years): 11 to 14 hours each day.
- Preschoolers (3 to 5 years): 10 to 13 hours each day.

Over three years old.

Parents who complain of sleep problems when their children are three years old or older find their problems eventually solved when their children begin school. Going to school forces a child to get up early, which also means going to bed relatively early unless the child takes a long nap during the day. Again, utilizing a routine chart will eliminate many bedtime battles.

When a child is verbal, involve them in the process of making the routine chart. Take pictures of the child doing the various tasks at bedtime and then work together to paste the pictures in order. It is critical that the parent collaborate with the child and include as much input as possible from the child, including allowing the child some choices in the order of tasks or the timings.

Morning, After School, & Evening Schedules

Most of the challenges at this stage of development (p. 52) can be resolved by establishing Routines (p. 137) and systems. The key to routines and systems is parental Follow Through. If a parent tends to haphazardly follow a routine, the child will recognize the inconsistency and will challenge the parent daily. A child that does not know what to expect will nag, whine, and question while a child whose life is governed by routines will follow the family systems with minimal resistance. Routines provide a sense of grounding and security for children.

Temper Tantrums

Temper tantrums are the dramatic way toddlers explore the world. Parents may wonder, "What are my children exploring when they are yelling, screaming, kicking, and embarrassing me?" Children are actually exploring the limits of their influence over their environment which includes you, the parent. They are asking, "Can I affect the environment to get what I want?" Nonetheless, it's rare that parents hear this message. Parents tend to feel helpless, frustrated, and angry. More importantly, parental reaction to tantrums sends one of the earliest lessons children learn about their place in the world. Sadly, sometimes the message sent is unintentionally injurious to the child's sense of self. Table 6.1 details the potential messages children receive based on parenting styles.

The self-theory children develop about the world is the result of millions of interactions. It is the collective response to the child that will determine which messages the child ultimately internalizes. Accordingly, if you recognize your reaction in one of the first two columns, you need not fear that you "have ruined your child for life." You have the power to change your reaction immediately and begin the process of influencing your child's misguided perceptions. It's never too late.

Suggestions for dealing with Temper Tantrums.

- Over the next week begin to observe the triggers for tantrums. Some children have a harder time containing their emotions when they are hungry or tired. Observe, analyze, and think of solutions to mitigate the triggers.

- Formulate a plan of response. With a preconceived plan, you will be pleasantly surprised to discover that your own reaction to a tantrum is calmer and firmer.

- Avoid reasoning with a child during a tantrum. The rational brain is turned off during such times and talking usually exacerbates the problem.

- Avoid giving in to your children's demands when they engage in tantrums. The sooner children recognize that tantrums are not effective manipulators, the sooner they will stop using tantrums. Be patient, consistent, and firm. Ultimately, your child will get the message.

- Different children have different temperaments, needs, and tolerance levels to stimuli. Accordingly, a family may have a child who does not engage in tantrums while a sibling may use it all the time.

- When the inevitable tantrum occurs in a public place be calm, take your child away from the scene, find a private spot, and say: "I see you are very upset right now because… Once you have calmed down we can go back and…" Sometimes it may be necessary to actually leave entirely.

- When tantrums occur at home try the following:
  - Always begin by Mirroring (p. 118) feelings, "I see you are very upset because…."
  - Use the tool Hugs When Upset or Not (p. 107) "Would you like a hug?"
  - Use the tool Distraction for Younger Children (p. 86) Creating distractions and redirecting work wonders to de-escalate tantrums. "Let's go and play…"

- Invite them to use the Positive Time-out (p. 131) tool the Jane Nelsen way: "Would it help you to go to…?" If the child says no, ask, "Would it help you if I went with you?"

- Ask, "What would help you calm down right now?"

- Use the tool Wheel of Choice (p. 152).

- If none of your strategies are working say, "I see that you are very upset right now. It's perfectly OK to be upset. When you have calmed down and would like to be with me, come and find me." Then walk away and do what you need to do. If you are upset yourself, take some time to calm down.

TABLE 6.1
Parenting Styles and Tantrums

Parenting Style:	Authoritarian	Permissive	Authoritative
How the Parent Reacts:	• Punishment • Spanking. • Yelling. • Locking them in their room. • Punitive time-out.	• Giving in to child's demands. • Bribing. • Cajoling. • Appeasing. • Reasoning.	• Mirroring feelings. • Asking child what would help them calm down. • Hugging them. • Letting them cry and telling them to find parent after calming down. • Positive Time-out.
Possible Messages Internalized by the Child:	• "I am bad." • "Something is wrong with me." • "Nobody loves me." • "They win this time but I will get what I want behind their back."	• "I'm the boss around here." • "I just need to cry and I'll get what I want." • "I simply have to bother them enough so they give in." • "Daddy doesn't like to see me upset. He'll give me anything I ask for."	• "I get angry when I don't get what I want." • "Mommy loves me even when I'm upset." • "I'm in charge of my emotions." • "When I cuddle in my blanket, I feel good." • "I'm not going to get my way all the time." • "It's okay to get upset, I just have to figure out how to calm down."

Touching Everything

Toddlers get into everything. This is normal behavior since their natural way of learning at this stage is through manipulation of objects. From a toddler's point of view, the environment is the new frontier that is awaiting discovery. Toddlers may love opening kitchen cupboards, splashing in the toilet water, playing with electrical outlets, or simply feeling the lovely crystal vase in the living room. Preschoolers test their physical and mental limits by creatively finding new ways to do things such as climbing on chairs to pull out chocolate or crackers from the kitchen cabinet.

Parents may experience daily struggles in their efforts to keep their curious, active, young children safe. Many have shared with me (Noha) that they spank their children in hopes of teaching the danger associated with all of these explorations. Then they tell me, "They keep doing it! They don't get it. I don't know what to do!" It's true. Young children do not make the connection between the spanking and the message the parent is trying to send. (See Spanking in the Islamic Context, p. 379). I invite you to channel your energy into preventing access to what you don't want your child getting into and you will end up with a less stressful day (Structure the Environment, p. 145). It will take some effort in the beginning to install all the necessary childproof gadgets, but it will save you a lot of frustration and anger.

Food Battles

Many parents complain that their children will not eat the food they make or will only eat one thing. Just as children explore their environments, they are discovering what flavors and textures of food they like and dislike. Parents model their relationship with food to their children who learn how food is used in the family—a meal to be shared, a snack eaten throughout the day, a comfort source when tired and upset, etc.

Parents know they cannot force-feed infants. Food items disliked by infants are typically spit out quickly. If the baby is not interested, nothing will work and usually parents stop feeding that particular food item. However, something changes when children become toddlers. Parents begin to use external behavior modification strategies to get children to eat: bribing with candy or dessert, threatening the loss of TV or park time, spoon-feeding while watching their favorite show, following them around with food as they play, preparing special dishes, etc. All of these behaviors stem from the belief that parents know what is best for their children and so they *must* force them to eat. Remember that children will not starve themselves. Hunger is a natural biological alarm clock for the need to eat. However, when parents resort to coercion and control, children become desensitized to their internal hunger signals and become dependent on parents to tell them when and what to eat. This is a tragedy!

If children have learned that food is a battleground, they will go hungry just to win the situation (for example, refuse to eat until given candy). Even so, they usually win because parents give in to their demands, fearful of the impact on the children's health. And the cycle continues. More worrisome are the long-term consequences of early food battles. "If you make too much of a fuss over food when (the child) is young, you may be setting yourself up for dealing with anorexia later" (Glasser, 1999, p. 215). Hence, we invite you to drop the battles early on and trust that your children will eat when they are hungry.

Deciding What You Will Do is at the center of eliminating food battles. Shifting focus from, "My son has to eat or he will not be healthy," to "I will do my part and allow hunger to do its job," liberates parents from unnecessary worry. When this shift occurs early (toddlerhood), children learn good food habits.

Examples of Decide What You Will Do.

• Offering healthy nutritious meals without pressure.
• Seeking input from children about weekly menu.
• Recognizing time limits and deciding what to cook without input from others.
• Dropping junk food from shopping lists.
• Having healthy snacks on hand (carrots, fruits, nuts, etc.).
• Letting children be the judge of whether they are hungry or not.

Example of Limited Choices.

• Parent decides what breakfast/lunch items are manageable in the family schedule.
• Parent writes them down.
• Every day, the parent decides which 2-3 items are going to be offered that day.
• Parent calmly asks the child to choose from the daily choices.
• If the child says, "I want..." which was not one of the options, the parent calmly says, "I am sorry... was not one of the options. Maybe we can have... on the weekend, but not today. So, what would you like to have,... or...?"

A word of caution is in order here. As the child grows older

Limited Choices become less effective because the child begins to be adamant about not choosing any of the options. When Limited Choices do not work, the parent switches to another Positive Discipline tool. For example, in a conflict about breakfast or lunch choices, the issue can be put on the Family Meeting (p. 96) agenda; the parent can decide which item will be prepared and allow the child the space to decide to eat or not; or, the parent can put the responsibility of preparing breakfast/lunch on the child.

Food battles around candy and chocolate can be eliminated by using the tool Structure the Environment (p. 145). Many parents today are very concerned about sugar intake. These parents are intentional about not buying any candy and chocolate. Their goal is to establish a low-sugar diet with their children, especially because studies have linked high sugar intake to higher levels of activity for children, obesity, and diabetes. There are other parents who are fine with their children having candy and chocolate as long as it is limited. Since very young children have difficulty understanding the rationale behind not having treats all the time or just before a meal, eliminating access to sweets can be the simplest solution (hiding them in a high cabinet or in the parents' room). However, parents need to have a clear system for when the child can have those treats. I (Noha) only bought chocolate or candy I approved of and my children knew they could only have dessert, candy, or chocolate after dinner. They also knew exactly how much they could have. Reflect on how you handle treats in your family, inform your children, and Follow Through.

Biting & Hitting Behaviors

Language acquisition to express feelings develops at different rates for children. Children who struggle with expressing themselves will resort to biting or hitting as a primitive form of communication. Parents cognizant of the frustration that belies biting and hitting are able to address these behaviors by using the tool Connection Before Correction (p. 80). The parent begins by saying, "I see that you are frustrated. You can feel upset and angry. But hurting others is not okay." The parent then encourages the child to empathize with the other child, "Look at her face. She is sad because you hit her. How can you help her feel better?" A child may need to learn how to make amends after such an incident. The goal is to train the child in emotional self-regulation (acknowledging feelings, controlling impulses to hurt others, calming down) and owning responsibility for one's actions by apologizing and connecting with others. When children are able to acknowledge their behavior they will be able to find solutions. This process will take time. Be patient as your child may repeat this behavior until the ability to control impulses is achieved. As children develop their language and social skills, they will be less likely to revert to biting and hitting and, instead, use words to communicate their needs.

Whining & Nagging Behaviors

Perhaps the most irritating behavior for parents is whining and nagging. Sadly, these are learned behaviors that children adopt to either get attention or get what they want. If they are not taught a more appropriate way to express themselves, it may become a habit that continues into the teen years and beyond.

To eliminate whining behavior, a parent begins by bringing it to the child's attention since children do not realize what they are doing. The parent says, "You are speaking to me in a whiny voice." This gentle reminder will first identify the behavior. Then the parent requests, "Please ask me again in a normal voice." Every time the child speaks in a whiny voice, the parent must respond the same way until the child learns to communicate appropriately. Inconsistent responses tempt children into escalating their whiny strategies since they work sometimes. Similarly, when children speak in a mature manner, it is important that parents respond positively so children know their efforts are noticed. A parent may say, "I noticed you used a normal voice just now! Thank you, I appreciate that."

Once a parent has responded to a child's request with a "No," and the child continues to nag, the parent can use the tool Statement of Fact (p. 143) to respond by simply stating the fact instead of lecturing or repeating what was said before. Again, the key with this tool is consistency and not caving in to demands. The parent says, "Did you ask me a question about... and did I answer it?" The child may respond with, "Yes, but ..." The parent then responds with firmness and kindness, "I will not change my mind no matter how often you ask. No means no. You have asked and I gave you my answer." The more the parent responds with consistency, the quicker the child will learn that nagging is not effective.

Buy Me More

Walk down an aisle in any toy store and you will inevitably see a parent and a child having a conversation similar to this:

Parent: No, I am not buying that. Please put it back.

Child: [Pulling it off the shelf] I want it!

Parent: I said no. Put it back!

Child: [Begins playing with the toy]: I really want it! Please buy it!

Then the tears begin and the story usually ends one of two ways: The parent yells at the child while the child throws a temper tantrum or the parent gives in and buys the toy. This scenario is so common because it reflects the normal behavior of young children who live only in the present moment. They lack the patience necessary to anticipate the future. Children will want new shiny things because these new gadgets are probably the coolest things they have ever seen in their short lives. They are curious, fascinated and intrigued by these items while knowing that their parents hold the power to bring these things home. Some children have learned that if they just plead and cry eventually they will get their way. Others simply don't understand why they can't have them. The concept of money is elusive. All they know is that their wants are being blocked by the parent, which is frustrating and unfair from their perspective.

Stores are also aware of how children react. This is why products are shelved at children's eye level. So, what are parents to do? Anticipating that children will be intrigued by what they see in stores is helpful. Parents can use these experiences to teach personal values about spending. Money management is a life skill that must be addressed in early childhood. Concepts for parents to teach include:

- Money (currency, checks, and credit cards).
- Needs versus wants.
- Money is spent, saved, and given.
- Patience versus instant gratification.

For children 0-3 years of age.

• Avoid taking children with you. For a couple of years, I (Noha) did grocery shopping after the children went to bed, thus avoiding the battles.

• Before going into a store explain your expectations, "We are going to the grocery store. I will not be buying any candy today," or "Today you may buy one piece of chocolate as long as it is less than one dollar."

• If your child throws a tantrum, simply say no, Mirror (p. 118) the child's feelings, and be firm. "I see how upset you are because you really would like to have this toy. Today is not a toy buying day."

• If a tantrum becomes too intense, carry your child and leave the store even if you have not accomplished your task.

• Sometimes you might buy what your child is asking for. Hopefully you will not establish this as a given because it could lead to entitlement. If you are planning to say yes, say it the first time your child asks for the item *not* after nagging and whining.

• Distract the child by pointing out something else interesting in the store like the music playing, a decoration at the entrance, etc.

For children 3-6 years of age.

Begin establishing an Allowance (p. 74) for your child. First decide how much you will give your child. Since young children have a difficult time holding their money, we invite you to keep their money for them. One envelope per child. Every month, add the child's allowance to the envelope. When the child asks for something, check the envelope to see if the child has enough money to buy the item. Children learn quickly if the parent is following through. Eventually the child will begin to ask the parent, "Dad, do I have enough to buy..." Beginning the allowance system this early teaches children a valuable lesson in buying only what they can afford. This lesson will be the solid foundation for informed decisions during the teen years.

Toilet Training

Training children to use the restroom can be one of the most trying times for parents. Using the toilet is a sign of independence and physical maturation. Since it involves training children to become conscious of what was previously an uncontrollable body function, the process is dependent on the child. Many parents choose when *they* are ready to toilet train (i.e. they are tired of changing diapers or pregnant with another child, etc.) rather than determining if the child is showing signs of being ready to use the toilet. Eager parents who rush to train toddlers when they are not ready realize that the toilet training process takes much longer with more accidents and power struggles.

Generally toddlers between two and three years old will show signs of controlling their bowel movements. They may be self-aware when they are soiling their diaper or are having fewer wet diapers in the evenings. They may show interest sitting on the toilet and express a desire to wear underwear. They may have developed the words for urine and stool. Observant parents will determine an appropriate time to begin toilet training.

Toilet training is the one piece of parenting I (Munira) always dreaded. When I tried to train my first child, I had no idea what I was doing and asked advice from other parents. I got so much contradictory information that it made me even more anxious and confused. Added to that, I got pressure from grandparents to toilet train my son at a young age because he was "too old" to be in diapers according to their cultural standards. I tried toilet training at two years old with epic failure. Then I tried again at 2.5 years old and encountered temper tantrums and power struggles—from both of us. Then, a month before turning three years old, we tried again and within three days my son was fully toilet trained.

I learned that my anxiety and emotional response played a large role in how my son approached toilet training. Even though he was only two years old, he picked up on my nervousness and began feeling the same way. I engaged in power struggles and frustration when I couldn't get him to cooperate. I focused on correction rather than connection and failed. Only when I finally became calm and unreactive did my son actually make progress. In contrast, my husband modeled confidence and composure. I was struck by how calmly he interacted with our son, and in response, how proud our son felt about his ability to be independent. My husband used the tool Take Time for Training (p. 147). He encouraged our son to use the toilet when he went, gently reminded him, was light-hearted and laughed with him, casually helped him clean up accidents, and loudly cheered when he succeeded. Following my husband's lead, this simple change in mindset brought me ease and strength.

Toilet training my first son taught me more about his temperament and how he learned best. It was also an opportunity to lean on my husband and better understand the role we each play when parenting our children. My husband went on to be super-dad and trained our other two sons with great success. He was always ready and encouraging of our children to transition to more independence. It started with toilet training and later he taught them to tie their own shoes, take showers, write their names, etc. The journey of toilet training is a bridge to independence and self-growth. I still don't like the process of toilet training and have sympathy for parents when they enter that stage. But, I remind them as a friend once said to me, "Toddlers will eventually learn to use the toilet and at their own pace — just look around, you don't see any teens in diapers, do you?"

School Separation Anxiety

Transitioning to school is a big change not only for children but for parents. Parents who show enthusiasm and confidence in their children will reassure them about their new experience. Parents can help their children transition to school by creating a morning routine, laying out clothes the night before, and packing a lunch together.

Going to school for the first time or returning to school after a long break creates anxiety in some children. It would be helpful for children beginning school for the first time to visit the school together beforehand and, if possible, meet the teacher. A child that is upset when dropped off can be consoled by the parent with a hug and comforting words, "It is hard to say goodbye. I can see you are feeling nervous about being in a new class," "I love you and can't wait to hear about your day when I pick you up." Parents should always say goodbye to their children rather than sneak away. Remaining firm and loving with a quick goodbye will show the child that the parent has confidence that the child will be fine and the parent trusts the teacher and school.

Some children react more intensely to leaving the safety of parents and home. They simply refuse to go to school or complain of being ill. Fear and panic persisting over a long period of time can impede the child's successful adjustment to school. Separation anxiety that persists in the form of severe tantrums, clinging behavior, or excessive worry and fear requires professional help for both the parent and the child. Counseling in these instances revolves around teaching the parents how to help the child with emotional self-regulation and transitions.

Seat Belts

It is very simple. No driving until everyone in the car is buckled in. No need to scream and yell. No need to threaten or reward. Simply establish the rule that you will not drive unless everyone is buckled in and stick to it. This means that sometimes you will be late to appointments. Consider leaving the house earlier to allow time to deal with tantrums, rebellions, and arguments. We invite you, especially when your children are capable of putting on their own seat belts, to sit in your seat, buckled in—waiting. Read or do a quiet activity until the children are in their seats securely.

If your children decide to take off their seat belts while you are driving, find a safe spot, park the car, and tell them you will not continue driving until they have put on their seat belts. Repeat this each time, if necessary. The time spent Following Through is a fraction of the time that is wasted on arguments and battles. It will also reinforce an important message: you mean what you say.

Some parents use the police as "the monster" to be feared when children resist putting on their seat belts. These children are told threateningly that the police will take them away if they are not buckled in. If fear-based parenting is established, your child may not learn to work or listen to rules unless there is the threat of punishment. Such children will not learn to do things for the good they bring but, rather, ask the question: "What will happen if I do not…?" Wearing seat belts is a safety procedure. If you shift the attention to the police as monitors, you detract from the core issue. The battle with your child could move to arguments over whether the police are nearby which is not the core issue. This approach erodes the trust of your child. Your child will grow up soon to discover that police give parents tickets and don't take away children. When they discover that fact, they will begin to wonder what other facts you've hidden from them. When that happens, you lose your child's trust. It will become difficult for your child to open up to you and connect with you. Lastly, the police force is dedicated to serving and helping the community. Using them as "monsters" will inhibit children from seeking their help when needed.

Play Time

Children naturally seek to play. The type of play they engage in is ever changing as they grow. When they are babies they play by exploring their environment, putting objects in their mouths, climbing on things, and watching what others are doing and saying. A baby's day-to-day existence is enveloped in these mundane activities, and parents may easily forget that babies learn through each of these experiences. As babies enter toddlerhood learning includes building with blocks, drawing pictures, and pretend play. During this stage, play is "serious work" as children create, imagine, and act out their thoughts and ideas. Preschoolers shift from individual play to group-play. They learn cooperation, teamwork, social skills, and reading emotions. We invite parents considering a preschool program to inquire about how play is emphasized and incorporated since it is the best learning strategy during these early years.

Use of Electronics

As with other aspects of family life, parents are the best role models for electronics use. Is the TV always on in the background? Are parents using cell phones at the dinner table? Are parents using electronics with limits? When electronics are a barrier to positive interactions with children, they are a problem for the entire family.

Since technology is ever evolving, long-term effects are only being predicted by researchers at this point. The research (cited in Ferguson, 2015) on the use of electronics with infants and toddlers is complex. For instance, the American Psychological Association found that parent-toddler interactions with media were vital for language development while the American Academy of Pediatrics advises no screen time at all for infants. However, most researchers advise moderation and suggest children use electronics with parents—not alone. This means parents should not use TV programs, videos, and games on their phones as a "babysitter" for their children. Creating a family rule that the use of electronics is supervised, deliberate, and for short periods of time establishes boundaries that children will continue to respect as they get older.

The issue of electronics will constantly be revisited in your parenting journey. I (Munira) found that with the birth of each of my children, abstinence from electronics became more and more difficult. With my first child, I limited television watching for the first two years of his life. Since he was born before the invention of smart phones and tablets, it was relatively easy. After his brother was born 18 months later, he began to watch educational programming for a limited time each day. This caused my second son to be exposed to the television at a younger age because of his older brother. Since they were close in age, I was still able to manage the content they watched so that it was appropriate and in line with our family values. On the other hand, my third son was born many years later, when his older brothers had begun playing games on tablets and consoles. It was nearly impossible to shield him from electronics. As a toddler he was not only exposed to TV, but to smart phone apps, console games, and movies. Whenever electronic use felt out of balance in our home, my husband and I would negotiate and Problem-Solve with our children. We would revisit the boundaries and what every family member could do differently. Although we didn't find perfect solutions every time, we were able to discuss our values and work together as a team. Each child is born within a context and, as the family grows, there inevitably will be changes. Showing flexibility and consciously redrawing the lines to adapt to the current context is necessary as children grow older.

Sibling Rivalry

All siblings fight. Sibling fights are actually instrumental in learning the art of compromise and negotiation. However, many adults recall childhood memories of jealousy, uneasy competition, and sometimes outright hate of their siblings. Blessed are those who remember their sibling interactions with love and affection. The key—to cultivating healthy sibling relations as a foundation for learning social collaboration—lies with the parent taking on a neutral role in sibling fights.

Begin early. With younger children, establish your role as a neutral observer rather than a judge or peacemaker. For example, when my (Noha) eldest was under the age of four and his brother was not yet three, fights began to occur. They were the simple fights over toys. I had read an article in *Parents* magazine about how critical it was to get children to solve their own problems. The article suggested putting each child in one corner of the room, facing one another, and asking them to discuss a compromise. Once they agreed on a solution, they could leave the corners and continue with their play. It worked like magic because I started this practice when they were young, and I did not have to supervise or even decide when they could leave the corners.

With older children who run to you to solve problems (or get siblings in trouble), facilitate the use of the tool Effective Communication (p. 87). Avoid having an opinion or siding with one child over the other—even when you know who is right and who is wrong! The goal is to get siblings to negotiate on their own. The focus is not on "who did what to whom" but, rather, on ensuring they are using the communication formulas. After they have shared their feelings and thoughts about the situation, ask the Curiosity Question: "What solutions would be helpful in this situation?" again ensuring that the children are the ones coming up with the solutions. If the children are fighting over something, and they have not yet come up with a viable solution, keep the item until they have come up with a plan. When the fight is physical, separate the siblings and send them off to different rooms. Once they have calmed down and are ready to talk, facilitate the discussion as mentioned above.

If you notice an emerging pattern with sibling fights, it might be necessary to establish or revise family rules and routines. For example, my husband (Noha) noticed that sometimes the children would be playing rough-and-tumble and it would escalate into a fight. After processing what happened several times, my husband invited the children to hold their hands up and say, "Stop. I don't want to play anymore." Looking back through the lens of therapy at what he did then, I recognize what a beautiful habit he established. In that simple suggestion he acknowledged their love for rough-and-tumble, did not deprive them of it, empowered the one who was feeling overwhelmed with a voice and the ability to stop what was going on, and taught the stronger party to hear and respect the other instantly.

Jobs

Jobs and chores are not reserved for adults in the family. Establishing responsibilities in the home can begin as early as toddlerhood. A child that helps with household chores develops a sense of belonging in the family, recognizes emerging abilities, and feels the satisfaction of helping others.

Toddlers can help with simple tasks like:

- Put away toys.
- Sort and match socks.
- Dust with a damp cloth.

- Put away kitchen items like plastic containers, wooden spoons, cups, etc.
- Place clothing in drawers and baskets.
- Push buttons to turn machines off and on.
- Dry spills, wet fixtures, etc.
- Scoop out pet food.

Once children reach preschool age, responsibilities can include:

- Set the table with utensils, napkins, and placemats.
- Move items from washer to dryer.
- Take laundry to hamper.
- Fold laundry and place in baskets.
- Fluff pillows.
- Wipe tables and countertops.
- Dust.
- Sort recycling.
- Empty small trash cans.
- Load/unload some dishes from dishwasher.
- Load soap into dishwasher/washing machine.
- Empty grocery bags.
- Peel vegetables.
- Water plants.
- Rake leaves, tidy a garden.

Exhausted Parents

Becoming a new parent is an exciting and exhausting experience all in one. Read the beautiful reflections about the birth of a baby and the lessons learned in the essay God Delivers (p. 303). First-time parents become fully consumed by the needs of their infant, and naturally become physically and emotionally drained. Many times they disregard their own individual and/or couple needs. Some parents feel "guilty" doing things they find pleasurable without their children, so they sacrifice their desires and focus on their children. Families that become child-centered create an environment where the needs of the children outweigh those of the parents. The result of such focus is unhealthy family dynamics where children feel entitled and lack empathy for others. Families must strive to remain couple-centered while raising their children. Their needs as couples and individuals must be balanced with their children's.

Juggling parenting, work, and social responsibilities leaves many parents stressed and exhausted. To counteract the negative impact of being pulled in many directions, parents need to practice self-care (Get a Life, p. 105). Nourishing oneself encompasses all areas of a parent's life, from the spiritual and physical to the emotional and intellectual. When parents recognize that self-care is not a luxury but a necessary ingredient of taking care of children, they will be more willing to allocate the time needed for enjoyable activities.

Examples of self-care activities.

- Personal time for reading, listening to music, or hobbies.
- Time for peace and quiet and contemplation.

- Regular scheduled time with spouse.
- Connecting with friends.
- Connecting with other parents.
- Participating in prayers and mosque activities.
- Spending time in nature.
- Maintaining a connection to Allah.
- Physical activities like exercising and walking.

Parents differ in their needs and how they recharge. What is critical is making self-care a priority as important as feeding one's own children. Self-care must occur daily. Thus, dedicating 20 minutes daily for rejuvenating activities is far more effective than engaging in a longer activity every now and then. (See Peaceful Families, p. 361).

Parental Frustration & Anger

The art of patience truly gets tested when one becomes a parent. Parents get angry no matter how good they are. It is a fact of life. Parents get angry for many reasons: loss of control, feeling tired, being challenged, doing too many things, getting overwhelmed, being criticized, doubting their abilities, etc. Anger is simply the state when all reserved energy has been extinguished and the parent is running on empty. When parents are angry, they forget four basic principles:

1. Their children are still young.
2. Their children are still learning.
3. Their children are trying their best.
4. Their children trust them to be mature adults.

I (Munira) had a very short temper and was very impatient when I first became a parent. I found myself feeling upset every day over minor things. I realized one day that I did not want to be remembered as an angry parent and so began the process of personal change. I actively worked to not "sweat the small stuff" in order to build my patience and emotional maturity. It took many years to change my beliefs about situations and to change the way I coped with situations. I am not perfect and can still revert to overreacting. But, in those situations, I have learned to forgive myself and actively work to recover and model more effective communication and coping skills with my family.

The tool Positive Time-out (p. 131) is excellent to use in times of frustration and anger. A parent can say to the child, "I am feeling very upset right now and I am going to take a Time-out to cool off," or "I am feeling angry right now and need time to think so I don't say something I will regret." Engaging in a self-soothing activity (reading, walking, cooking, doing the dishes, exercising, praying) which calms and grounds the parent is more effective than angry outbursts. Also effective is following the 4 Rs of Recovery (Nelsen, 2006):

1. Regroup ("I need to take time to calm down").
2. Recognize the mistake ("Oops! I overreacted!").
3. Reconcile ("I am sorry I hurt your feelings").
4. Resolve ("What can we do so this does not happen again?").

Following these steps empowers parents to recover from negative interactions with their children while, at the same time, own personal responsibility for their feelings and actions. Additionally, children learn from their parents' reactions how to handle mistakes and recover from emotional agitation as they grow. (See Attitude of Gratitude, p. 307).

Islam-the-Habit

During the early years, parents are transmitting Islam through their actions and words. Inculcating children with the ethos of Islam occurs vicariously: when parents order pizza with no pork sausage; when parents pray, fast, or go to the mosque; or when parents say "*Alhamdu Lillah* (all praise to God), *Allahu akbar* (God is the greatest), *subhan Allah* (glory to God), *la hawla wa la quwwata illa Billah* (there is no might or power except in God)." All of these are indirect ways through which parents introduce children to their faith-based worldview. What parents say and practice on a regular basis becomes Islam for the child. Begin with yourself. If you are not content with your practice of faith or view, you will need to evaluate it early because children see through empty words. Train yourself in the Islamic practices you cherish and your children will absorb them surreptitiously.

The first seven years are *no obligation* years. Keep them this way. Some parents, in their zeal for Islam, demand religious practice of their children before the age of seven (e.g. commanding the child to pray, forcing girls to wear the Islamic head covering, etc.). Please avoid doing that. This is an example of what the Prophet (pbuh) said: "Anyone who is overly austere in his practice of this faith will be overpowered by his practice" (Hadith, Bukhari, Muslim). Adopting faith is a process over time. It cannot be rushed nor forced. So, give your child the space, time, and training to come into faith. Preserve the first seven years without the pressure of obligations, as Allah intended them.

There are a few basic articles of faith that children must be introduced to from an early age. The most critical piece is connecting your child with Allah the Loving. Guide your child toward deeds that Allah loves. Instead of saying, "You should always say the truth because Allah will punish you if you lie," say instead, "Allah loves you and loves those who say the truth. And those whom Allah loves, He will protect and support." It's the same message about honesty, but one is wrapped in love while the other is steeped in fear (see Teaching Children Love of Allah, p. 373). There will be time later to talk about the Fear of Allah, *Shaitan* (Satan), and Hell. Daily in my practice, I (Noha) see the ramifications of raising children with only the fear of Allah. Young and old, their sense of worth has been tied to prohibitions, sins, and hellfire. They become encrusted in deep-seated shame due to the negative messaging they received as children. The injury to their psyche by such shame is difficult to eradicate (though it can be ameliorated in therapy) and will rear its ugly head whenever they run low on emotional energy. Gift your child those first seven years with the love—not fear—of Allah.

Nurture *shukr* (gratefulness) to Allah. In your daily life always invoke *alhamdu Lillah* (all praise to God). Model how grateful you are for all that you have in your life. Teach children to say *alhamdu Lillah* when they get something new or when something good occurs. Avoid the trap of saying, "Do good so that Allah will give you good things." Instead say, "Do good to show gratitude to Allah for his infinite bounties. Even when things are bad, we are Blessed." Allah did not promise a life full of material prosperity and success to those who follow His Path. Instead He promised his servants a good worldly life based on peace and contentment despite the difficulties of life. Many children raised with the idea that they will reap good because they are good come into therapy as angry resentful young adults because Allah has not Granted them what they want. As parents, the messages you send will go a long way in mitigating this sense of entitlement.

To counteract the sentiment, "Why is Allah doing this to me?" inculcate the idea that adversities are trials from Allah. Teach children to overcome difficulties with spiritual success by facing them with patience, action, and perseverance. Avoid presenting misfortunes as the results of sins. When children are told that negative events are the results of what they have done or said, they internalize a negative self-worth that colors the rest of their lives with shame and guilt. Emphasize the Islamic view of hardships: "We have Created humans in constant turmoil," (Quran, 90:4), "The greater the trial, the greater the recompense. And Allah tests those whom He loves. Those who respond with composure gain contentment. And those who respond with anger are consumed with discontentment," (Hadith, Tirmizi). Hence, with tribulations, focus your children's attention on how they will deal with the situation rather than connecting the event to their worth. (see Fragile Adults Syndrome, p. 393).

Practices to initiate before the age of seven:

- Introduce Allah and his Prophets
- Teach children to say *bismillah* (In the Name of God) before eating and *alhamdu Lillah* (all praise to God) after eating.
- Teach *duaa* (supplication) before eating.
- Let them know Muslims don't eat pork nor do they drink alcohol.

- Teach them the Islamic etiquette surrounding the use of the toilet (sitting, avoid soiling seat or clothes, cleaning soiled toilet seat or clothes, cleansing with water after urinating or defecating, and washing hands afterwards).

- Share Islamic songs and stories.

- Begin teaching children the Arabic language to have direct access to the Quran. In connecting children to the Quran, focus on understanding and application.

- Help children memorize a *surah* (chapter) of the Quran. The most important *surah* to memorize is *al-Fatiha* (the opening chapter of the Quran) as it is the core of obligatory prayers.

- Recognize that children will differ in their ability to memorize. For some it comes very naturally. For others it's a struggle. Accordingly, encourage memorization but avoid shaming children. Find a teacher who teaches with love and respect, not fear and punishment.

- Connect children to Allah through His beautiful creations. Spend time in nature appreciating animals, mountains, trees, water, deserts, etc. These experiences will help them develop appreciate the interconnectedness of the universe. Teach them to express their awe by saying *subhan Allah* (glory to God) for the beauty of His creations.

- When your children show interest in performing any of the obligatory practices, encourage them to do small steps and emphasize that it's not obligated yet. See the subsequent stories in "Community Connection" of two parents and how they handled fasting with their children when they were younger than seven years old.

Community Connection

My 5-year-old wakes up for suhour (pre-dawn meal) every morning with us and decides to fast until breakfast at 8:30am. After breakfast he chooses to fast again until lunch at noon. Subhana Allah (glory to God), a few days ago he mentioned how we need to give A LOT of food to the poor so that their tummies don't hurt like his does between breakfast and lunch. Masha Allah (May God protect him). What does he do about it? He puts $1 in each pocket of his Ramadan calendar and decides (with his 3-year-old sibling) to give $30 at the end of Ramadan to the poor in India—that is where we are going after Ramadan insha Allah (God willing). Alhamdu Lillah (all praise to God)!

Farah Ruknuddeen

Yesterday, my 6-year-old son said, "Mommy, I really want to fast to make Allah happy with me." I was, of course, so touched and told him that Allah is already happy with him and that children don't have to fast. But if he really wanted to, maybe he could fast for part of the day. I then asked him how long he would like to fast. He said three hours. So we decided that the best time was between 5-8 pm so that he could break iftar (meal breaking the fast) with us. I told him that he should listen to his body and let me know if he felt tired, hungry or thirsty and it was too much for him. He assured me he could handle it.

At 6:30pm, he came upstairs pouting. I asked him what was wrong, and he said that Baba gave his favorite snack to his little brother. He really wanted to have some too, but he felt bad about breaking his fast. He started to get teary-eyed and felt like he had failed. So, I told him that he had done really well and showed so much willpower by not giving in. We calculated that he had fasted for 2 hours, which was great for his first fast, and I suggested he could gradually do more when he was ready. He wiped his tears, smiled, and ran downstairs to enjoy his snack!

Hosai Mojaddidi

These first five years are full of rapid change and growth. However, families who have established routines and systems during the early years of childhood commonly enjoy what are called the "golden years" of childhood in the next stage. The middle childhood years bring into focus the unique innate strengths (p. 44) of children. The next chapter is full of ideas that will foster an encouraging home environment thus supporting the emerging identities of children.

CHAPTER 7

MIDDLE CHILDHOOD YEARS (6-12)

In this stage of development (p. 52), the child's life revolves around school and friendships. Solutions that have been established when children were younger will need to be revisited and revised. Parents continue to have the greatest influence on their children's habits and values while children continue to seek the guidance and approval of their parents. Children's perception of themselves expands as they interact with teachers, coaches, and peers. For some families these years are considered the "golden years" of parenting with smooth parent-child relations and a less hectic lifestyle.

Disrespect & Talking Back

At some point all parents will have heated exchanges with their children involving talking back. The first time it occurs many parents are taken aback and shocked that their children could respond in such a negative tone. Many times parents quickly react with anger. This may lead to a power struggle between the parent and child and a subsequent breakdown in the relationship. Therefore, it is important to understand the common reasons behind talking back and the best way for parents to respond.

Common reasons for talking back.

- Repeating or mimicking how adults speak.
- Trying to get a reaction from the parent.
- Seeking attention.
- Feeling discouraged and powerless.
- Testing their own power in the relationship.

Conversations with spouses, friends, store clerks, and co-workers are all opportunities to teach respectful listening and speaking skills. Parents model how to speak to other people. The tone and words used by parents will inevitably be absorbed and repeated by children. If a child speaks with disrespect, it is helpful to begin with self-reflection. Listen to yourself the next time you request something from your child. Do you use respectful speech? Are you sarcastic? Condescending? (See Effective Communication, p. 87)

The biggest challenge is how parents handle their emotions and what they say when they are stressed or frustrated. For example, a parent who feels rushed may say, "Hurry up! I can't believe we are late again! What are you doing? You always make us late!" This type of exchange may later be thrown back at the parent by the child saying, "I can't believe you forgot to pick up milk today! What am I going to eat for breakfast?" A Positive Discipline parent will say instead, "I need us to work together quickly because we are short on time. I know it's annoying to be rushed, and I am sorry that's the case right now. Please help me make this work." With the first statement, the parent is externalizing personal frustration onto the child with blame and accusation. In the second statement, the parent is acknowledging the situation and asking the child to be an ally in helping alleviate it. (Mutual Respect, p. 121).

In a heated conversation with the child a parent has two choices: either respond in an equally hurtful way, or set limits with the child. When parents internalize the words of the child, they feel attacked and may respond to the child by saying, "How dare you speak to me that way! Fine! Don't help. See what that gets you!" This is not helpful for the parent or child. However, parents who are able to externalize the comments will be able to understand the "hidden message" the child is sending (Belief Behind the Behavior, p. 83).

The best response to talking back is emotional Mirroring (p. 118) and setting limits. The parent can say, "I see that you are very upset. I feel disrespected when you speak to me like that. I will give you space to cool off, and we can talk about this later." When the parent responds to the child with respectful limits instead of talking back or punishing the child, the parent chooses not to engage in a power struggle. The parent models emotional regulation and the child learns that needs will be met, not through manipulation and anger, but through cooperation and respect. Parent and child can engage in further problem-solving after the child calms down.

Enabling

The middle childhood years are the opportune years for teaching children valuable skills for life. Sadly, some parents rob their children of these opportunities by shielding them from the realities of life. This phenomenon is called enabling. Parents do not intentionally set out to weaken their children's resilience and perseverance. They actually believe they are doing what is best for the children. They believe that by doing for their children, they are showing them how much they love them and are willing to sacrifice for them. (See Building Resiliency, p. 357).

Some parents do things for their children because they can do it easier, faster, or better than their children. Efficiency becomes more important than teaching and mentoring. Sometimes parents are simply avoiding "battles." Parents become cautious in their engagements with their children and focus on reducing conflict at the expense of teaching or expecting more from the children. In this dynamic, children hold the power, as parents fear temper tantrums or worry about their children hating them. Parents may also do for their children because they want them to look good for others. They believe the only way they can have their children meet society's expectations is to do it for them.

Some parents wish for their children to succeed in a competitive world and so they "brand" their children in the best light possible by creating facades. These children become badges of honor for their parents and a reflection of what parents want others to see in their children. Other parents "clip their children's wings" out of fear. Their goal is to protect their children from perceived harm, pain, or disappointment. Typically, these parents believe that their children are incapable of handling challenges or think they are still too young. These parents miss the fact that, just as the butterfly strengthens its wings breaking out of the cocoon, children build their own emotional muscles when they face challenges.

The long-term result for these children is failure to launch into adulthood. Just as the butterfly that did not break through its cocoon on its own fails to fly off, these children, as adults, fail to stand on their own. The parents then feel obligated to continue with their emotional and financial support because, in fact, they were the ones who created the over-dependence by clipping their children's wings in the first place.

Entitlement

Many families in Western societies are facing a new 21st century challenge—children who feel entitled. According to a poll conducted by *Time* magazine and CNN, two-thirds of American parents think that their children are spoiled (cited in Kolbert, 2012). Many parents shake their heads in frustration and are resigned to this reality. Sadly, they feel defeated and unable to correct the problem.

A combination of shifting socio-economics, roles, and values has contributed to the current rampant entitlement attitudes. Living in a time of prosperity and excess has created opportunities for over-consumption by adults and children, alike. Values have shifted from a focus on hard work to a lifestyle focused on materialism and fun. Cultural norms have changed parental roles from guides to super-givers. Parents living a life of ease and comfort no longer expect children to contribute to family life. These trends have been normalized as the path to success and happiness.

Entitlement in children is the direct result of parents who love their children too much. They misperceive their parental responsibility to include doing everything for their children, protecting their children from the slightest difficulty or pain, and giving them everything they ask for. What ensues is a dysfunctional dynamic wherein children expect people around them to give, do, and help at any cost. In the process, important life lessons are lost.

Examples of beliefs held by entitled children.

• Others will shield me from pain and disappointment.

• Others should take care of me and my needs.

• I just have to ask the people around me for what I want and they will get it because people don't want to say no to me.

• Everyone around me should make me happy and content at all times.

• I deserve to be happy all the time.

• My parents will bail me out of any situation.

Several tools are instrumental in counteracting the entitlement wave: Empowering (p. 90), Encouragement (p. 94), Letting Go (p. 111), Jobs (p. 109), Allowance (p. 74), Logical Consequences (p. 114), Natural Consequences (p. 125), Mistakes are Opportunities for Learning (p. 119), and Family Meetings (p. 96). By implementing all of these tools, parents gradually stretch their children's capacities to deal physically and emotionally with the realities of life. Children learn that to be successful they must own responsibility for their lives and have the patience to deal with the challenging non-fun aspects of living. When children recognize that it's up to them to decide what kind of life they want to lead, they will resist the entitlement wave.

Jobs

School aged children can take on bigger jobs and responsibilities in the home.

Examples of jobs that are appropriate for this age.

- Set the table.
- Prepare a meal.
- Peel vegetables.
- Wipe tables and countertops.
- Wash dishes.
- Load/unload the dishwasher.
- Empty grocery bags.
- Pack school lunches.
- Take laundry to hamper.
- Place laundry into washer.
- Move laundry from washer to dryer.
- Fold laundry and put away.
- Change bed sheets and towels.
- Take out the trash and recyclables.
- Dust.
- Vacuum.
- Mop floors.
- Water plants.
- Rake leaves, tidy garden.
- Wash windows and mirrors.
- Wash the car.
- Shovel snow.
- Feed pets.
- Clean pet cages/crates/bedding.

Technology

Fifteen years ago, parents worried their children watched too much television instead of playing outside. Today, technology has evolved to the point where children are glued to not only television screens, but tablets, computers, phones, game consoles, and the Internet—rarely playing outside or interacting with others face-to-face. The advancement of technology has had both positive and negative effects. Researchers (cited in Taylor, 2012) found positives such as improved hand/eye coordination and problem solving skills. Games and apps have also become an engaging platform for children to learn, create, and innovate ideas.

Nonetheless, technology has negatively impacted children's cognitive processes in areas such as attention span, decision-making, memory, and learning. Researchers (cited in Summers, 2014) at UCLA found that children who were removed from their devices for a period of five days were better able to read facial expressions and nonverbal cues compared to children who were continuously plugged into media. The study showed that children need face-to-face interactions to build empathy and connection.

Disconnecting children from electronics completely is neither practical nor possible. Electronics are an integral part of people's lives now. Balance is the key. Families must manage their use in a healthy way. Family Meetings (p. 96) provide wonderful opportunities to discuss and decide how much time to spend on electronics. I (Munira) have reviewed and revised our rules regarding electronics at Family Meetings many times in our home. We would brainstorm what everyone felt was reasonable and develop a plan when we found using the computer for homework spilled over to computer games. Many times my children would want to set up specific time limits for specific electronics. Our final decisions always balanced electronic time with extracurricular activities and unstructured play time. It was always a work in progress. It also required that my husband and I model our values by not being connected to our own electronics all the time. Each family has to find a balance that works for them.

We invite you to find a space in your home where all electronic use is done in an open area so that you are aware of what your children are watching, playing, or listening to at any given time. When technology consumption is a "public sport," children are less tempted to engage in media that is inappropriate. In our family computers and cell phones always stayed in the family room and were never allowed in bedrooms. Researchers (cited in Whiteman, 2013) have found that children who had televisions and computers in their bedrooms went to sleep later and had shorter sleep patterns, which negatively impacted their schoolwork and psychological growth. Electronics should be "parked" during meals, Family Meetings, family nights, and at a specific time in the evenings. By enforcing these types of rules, parents teach children self-control and the balanced use of electronics.

A word of advice: Children can be introduced to phones and computers with "basic models" instead of the latest and greatest. As they learn to be responsible for their items and their appropriate use, they can "graduate" to better phones and computers. As children get older and show more responsibility they can also contribute toward purchasing the more expensive items they want with the guidance of parents.

Internet Safety & Media Literacy

Just as parents do not hand their children the keys to their car without training, parents should not allow their children online without teaching them Internet safety. The Internet and media have progressed so quickly that most people can't keep up with the latest innovations. The Internet is a huge source of information, entertainment, connection, and efficiency. So, it will continue to play a major role in families' lives.

Good practices to teach Internet and media literacy.

- Install parental controls which limit exposure to inappropriate content on the Internet.
- Explain that not everything they find online will be true or good.
- Teach children how to use search engines by using critical thinking skills.
- Caution children about clicking advertising bars and buttons.
- Empower children with what they can do when inappropriate images pop up on the screen instead of seeding guilt and shame.
- Encourage children to seek help when they are uncertain what to do.
- Instruct them to avoid sharing personal information (age, where they live, or where they go to school) with others online.
- Be firm about not trusting people they have only met online since they won't really know who they are.
- Teach children to create non-identifying usernames to

protect their privacy.

- Explain what junk mail is. Warn them of inappropriate messages sent as spam and instruct them not to open them.
- Invite them to reject friend requests from people they don't know.
- Discuss the ramifications of posting photos or comments to online forums.
- Explain what "digital footprints" are and how they can impact major life decisions.

As a parent in the 21st Century, be aware and connected to current trends in smartphone apps, social media and Internet sites. Children's likes and dislikes in computer games, apps, websites, music, and movies will evolve as they get older. Whatever media your children find interesting is an opportunity for you to learn, teach, and engage with them. Engaging with children at their level, discussing what they are experiencing, and advising them along the way will keep parents aware of their online activities.

Have conversations about your values, what is age-appropriate, and why you are limiting their exposure to media that is violent and/or has sexual content. Children need to understand what their parents value and why. Doing so will empower them to make healthy choices when they are away from parents and when they are older with more access to technology. Families can have regular discussions about the messages learned from media consumed. This creates intentionality and consciousness about the entertainment consumed and reinforces family values.

Struggles at School

With children attending school an average of six hours a day, their academic and social experiences imprint their sense of self and their abilities. A strong partnership between parents and teachers becomes vital for success in school, as studies (Olsen & Fuller, 2011) show children do better in school when their parents are involved in their school experience. Struggles in school can range from minor to severe and from short-term to long-term.

Common challenges related to school attendance.

- Poor academic performance.
- Lack of motivation.
- Disruptive behavior.
- Poor relationships with classmates or teachers.

There can be various factors, both personal and school related, that contribute to a child's struggles at school.

Examples of personal factors.

- Developmental difficulties (Down syndrome, cerebral palsy, etc.)
- Cognitive difficulties (dyslexia, attention deficit disorder, autism, etc.)
- Psychosocial difficulties (poverty, immigration, conflictual divorce, drug use, etc.).
- Chronic illness (cancer, rheumatic fever, diabetes, etc.).
- Trauma (wars, natural disasters, death in the family, abuse, etc.).

Examples of school factors.

- Bullying.
- Disconnection from peers, teachers, or school culture.
- Mismatch between student's ability and academic standard—over or under challenged.
- Lack of academic support.
- Competing demands of extracurricular activities.

Struggles such as these need to be addressed by parents and teachers as soon as possible. The experience children have in school has a major impact on their general well-being. Problems not addressed early lead to poor self-esteem, mistrust of others, and disinterest in learning. Sadly, when parents and teachers label students as "troublemakers" or "easily distracted," children succumb to deep feelings of inadequacy and shame. Academic and behavioral struggles are a sign children need support not labels and blame. Every child's situation will be different. However, it is critical to focus on solving problems, uncovering the child's hidden strengths, and asking for help from teachers, administrators, psychologists.

Homework Battles

Completing assignments and projects at home can turn after-school hours into a challenging time for parents. Thinking about homework as a positive activity that is the responsibility of the child can change the family dynamics. Homework is for the child not the parent. A parent's responsibility lies in creating an environment at home that encourages independence and personal responsibility.

Many of the common struggles with homework can be managed with Routines (p. 137). Develop a written after-school routine delineating homework time and other activities. Some children need time to decompress and snack before studying. Others may get straight to it before doing anything else. Whatever the routine is, make it one that satisfies both the child and the parent. A parent's responsibility is to protect that time from other tasks such as running errands or rushing from one activity to another.

Tips for a productive homework routine.

- Create a quiet work area where all supplies are ready and available for the child to work independently.
- Use Timers for Young Children (p. 148) to teach children how to manage time and take appropriate breaks.
- Create clear enforceable rules about the use of electronics. Some parents choose to have phones in the "parking area" while children are doing homework. Others allow children access to their phones for a limited time every hour.
- Be consistent with bedtime routines *even* when homework was not completed. An empowering statement would be, "It seems that your choices today did not work for you. *Insha Allah* (God willing) tomorrow you can make better choices about your homework. If you would like, you can wake up earlier to do your homework. Right now it is bedtime."
- Do not correct the homework for the child or ask the child to redo it. If the parent is dissatisfied with the quality of the work, ask the child, "Are you satisfied with the work you have done?" This allows children to reflect on their own

personal work standards and make decisions based on the values they are developing.

- Absolutely refrain from reminding children to do homework.

Some children will ask their parents for help with their homework. Some will ask their parents to sit with them while doing homework. This robs children of the space needed to be independent and responsible. Parents can review the directions with the child and clarify any questions. Then they can show faith that the child can do the work independently by leaving the child to complete the assignment. If a child is struggling with a concept and does not understand the assignment, a parent can choose to re-teach the assignment to the child or can leave a note on the assignment for the teacher, explaining that the child needs more help with the concept. Also, encouraging the child to ask the teacher directly to further explain the concept will create open communication between teacher, student, and parent. Review the tools Dealing with the Belief Behind the Behavior (p. 83) and Empowering versus Enabling (p. 90).

Forgetting Things

Children learn important life skills preparing for school, completing homework, returning permission slips, and taking their lunch. With every school year, there are greater demands, experiences, responsibilities, and expectations. Inevitably, one day they will forget something and it will probably be something important. Many parents will rush to fix the problem by quickly going home to retrieve the item or speaking to the teacher to grant an excuse. However, when forgetting items becomes a constant problem, parents become frustrated by their children's irresponsibility. Forgetting things is an excellent opportunity to teach a child personal responsibility.

Deciding What You Will Do (p. 85) is the tool of choice for this challenge. The first time children forget something, parents can reflect with them how to prevent the situation from repeating itself and the Natural Consequences (p. 125) if it happens again. Forgetting items was common with my (Munira) children, to the extent that one of my sons once got into the car without shoes, and not until we were pulling up to the school did it occur to him. In that moment, not knowing if I should scream, laugh or cry, I turned the car around to retrieve his shoes and we discussed what needed to happen in the morning to help him remember his shoes. He never forgot his shoes again, but my sons have forgotten lunches, homework, permission slips, projects, jackets, etc. The agreement that I made with them was this: The first time they forgot something, I would get it for them. Any time after that they would have to figure it out on their own. I told them I had faith that they would find a way to resolve the problem and be responsible.

Follow Through (p. 104) will be important in these situations. It is easy to make the agreement with the child, but not so easy to Follow Through. When you get to work and look in the back seat and see your son's lunch sitting there, what will you do? When your daughter calls you to tell you she left her project at home, what will you do? You will remind your children of the agreement, empathize with their struggle, show faith and then do nothing. They may be a little uncomfortable at school that day or it may affect their grade, but the Natural Consequences (p. 125) will be remembered. After many experiences like these, my own children learned to be responsible. So much so, that when my son was in middle school and forgot something at home, his teacher told him to call his mother to get it, and he responded, "No, she won't come. It was my responsibility."

Friendships

Having good friends is an important part of life. Helping your child value positive friendships can be a great comfort throughout life. Researchers (Berndt, 2002) have found that children's classroom friendships significantly impact their well-being, affecting both adjustment to school and psychosocial development. Friendships move beyond the pre-planned play dates of early childhood to where children begin to choose their friends. Their personalities flourish in school. The extroverted child gathers friends for games on the playground while the introverted child plays on the swings with one other friend. The number of friends and the types of friends will be different for every child. Chosen friends usually reflect where children are at a given time in their life.

Once parents realize that their children's social circle can have both a positive and negative influence, they may seek to control it. When parents attempt to control or criticize the friends children choose, they send the message that children have poor judgment and can't make good independent decisions. This lack of faith in the child usually stems from the parents' anxiety about the child making wrong choices. Friendships, even when parents disapprove, can be opportunities to teach children valuable relationship lessons. In the process, the parent-child relationship will strengthen. If the parent-child bond is strong, parents will exert greater influence on their children's development than the peer group they interact with.

Parents cannot control whom their children choose to befriend, but they have a lot of influence by modeling healthy friendships, teaching how to choose friends, sharing observations they notice about friendship dynamics, and building good relationships with their children's friends. Beginning when a child is very young, parents can engage in general conversations about friendships by asking the child, "What makes someone a good friend?" "Are you a good friend to others?" Parents can also reflect on their own friendships and share with their children how they met their friends and why they have remained friends. This creates an opportunity to share family values regarding healthy friendships and character traits. For example, discussions can include what friends have in common, how they treat each other with respect, are dependable, are fun to be with, are trustworthy, etc. In addition, children are encouraged to be good friends and embody good character in their interactions with others. "Mix with the noble people, you will become one of them; and keep away from evil people to protect yourself from their evils" (Hadith, Bukhari, Muslim).

Tips to help children with friendships.

- Show Faith. Parents can show confidence in their child's ability and character by saying:
  - "I know you are friends with people who share your values."
  - "You have many things in common. I can see how you are friends."

- "You can be a good influence on one another."

- Communicate. Ask your children what they specifically enjoy about their friends so you have a better understanding about what need the relationship is fulfilling for them. Clear, open, and non-judgmental communication with your child will strengthen the respect and trust between you.

- Empower. Show an interest in your children's friends and encourage them to invite their friends over so that you can also build a positive relationship with their friends. Create a home environment where your child feels comfortable inviting friends into the home.

- Listening. When children have conflicts with friends, use Listening (p. 113) skills to hear their complaints, worries, and experiences. Do not interfere or solve their problems for them. Have faith they can handle disagreements on their own, and they will seek your advice if they need it. Mirror (p. 118) to your children their worries and complaints by saying:
    - "You are feeling really upset that Ahmad said that to you."
    - "You are really worried Aisha won't be your friend."
    - "You are hurt Bilal treated you this way."
    - "What do you think will happen next?"
    - "What will you do tomorrow?"

Social experiences help children grow and learn about what they value and how to build healthy relationships with others.

Bullying

According to the National Center for Education Statistics (2013), 22 percent of students aged 12 - 18 reported having been bullied at school. Bullying is intentional tormenting of someone physically (hitting and shoving), verbally (name calling), or psychologically (mocking, intimidating). Bullying can also be done subversively by shunning, taunting, or spreading rumors via social media and texting. All forms of bullying are detrimental to a child's well-being, safety, and self-esteem. Parents may be unaware a child is being bullied unless they see physical injuries or the child shares the incident. However, any of the following symptoms could signal a child is struggling with bullying: increased anxiety, poor sleeping and eating habits, withdrawal from activities, or avoidance of people and situations.

Since bullying takes many forms and ranges in severity, there is no one-size-fits-all approach. Factors such as the child's age, language skills, type of bullying behavior, and severity of the situation will determine the best course of action. School officials and police authorities take bullying seriously because all students should feel safe going to school.

Tips for responding to bullying.

- Curiosity Questions. Find opportunities to bring up the issue of bullying. For instance, if you see a situation on a TV show or in a book, use it as a conversation starter. Ask your child:
    - "What do think of this?"
    - "Have you ever seen someone get bullied at school?"
    - "What was that like?"
    - "What do you think the person can do?"

- Teach Children What to Do. Ask them how they could respond if they are bullied or see it happening to someone else. Encourage children to tell an adult if they see bullying happening or if it happens to them.

- Listening. If your child tells you they are being bullied, listen calmly and offer comfort and support. A child may feel embarrassed, ashamed, and worried that you will be upset, disappointed, or angry. You must remain calm and practice active listening.

- Mirroring Feelings. Children who share they are being bullied are vulnerable and need comfort and understanding from their parents. Children may believe the bullying is their own fault and be scared of telling lest the bully finds out and makes the situation worse, or be worried that you won't believe them or won't do anything about it, or be anxious you may urge them to fight back.

- Encouragement. Commend children for being open and sharing this information with you. Remind them that bullying behavior has more to do with the bully than with them. Avoid saying, "Be strong." Say, "It's natural to be scared. Courage is about facing your fear."

- Problem Solve. Discuss with your children how you can help them feel safe at school. Have your children decide if they want to speak to a teacher about the situation, or if they want you to come to the school and help them share the situation with their teacher. Encouraging children to speak to their teacher or administrator empowers them and shifts the locus of control to them.

- Empower. Giving children tools for how to deal with

bullying will shift the locus of control back to them and give them solid responses. Examples include: avoiding the bully and using the buddy system at school; walking away and practicing self-soothing strategies when they are angry; acting brave and ignoring the bully; blocking the bully from their social media and texting; and seeking the help of an adult.

• Decide What You Will Do. Continue to check in with your children about the effect bullying is having on their academic and social environment at school. Evaluate and decide what the long-term solution will be if the problem is not resolved effectively. Sometimes changing environments may be the only way to eliminate the bullying experience.

Islam-the-Habit

In the Islamic tradition, children are blank slates until they reach puberty, after which their deeds, both good and bad, begin to matter. More importantly, at the time of puberty they become accountable for their religious practices. However, puberty is not an instant switch. Puberty is a critical point along the path of training children in Islam-the-Habit. It's the point at which a parent tells a child, "Your religious practice is now a real responsibility. What you do with this responsibility matters in the sight of Allah, so be aware of how you move forward with your faith. I love you. I am here to help and support, but the power is in your hands."

Parents are Allah's messengers to their children. While humans are created in a state of *fitra* (a pure state that is capable of knowing Allah if unhindered), living life can be a major distraction from knowing Allah. Hence, how parents lead their lives either enhances or hinders the connection with Allah. The initial teaching and guidance establishes Islam-the-Habit, while the shift to Islam as a personal choice and a way of life, develops in adolescence and beyond. No one can predict when a child has shifted from Islam-the-Habit to Islam-the-Choice (discussed further in the teen section). A parent's sole responsibility is passing on the message and it is not tied to the results.

Prayer and fasting are religious obligations at the time of puberty. Prior to that age, scholars suggest parents invite children to pray and fast when they are between the ages of seven and ten. Encouraging children to fast and pray does not mean to force, coerce, or worse, punish (see Spanking in the Islamic Context, p. 379). Rather, guidance in the early years about prayers, as well as the significance of Ramadan, should be in the spirit of sharing Islamic values with love and respect. The following discussion addresses concrete steps for training children in Islam-the-Habit during the middle childhood years.

Prayers.

Rituals in Islam are opportunities to nurture a child's spirituality. A parent's actions will speak far louder than lectures and demands. Children that see their parents pray will naturally emulate these rituals. Notice how pre-verbal toddlers raised in practicing homes will mimic the acts of prayer simply by hearing the *athan* (call to prayer). Allah has created humans with this innate ability to learn vicariously. However, in order for the rituals to have meaning for children, parents must share the deeper spiritual meaning behind the acts of worship: Why is prayer important to them? What do they pray for? How does prayer connect them to Allah? As children mature and prayer time becomes a valued habit in the home, they will take personal responsibility for their prayers with little reminding. I (Munira) offered my children a choice to pray or sit quietly as part of their spiritual development. When they chose not to pray, our family rule was they had to sit quietly in contemplation reflecting on what they were grateful for while we completed our group prayers. I reminded them that they were not praying for my sake. Rather, their prayer was a time to talk to Allah and connect with their Creator so they can be grounded spiritually and have a focused and purposeful life. (See Nurturing Spirituality, p. 367).

Ways to establish the habit of prayers.

- Evaluate what you are modeling. Your children will be empowered by what they see you do and practice on a regular basis. Asking them to do what you personally don't practice is not effective.

- Teach your child how to pray. Teach the components of prayers: *wudu* (ablution), *al-Fatiha* (the opening chapter of the Quran), *tahiyat* (salutations), *tasbeeh* (glorification of God), how to pray, number of prayers, numbers of *rakat* (prayer cycles). Let them model the steps out loud or lead prayer with siblings.

- Create your home-mosque. It does not need to be a full room, nor does it need to be a big space. Simply a clean and beautiful area at home that can be dedicated for prayer where all prayer rugs and prayer clothes can be found. *Alhamdu Lillah* (all praise to God) I (Noha) created such a place in my home. My niece, who was living with us, reflected that praying in that space was different than praying in her own room. I have personally felt the difference in ambience between spaces consistently used for worship and non-worship spaces.

- Project the *athan* (call to prayer) at home. With changing technology, ideas come and go. Choose one that works for your home.

- Go back to the basics. Obligatory prayers are the five daily prayers. Focus your effort on these. Teach your child about the *sunnah* (voluntary) prayers and relay their value in connecting with Allah. But we encourage you to avoid pressuring your child to pray them. Focus on establishing the habit of the five prayers. We have observed children who felt overwhelmed because of all the *sunnah* prayers that were emotionally imposed on them to the point that some chose to let go of all prayers, including the five obligatory ones.

- Pray together as a family. Have a Family Meeting (p. 96) where you discuss the details of praying together: When will you pray? Who will call the prayer? Where will you pray? We invite you to establish the mosque rule in your home. At the mosque, prayer does not wait for people. Prayer is what gets people to come. Enact the same rule at home. Once the family has agreed on when and how to call to prayer, start the prayer even if some family members are missing. It is surprising how this simple rule gets people to come hurriedly, much more so than reminders and coaxing.

- Connect with the mosque. When possible, attend the congregational prayers, thus connecting children with the larger Muslim community.

- Practice prayers when out and about. Model maintaining

prayers when going about your life, e.g. when spending the day at an amusement park, at the mall, while traveling, etc.

Encouraging a child in the early years can be done in different ways. Some examples are hugs and kisses after prayers are done, saying, "May Allah be pleased with you as I am pleased with you." And catching children remembering the prayers on their own and saying, "My heart fills with joy whenever I see you being responsible for your prayers. May Allah bless you in this life and the hereafter."

Avoid criticizing the way your child prays. Your role is to help your child establish the habit early on. The fine tuning of the prayer itself is a personal mission that will certainly take time and will be different from one child to another. Some parents demand the repetition of prayers because they did not like the way the child prayed. Please avoid doing that. In situations where the child is praying erroneously we invite you to utilize the following approach: "Are you open to hearing an observation I have about your prayer?" If the child says, "No," respect that. If the child is open to hearing your comments, continue. "I have noticed that you touch the ground in *sujood* (prostration) before the *imam* and I wanted to let you know that, since we are following the *imam*, he needs to be the first one to touch the ground. Do you have questions about this? Do you have questions about prayers or anything else?"

We invite you to let go of all material incentives for prayers. Avoid establishing reward systems to motivate a child to pray. Some parents associate every prayer with a monetary reward. Some have a prayer chart; when the child prays a certain number in a week, the child gets a gift. These parents are coming from a place of love. However, there is danger when children associate their actions and performance with immediate gratification. Rewards can easily become the focus instead of the prayers themselves. When a child works on their prayers for the sake of the material reward, they are more likely to resist maintaining the prayers when they don't like the reward. From the beginning, associate prayers with seeking a connection with Allah, nothing else. In turn, link the connection with Allah to the delayed gratification of living a good life in this life and the hereafter. "Whoever works righteousness, man or woman and has faith, verily, to him will We give a life that is good, and We will bestow on such their reward according to the best of their actions" (Quran, 16:97).

If there is a need, keeping a chart to track the child's progress is fine as long as it's not associated with any reward. Some children need a visual tool to see how well they are doing in keeping up their regular prayers. Other children do not need such a chart. Collaborate on the tracking chart only if the child is interested in one and will be responsible for filling in the chart themselves, as opposed to the parent doing so.

If you notice that some members of the family are not being consistent in prayer, engage them in conversations seeking to understand, not to shame or lecture. For example, say, "I have noticed you are having a hard time praying consistently. I am wondering what is going on. Prayer is an important piece in our connection with Allah and it takes effort to maintain. I know it's not easy. What would help you? How can you work around this challenge? How would you like me to support you?" For some children practicing prayers will be easy and smooth. For others, it will be a life-long struggle. Remember your role is not to coerce; rather, your role is to teach, guide, and support.

If one parent prays and the other does not, we invite the parent who prays to be the one in charge of the task of prayers. In my practice, I (Noha) have observed families where the praying parent exerts pressure on the non-praying parent to take charge of this responsibility with mounting tension and resentment. It's not gender specific. I have seen fathers pressuring non-praying mothers and vice versa. Children will ultimately observe the discrepancy in the practice between the two parents. Parents can avoid labels and judgment and use rationales that touch upon struggle. Instead of saying, "Your Mom/Dad is not a good Muslim because he/she is not praying," say, "Your Mom/Dad is working on making prayer a priority in his/her life. We will pray for him/her so Allah will make it easier for him/her." Remember that, ultimately, establishing prayers is an individual responsibility. Your role is to teach, support, and encourage.

Fasting.

Another religious obligation that parents seek to nurture is fasting. Fasting can be a very difficult exercise for children since most can't imagine being without food and water for extended periods of time. In the Arab culture, the process of taking small steps to train a child to fast is called "Steps of the Minaret." Just as one ascends to the top of the minaret via steps, so does one reach the full fasting day through tiny steps. Children between the ages of seven and ten are invited to fast a few days or half days. I (Munira) have found that encouraging my children to begin fasting after lunch time (rather than the morning time) until *iftar* (meal breaking the fast) is rewarding for them as they get to break the fast with the family. Some children may choose to fast only on weekends in Ramadan, while others may choose to abstain from food but drinking only water. As children get older, allow them the space to decide when they are willing to try fasting whole days in Ramadan. When children are feeling weak during the fast, acknowledge the difficulty of fasting and invite them to find ways that would help them persevere to the end of the day. All forms of fasting for children should be celebrated and encouraged as these are stepping stones to build their endurance for fasting the month of Ramadan.

As with prayers, avoid associating any rewards with fasting. The lasting joy of accomplishments far exceeds the transitory excitement of rewards. One of my children (Noha) to this day is very proud of the fact that he fasted the whole month of Ramadan at the age of seven. It was his choice, and he felt capable and accomplished at the end of that Ramadan.

Remember that religious obligations are individual responsibilities. Avoid shaming children if they choose to break their fast some days. Instead, encourage them by saying, "It seems you had a hard time fasting today. I wonder what happened? What is different today? What can you do to help yourself fast tomorrow?" If a child says, "I don't want to fast," engage the child in a conversation of understanding by saying, "Tell me what is going on. What is the difficult piece about fasting for you? How can you work around that? What would help you? How can I help you?" Validate the child's feelings. Avoid dismissing or minimizing these feelings by saying, "Oh! That's not a big deal! I know you can do it!" Instead say, "So, fasting is very hard for you.

You feel tired and hungry all day. I can see how difficult it is for you." Be sure to send the core message that "fasting is between you and Allah. He Cherishes those who fast so highly; and He has promised them infinite rewards."

In Muslim-majority countries, the month of Ramadan transforms the whole country: work and school schedules change, mosques swell with *taraweeh* (night prayers) attendees, special food items are prepared, shopping hours change from day to night, even media companies create special 30-day TV programs. Children raised in these countries absorb the significance of Ramadan effortlessly. However, in non-Muslim majority countries, individual families create the Ramadan atmosphere. In the U.S., Ramadan has become a month of festivities associated with decorating the house, community *iftars* (meal breaking the fast), attending the mosque nightly, gathering with friends and family, and participating in homeless feedings and toy drives. Families can actively create unique memorable traditions that make the month extra special for children living in non-Muslim countries.

Ideas for memorable traditions.

• Prepare special appetizers for the month.

• Make a paper chain to count down to Ramadan and/or Eid.

• Use special serving dishes for meals.

• Hang a Ramadan calendar to track the days.

• Keep a good deeds journal.

• Create a charity collection jar.

• Have *suhour* (pre-dawn meal) at a 24-hour restaurant.

• Bake cookies for neighbors.

- Prepare Eid cookies with family members.
- Read and discuss the meaning of Quran as a family.
- Listen to the Quran in the car and at home.
- Share an *iftar* meal with non-Muslim friends.
- Visit the holy cities of Makkah and Madina.

Empower your children in suhour.

Suhour is a *sunnah* (voluntary) not *fard* (obligatory) and adults differ in how they engage with it. Some people eat before they sleep and others wake up for the pre-dawn meal. Keeping these facts in mind empowers parents to grant children the space to make their own decisions about how they want to handle *suhour*. It is unfortunate that *suhour* has become a major struggle in some families. Invoking the Prophet's (pbuh) tradition, have a Family Meeting (p. 96) to transform *suhour* into an empowering experience:

- Share the Prophet's (pbuh) recommendation: "Have *suhour* for there are blessings in *suhour*." No lecture is necessary. Just a statement of the hadith.
- Explain that it's a *sunnah*, not *fard*, intended to strengthen one's ability to fast, especially during long summer days. No lecture is necessary. Just a Statement of Fact (p. 143).
- Explain the two major ways of managing *suhour* as mentioned above (before sleep vs. wake up before *fajr*, dawn prayer). Invite your children to choose which way they want to follow (Limited Choices, p. 112).
- Invite those who choose to wake up before *fajr* to think about how they will wake up. Invite children to wake themselves

up. If necessary, buy an alarm clock.

- If children want you to wake them up, establish the rule that you will go into their room only one time. Be firm about not going in again and again to wake them up.

- Ask the question, "What's going to happen if you don't wake up for *suhour*?" Allow them to reflect.

- If your children miss *suhour*, please don't panic. They will be fine. They may feel hungry and tired, but that is what fasting is about. They will survive the day and learn more about the impact of hunger on the body and psyche.

- Invite children to tell you what they would like to have for *suhour*. However, you have veto power. If it is something you don't want to spend your time making, gently say, "I know you love… However, this dish takes a lot of effort and time and it will be difficult to make for *suhour*." Or offer to make it one time during Ramadan.

- Expect children to be active in making and preparing their own *suhour*.

- Ask what items family members would like to always have on hand during the month and make them available.

- Avoid the practice of feeding your children in their bed while they are half asleep. Let them take responsibility for their fasting and *suhour*.

Modesty.

Parents teach children the value of modesty in all aspects of their life, from how they speak and behave to the clothing they wear. In Islam, modesty is a topic that applies *equally* to both boys and girls. Modesty is a way of life that begins in early childhood.

Parental values that are modeled and taught become the compass for children into adulthood.

I (Munira) was raised in a home where modesty was expected in my actions and words. While the *hijab* (head covering) did not come up in my home, neither as a requirement nor as a non-requirement, I was, nonetheless, expected to dress with dignity and self-respect. Most importantly, I was invited to interact with others with ethical fortitude. My parents' expectations revolved around modesty of behavior—don't flirt, speak with respect, don't swear. In short, my parents picked their battles, and what I wore simply was not one of them. When I was in college, I was intrigued and influenced by the outward forms of modesty I saw in my Muslim friends, I and gradually moved towards wearing longer clothes until I decided to wear the *hijab* myself.

Similarly, in raising my own sons, I taught them the value of modesty by focusing on how they behave and speak with others. I focused on modesty as a dimension of their character. Put-downs were never acceptable, and speaking respectfully to elders was always expected. Kindness and good manners towards their friends, siblings, and teachers were outward manifestations of their modesty. I also raised them from a young age to be aware and protective of their bodies. For instance, when they went swimming, I insisted they wear long shorts and rash guard shirts. This was partially to protect them from the sun, but also to build in them a sense of personal modesty. One of my sons loved to wear shorts all the time. I respected his preference while emphasizing the need to have shorts that cover his knees for prayers. These were small ways I encouraged them to maintain modesty in their appearance while always upholding modesty in their behavior and speech. I taught them that modesty begins with their heart and ends with their clothing.

The issue of *hijab* is a source of much debate and varied opinions. The views women hold about *hijab* fall into four general categories (Shabbas, 2006):

1. Those who believe it's a *fard* (obligatory practice) on every woman and practice it.

2. Those who believe it's a *fard* on every woman but choose not to practice it for various reasons.

3. Those who wear it because it's a cultural norm and have not made the conscious choice to wear it as a religious practice.

4. Those who don't believe it's a *fard* and are against wearing it for both cultural and religious reasons.

The following reflections are intended for the first category who believe in the practice of *hijab* and seek to train their daughters to wear it. I (Noha) am a believer in the practice of *hijab*. *Alhamdu Lillah* (all praise to God), I made the decision to practice it at the age of 12. However, the social norms of my family and my Arab culture at the time did not view *hijab* as a religious obligation. It was seen as a cultural practice. Accordingly, my decision to wear it was met with resistance in my family. It took me two years to get my mom, in particular, on board. My mom (may Allah bless her in this life and the hereafter) was worried that it would deprive and restrict my life. She wished that I would enjoy life free of the bounds of *hijab*. I am grateful to Allah that I was firm in my resolve and finally began wearing it at the age of 14. *Alhamdu Lillah* (all praise to God) I have not regretted that decision at any time in my life. On the contrary, I personally believe wearing it so early protected me from obsessing over how I looked and what people thought of me. I was able to direct my energy away from seeking the attention of others toward cultivating my inner peace.

That was my personal journey. When Allah blessed me with two lovely daughters, I had to think about how I would handle the issue of *hijab* with them. It was important for me to establish the habit with them, but I did not want to force the issue. In my conversations with my daughters I would casually say that when they reached puberty, they would wear *hijab*. In this way they began to visualize themselves in *hijab* and they knew my expectation. We were blessed with a group of friends who all practiced *hijab*. So my daughters had other role models wearing *hijab* in our social circle. When the issue came up about women who don't wear *hijab*, I would mention that some women have a difficult time with *hijab* and that does not diminish their worth, as Allah Knows the struggles of everyone. I chose not to encourage a "training period" for *hijab* where they wore it before it became obligatory.

As my daughters neared the anticipated time of puberty, I suggested they begin the new school year wearing *hijab*, only at school, so that when puberty hit sometime during the year, people at school were already used to them with their *hijab*. However, there were many girls in our social circle who chose to wear the *hijab* only once they reached puberty even if that occurred midyear and they managed fine.

My focus with *hijab* was the basics, which meant I didn't insist on a specific style of *hijab* but gave my daughters the freedom to choose how they would wear it within some broad limits. While I tend to wear dresses and skirts, my daughters chose to wear pants and shirts. I certainly vetoed some items. But, in general, my attitude was that of training and granting them the space to figure out how they wanted to navigate this journey with Allah.

One day on our way to class, Munira was wondering how mothers of girls handle the *hijab* issue, especially considering today's climate when Islam is being undermined from many directions. I explained to her what I did with my girls. In response she wondered if what I did was forcing them, since they did not come out and say they wanted to wear it, and since I did not posit the *hijab* issue as a choice. I had not thought about my strategy as such and, after some contemplation, I realized that what I did was set an expectation that my girls did not question because of our own lifestyle. I don't consider that forcing; rather, I nudged them in the direction of *hijab*. To force a girl into *hijab* would be to coerce her when she clearly does not want to wear it. It does not mean my daughters loved wearing the *hijab* at the time. It was a struggle, but one they did not reject. I remember telling Munira that setting the expectation for my girls fulfilled my duty as a parent—guiding and initiating the training process. What the girls do with their *hijab* later in life is their decision. I did not realize that those words would haunt me later on. In her freshman year of college my youngest daughter chose to take off her *hijab*. It was a difficult time for me. However, because I differentiated between my responsibilities (teach and encourage) and her responsibilities (choose her actions), I was able to accept the fact that I did my part, and it was up to her to walk her own spiritual journey.

I share with you my personal strategy for *hijab* with my daughters because it's difficult to predict what will work in a family without knowing the family's dynamics or context. Every family is different. Every family will need to decide what works for them. Between the time we began writing this book (2013) and the time of publication (2016), I have noticed two major shifts in attitudes toward *hijab* in the American Muslim community. One, there is a wave of young women who are choosing to take off their *hijab* because it does not hold a spiritual meaning for them. Secondly, among practicing parents, some are presenting *hijab* as a personal choice to young daughters instead of expecting them to wear it.

General guidelines.

- Reflect on your personal belief and practice about *hijab*.
- Reflect on what message you would like to convey to your daughter.
- Observe the current social norms regarding *hijab* in your community. What do you like? What do you not like?
- Ask your friends and people you respect how they choose to handle *hijab* in their families.
- Come up with a plan early. Don't wait until your daughter has reached puberty to start thinking about it.

Differentiate between nudging and forcing. Nudging is setting the expectation and working through your daughter's concerns step by step. Nudging is listening and validating her feelings then working on possible solutions. Forcing is refusing to hear any discussions or entertain any compromises. Forcing is using threats when the girl has clearly stated she does not want to wear *hijab*. Forcing is saying and behaving in a way that sends the message, "My way or the highway!"

Some parents are wary of nudging their daughters toward *hijab* because they are afraid they will take it off later in life. Some people believe that it's worse to put on the *hijab* and take it off than not wearing it in the first place. I do not agree with that sentiment. My mom just recently reminded me of the promise she extracted from me before agreeing to my request to wear the hijab: I was never to hesitate in taking it off, if I chose to later on in life. My amazing mom liberated me from the shackles of worrying about what people might say and invited me to be authentic and genuine. In life we encounter random windows of spirituality that, if not taken advantage of, are lost to us. *Hijab* is a practice that requires patience and time before it becomes a spiritual practice. If your daughter is interested in wearing it, avoid telling her she must be certain she will keep it on for the rest of her life. Celebrate her spirituality burst, encourage it, and then pray that it will become a lifelong practice for her. None of us can guarantee that. But if we don't start at some point, despite the uncertainty, we rob ourselves of the chance to do it. *Bil tawfiq* (with divine success).

Islam for life.

Many Muslim parents focus on the ritualistic aspect of Islam and lose sight of instilling a solid foundation of *aqeeda* (articles of faith). What is prayer, charity, fasting, *hijab*, if not stemming from a connection with Allah? Therefore, we invite you to dedicate energy and effort to teaching children about Islamic tenets that pertain to the meaning of life: Islam for living a spiritually satisfying life. There are many ways to transmit these messages: Islamic schools, weekend schools, private teachers, study circles, youth groups, conferences, podcasts, YouTube videos, etc.

However, the most influential teachers are you, the parents—through how you live Islam on a daily basis. Based on our observations of how children relate to Islam, we invite you to cover the following areas of Islam with depth and understanding:

- Loving Allah.
- Purpose of creation and life.
- Islamic view of who Allah is and his attributes.
- Islamic character, ethics, and morality.
- Prophet Muhammad (pbuh): his story and character.
- Love and responsibility toward others: family, friends, neighbors, community, humanity.
- Racial, gender, and social equality.
- Self-worth defined by a connection with Allah.
- *Qadar* (divine preordination of good and evil events).
- Stories of other prophets.
- Stories of early Muslims.
- Angels.
- Quran and Holy Books.
- Death and afterlife.
- Trials as an integral part of life.
- Intentionality in all actions.
- Generosity in various forms.
- Compassion towards Allah's creations.
- Positive mental attitude.
- Balanced living.
- Gratitude for everything perceived as good and bad.

While the middle childhood years are considered the "golden years" of parenting, the next stage is referred to as the "turbulent years" or the "family team years" depending on family dynamics. During the teen years children begin to separate and individuate from their parents. This natural process can be fraught with tension and resistance in some families. For others, those years showcase powerful collaboration and teamwork. In the next chapter we cover common areas of conflict, invitations to shift perceptions, and specific ideas for how to navigate these significant years.

CHAPTER 8

THE TEEN YEARS (13-18)

Adolescence is the transitional period between childhood and young adulthood. Teens experience profound biological and emotional changes. As their neural pathways rapidly expand and restructure, they exhibit random mood shifts and behavior changes. They begin the necessary process of separation and individuation while striving for a deeper understanding of who they are and what the world is.

In connected families, the role of the parent shifts at this stage to that of a mentor. The strong relationship established with the child in earlier years becomes the foundation from which the teen springs forward to navigate social circles and make independent decisions. The teen relies on the support and encouragement of the parent while seeking autonomy to explore and learn. While remaining present and available, parents begin the process of letting go and allow space for teens to forge their own paths into adulthood.

During adolescence, parents will fully experience the impact of their earlier parenting style. The negative ramifications of dysfunctional dynamics (such as permissive and authoritarian parenting styles) dramatically come to the forefront resulting in many families seeking help and counseling. In households where authoritative parenting was utilized, there will be a strong family connection that will weather common teen challenges successfully.

There is no way for us to predict where you are in your relationship with your teen. Therefore, some of what is shared in this section may sound impossible, ridiculous, trivial, or nonsensical. The suggestions outlined in this section will be easier for parents who implemented the authoritative style (Positive Discipline parenting) from an early age. This does not mean that parents with other parenting styles need to give up. It is never too late to change course and utilize a different parenting style. In reality, it is the only option available if a parent is interested in changing the family dynamic.

Parenting an Adolescent

By the time a child is a teen, an authoritative parent has learned that the child is an independent person and not merely an extension of the parent. While the early years have cemented the parent-child bond, they have also provided space for the parent to begin the process of letting go gently and slowly. Authoritative parents know that these will be the final years before the real "letting go" occurs in early adulthood. Contrary to the stereotypical description of the teen years as troublesome and miserable, many authoritative parents share that the teen years are beautiful. These parents feel connected to their teens. They also feel pride and joy as their teens exhibit independence, responsibility, accountability, integrity, etc. Connected families typically cherish these "family team years" as a result of all the hard work exerted during the early years to establish a strong spirit of collaboration and respect. This does not suggest that teens of authoritative parents are "perfect" or without challenges. They are teens, after all! However, the connection, mutual respect, and focus on solutions empower these families to weather the difficulties of adolescence.

Authoritarian parents, on the other hand, enter the teen years with the expectation that their children will be a younger reflection of them. They believe that their teens' behavior and thinking must be in exact alignment with theirs. When parents and teens share the same worldviews, parents believe they have the "perfect" teen. However, problems arise in authoritarian households when the teen's worldview not only does not align, it collides. These parents experience the commonly termed "turbulent teen" years.

Permissive parents may not expect their teens to be a replica of them, but they do expect them to follow their guidance out of pure love. It comes as a shock to them when their teens continue to forge their own paths, even to their own detriment and with disregard to parental guidance. Permissive parents mistakenly believe that loving their children without establishing boundaries when they are young will garner obedience from these children as teens. It's true that, in these families, the loving bond may be strong during adolescence, but the parental influence is weak. Permissive households experience challenges with teens that could include self-destructive behaviors, impulsivity, and poor social skills.

In my professional role as a family therapist, I (Noha) have found that authoritarian or permissive parents tend to struggle more intensely with adolescents. In addition to the tumultuous social, emotional, and developmental process of adolescence, ineffective parental attitudes and expectations as described above contribute to the havoc of adolescence. On the other hand, authoritative parents generally have learned and adopted positive skills and tools during their parenting journey that help them navigate this time more effectively. For example, parents who have learned and taught their children how to self-regulate emotions will succeed in weathering the normal moodiness of teens.

Priorities When Parenting Teens

From our observations of families with adolescents, we have noticed that parents who focus their energy and time on the following three priorities were better able to handle emerging challenges. Whether the challenge is minor (talking back) or more serious (drug use) these priorities are the key.

1. Connect with your teen.

The most critical practice for parents is to focus on connecting during good and bad times. If a parent wishes to have even a small influence, it needs to be based on a foundation of connection. This is what will soften a teen's heart to take notice of what is important. Connection is when teens know that their parents' love for them is not conditioned on being "perfect," when they know their parents love them for who they are with their idiosyncrasies and uniqueness. Connection is in place when parents distinguish between correcting the behavior from the intrinsic worth of the teen. Connection is expressed by saying, "I personally don't like this shirt, but since it's Islamically fine and you like it, I am fine with you wearing it," "I am worried about you. Your grades are not reflecting your abilities," "I love you, but I don't agree with what you are doing," "I love you. I am sad about your decision to…" Connection is loving with limits: "I understand how important it is for you to buy this game, so, you will need to save your allowance for that. You know the rule about me lending you money," while at the same time loving without conditions, "I love you even though I don't like what you are doing."

2. Pick your confrontations.

As teens attempt to define their identities, they may behave in ways that are alien to the family culture. Every teen is different. Even in the same family, some will struggle more than their siblings in the search for who they are. When parents struggle with multiple problems at the same time, it becomes critical to choose which issues to focus on.

We invite you to write down a list of all the challenges you are facing with your teen at the moment. Arrange them in order of seriousness. For example, if a teen is using drugs, this challenge supersedes the teen's below-average academic performance. After listing all the challenges, begin tackling one or two issues at a time—not everything on the list. When you feel one issue has been contained, move to another and continue in this manner. Battles over multiple issues can be overwhelming for both parent and teen, creating helplessness and distance. Choosing to address the most serious issue at hand channels the available emotional energy and effectively bridges the disconnection in the family.

3. Work with what is under your control.

Parents unwittingly let go of what they control in a futile effort to control what they cannot. For example, a family is struggling with their son's excessive use of his smart phone. The parents have noticed that he is staying up late at night and struggling to wake up in the morning. In the last 3 weeks he has been tardy 7 times because of his sleep schedule. His parents have talked to him, threatened to take away his smart phone forever, and offered him $10 every night he sleeps on time. Nothing is working because they are not focusing on what they control directly.

For example, after stating (not lecturing!) the importance of getting a good night's sleep and establishing limits on how many tardy arrivals they will excuse every semester (see p. 115), they work with him to set a nightly phone curfew. They establish the expectation that at that time the phone will be parked in the parents' bedroom for the night. The parents will need to Follow Through by going to their son at the appointed time and extending their hand in a silent gesture to get the phone. In situations where the teen is still not collaborating, the parents can limit access to the Internet using the router's parental controls. Such interventions are directly enacted by the parents. With teens, directing energy toward what parents can do rather than waiting for the teen to do their bidding is crucial.

Shifting Independence & Responsibility

When the child was an infant, the parent carried great responsibility for the child's life. As the child grew, the parent continued to train the child whose responsibilities expanded. During the teen years, the shift becomes even greater. The goal is that, by the end of adolescence, young adults bear full responsibility. Figure 8.1 showcases the ideal gradual shift of responsibility from parent to child throughout the parenting journey.

Parents who are unconscious of this natural shift are caught unaware during adolescence when teens demand their autonomy. Parents who reject the independence and shifting responsibility will encounter power struggles and conflict with their teens all the way into adulthood. The teen years are "practice years" under the guidance of parents for developing life skills for adulthood.

FIGURE 8.1
Shifting Independence

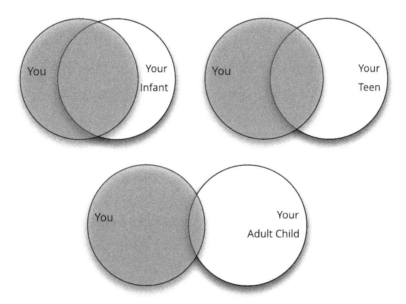

One of my (Munira) sons once shared a poignant analogy with my husband and me. We were talking to him about our role as parents now that he was a teen. He said, "You are like coaches standing on the sidelines of the field. You can give me advice when I get into the locker room, but coaching from the sidelines distracts me and doesn't help—especially yelling from the sidelines if I do something wrong." This was a fantastic analogy. Adolescence is a time to let teens play the game (life) on their own, while they try to implement all the coaching they have received. Parents watch them play, encourage them, correct them privately when they make mistakes, and let them get back on the field to try again. The responsibility of the coach is limited. Teens know parents are watching and supporting, but the field is theirs, and they are the ones who must decide how to play the game.

Identity Formation

The deeply personal journey of self-awareness begins at this age, with questions of "Who am I?" "Am I normal, competent, lovable?" and "Where am I going?" These questions continue to be asked into adulthood as one's identity crystalizes. Adolescence begins with teens thinking in concrete terms and progresses into comprehending abstract concepts and ideas.

Erik Erikson (Newman & Newman, 2003), the father of the psychosocial theory of development, normalized the process by which teens formulate their self-concept. He stipulated that part of the normal psychological development is a period of questioning and discovery culminating with identity formulation. An identity is a self-theory that answers personal questions for the individual. Erikson posited that the identity formation process begins in adolescence with the majority of teens successfully coming to terms with who they are by early adulthood. However, he stated that some teens experience confusion and loss and may not resolve their questions of identity until later in life. Erikson emphasized the role of family, social group, culture, biology, and historical events in impacting development. Some of the universal questions defining identity include:

- Who am I?
- Which group do I belong to? (ethnic, social, religious, national, gender, etc.)
- What do I believe? (religious, spiritual, economic, social.)
- What is the meaning of my life?
- What are my goals and aspirations?
- What kind of life do I want to lead?
- What brings me happiness?

The first three questions typically lay the foundation for the remaining questions. Teens 12 to 18 years of age commonly work out the questions concerning group belonging: Who are my friends? What is my nationality? What is my race? Which community do I belong to? Young adults, between the ages of 19 to 25, struggle with the question of values and beliefs: Do I believe in Allah? Does Islam answer my existential questions? Do I want to practice Islam the way my parents do?

It is inevitable that the first step to formulating an individual identity is comparing parental identities to those of others in the teens' social circle. Teens will compare their parents to aunts and uncles, their friends' parents, teachers, and coaches—anyone who is in their lives. They compare values, beliefs, and ideas about the world, behaviors, gestures, and manners. While in the beginning parents constitute the benchmark for their children (which is normal), only in well-connected families do parents continue to be a significant standard for their children. These parents typically maintain great influence on their children throughout life. On the other hand, in disconnected families, parents lose their status and influence as teens choose other role models from their social circles.

During this process of comparing models, teens typically engage in critical thought, adopting and rejecting values and ideas. They experiment with new behaviors, beliefs, opinions, styles of dress, habits, norms, and fads. They will certainly differ in the degree and intensity of their explorations, but all teens will define themselves as separate from their parents in some way or another. For some, the distinction and separation is grave and tremendous. For others, it's subtle and minor.

The most important parental shift, at this stage, is accepting the idea that teens will have a separate and unique identity from that of their parents. We invite you to consider that forging a different path than yours may be the choice your teen makes. We invite you to accept and accede the limits of your influence on their thinking and lives. Paradoxically, the stronger the bond that you had, before this transformational phase, the more influence you will have.

In my (Noha) practice, parents constantly ask me questions like, "Why is my teen not listening to me?" "My son wants to wear shorts to the *masjid* (mosque)!" "I don't understand why my daughter wants to dye her hair purple!" "It was not like that during my teen years! We listened to what our parents told us. We cared about what our parents said, but our teens don't! What's going on? Why aren't our teens conforming to our ideals and values?" I have been reflecting on these questions for a while and what follows are some of my thoughts.

For parents who rebelled against their family's social norms, what their teens are doing is understandable, albeit painful. Parents who were conformist when they were teens themselves cannot fathom their teens' need to be unique and different. They tend to blame themselves for the way their teens are behaving and they ruminate over "if only…" We invite these parents to understand that this non-conformity to your family culture is part of the normal process of development. Work with it instead of fighting it.

We live in the era of "relativity" which eschews black-and-white thinking. It promotes unconventional ideas and notions and stamps new concepts with validity as long as a person likes it, wants to follow it, and is not hurting anyone in the process. This "anything goes" paradigm is at the root of the lack of conformity that is prevalent globally. In previous generations, teens may have felt social pressure to conform publically, even if they secretly did not. Today emerging global cultural norms are sending the message, "Question everything. Reject what you don't like. Figure out what you want to do. You are fine even if you go against the status quo. You are fine even if you go against your parents' values." Currently, conformity is not a celebrated virtue (see Blind Birr, p. 385).

Teens throughout history have always chosen a different identity than their parents. This is not an unusual trend, and it is actually part of the Islamic tradition. For example, Imam Ali bin Abu Taleb, the cousin of the Prophet (pbuh), was only a boy when he accepted Islam. He certainly chose a different path than that of his tribe. It's only now, because Muslims believe that Islam is the true religion, that we can't see how accepting Islam at that time was choosing a different unique identity. Another example is Salman Alfarisi, who, as a teen, migrated from Persia to Medina through Syria, rejecting his local traditions, in search of the Truth.

Teens living in non-Muslim majority cultures struggle with upholding their parents' values and norms. Some Muslim teens are the only Muslims in their school or in their community. Upholding Islamic values amidst peers who don't understand why they behave and dress the way they do becomes a perpetual challenge. Every Islamic ritual they practice demands explanations and requests for special accommodations. When compared to teens living in a Muslim-friendly environment where no explanations and no special requests are required, Muslim teens in the West face great social and emotional pressures. In their effort to diffuse such enormous pressures, teens sometimes adopt behaviors and styles that follow the social norms but go against the family culture.

Teens living in the West are capable of separating from the family earlier and faster, emboldening them to resist and reject family norms they don't like. For example, in the U.S., when teens turn 18 years old, they are capable of moving out legally and culturally. However, teens who live in the Middle East or Asia won't be able to separate from the family until later in adulthood due to financial constraints and social norms that reject such a practice.

When my (Noha) children were going through the teen years, I navigated many challenges by adopting the following strategies:

- I accepted the fact that my children were their own individuals with their own ideas and beliefs. I reminded myself that my responsibility was to guide and teach but not to coerce or control. They could choose to accept or reject my guidance. Accordingly I would say something like, "I think it's important to have breakfast in the morning, but it seems you don't think so. I trust you will figure out what works for you."

- When it came to Islamic practices, I utilized the breadth of Islamic rulings rather than focusing on one specific opinion or school of thought. I also did not ask my children to practice Islam as conservatively as I did. As long as their practices were clearly within the permissible range, I did not even raise the issue. I understood that practicing Islam falls on a continuum and not everyone will practice the same way. I also knew from my own life experience that practicing Islam is a journey that does not end until we die.

- I understood that some of my cultural practices were outdated and needed adjustment. For example, I grew up in a family where men did not help around the house. I made it a point early to involve my sons in jobs around the house—including cooking.

- I did not take their divergent ideas, behaviors, or customs as a reflection of my failure as a parent. I understood that they are divine *amana* (trust) for me to nurture and guide, but not to force into a rigid mold.

Peer Pressure

Influence from peers is a necessary and normal part of the psychosocial development of children. It is usually identified as a problem when it leads to negative behaviors rather than positive ones. The biggest protective factor against negative peer pressure is a positive relationship with parents at home because that boosts the child's self-confidence and self-worth.

The need to fit in a group is an extension of *finding belonging*. It is a normal need but could be exacerbated in children who struggle to belong at home or in their community. Those who are starving to belong may fulfill this need by going along with a peer group, even if it goes against their family values. The strong desire to be liked and the fear of being made fun of, can lead a teen to succumb to peer pressure. For others, the curiosity of trying something new may motivate them to follow the peer group and dismiss "common sense." Others may feel inspired and motivated by the accomplishments of a peer group and seek to emulate and join them.

Parents will gain a deeper understanding of why a child is succumbing to peer pressure by asking Curiosity Questions (p. 82), "Help me understand what is going on. What is so special about this group? When do you meet? How do you feel when you are with them? What is your assessment of what happened?" Many times teens are simply trying to fit in. They are not necessarily thinking about moral values or rebelling against parental values. Parents empower teens by inviting them to listen to their "internal compass" and pay attention to their feelings and beliefs when faced with peer pressure. Parents also encourage teens to make the best decision for themselves when put in difficult situations by having discussions: Will they be able to say no and walk away? Do they have friends who can help them? How can they ask their parents for help?

Parents can share their own experiences of how they coped

with peer pressure as teens and now as adults. Explaining that peer pressure is something adults also struggle with can validate a teen's experience. A parent can say, "I felt that pressure when I was in high school too. It must be really hard for you to say no when everyone else is doing it."

In situations when peer pressure leads to negative ramifications, utilizing Mistakes are Opportunities for Learning (p. 119) changes the situation to a valuable life lesson. Parents can help teens reflect, learn from the experience, and identify how they can do things differently next time. It may mean that they find new friends or become more assertive and vocal in their personal views.

Risky Behavior

Teens experience intense intellectual and emotional changes as they begin to discover who they are in relation to the world. In this quest for deeper understanding, teens may engage in risk-taking. Risk-taking varies from small things like trying new tricks on their skateboard or dyeing their hair, to using drugs or premarital sex. The reasons teens engage in risk-taking are different for every teen. Some succumb to peer pressure, others may have a tendency to seek out extreme sensations, while some struggle with emotional difficulties. The part of a teen's brain responsible for impulse control doesn't fully develop until the age of 25 which explains their quick dismissal of consequences and ramifications. What can parents do?

Studies (cited in Szalavitz, 2012) found that parents who maintain a connection with their teens reduce their risk-taking behavior. Parents must pick and choose their focus areas. When parents focus on Connection before Correction (p. 80), they will have greater influence. Some activities teens choose may be disliked by the parent, but are not necessarily harmful or destructive: e.g. wearing mismatched clothes, taking a million selfies, or staying up late. In these instances parents need to let go and allow Natural Consequences (p. 125) to occur.

Researchers (cited in Szalavitz, 2012) have found that discussing potential negative consequences of different types of perilous activities reduces participation in risky behaviors. If the risk is known, the teen engages less frequently. If the risk is unknown, the teen is prone to try it because teens have a greater tolerance for uncertainty than adults. When the parent-teen relationship is positive, discussing with teens the costs of risky behaviors while establishing agreements, clear limits, and expectations empowers them to make better choices. Parents can ask teens questions like, "What are the chances this will turn out well, and what are the chances something might go wrong?" "What do you think might happen if you choose to do this?"

Parents set limits after listening to what their teens have to say, "I know how important it is for you to be with your friends until the early morning hours. However, our curfew is 11 p.m., and I expect you to abide by that," and "You have explained to me that the joint I found in your room was a one-time thing. However, I want you to know that I will be looking in your room regularly since I am worried about you smoking weed."

Trust

A concern many parents have with their teens is trust. Can they or should they trust their teens? In general, parents who give their teens increasing amounts of independence in some areas of their lives notice that their teens explore without resorting to dishonesty and rebellion. Teens who resort to dishonesty are actively disengaging from their parents to protect their ego and maintain their independence and freedom. Parents need to set limits and make agreements with teens to build trust. As teens meet expectations and show responsible behavior, they build trust and earn more independence.

The foundational elements of trust and honesty are established in early childhood. Parents model honesty, or lack of, through their own behaviors. Teens emulate these early values in their social interactions including those with their parents. Teens also know if it is safe to share their thoughts and feelings with their parents. Will they feel attacked or encouraged when they speak? The anticipated reaction of parents will dictate whether teens will honestly share or lie about their behaviors. Families where mistakes are seen as opportunities to learn will inspire honesty and trust. On the other hand, families where mistakes are immediate triggers for punishments and shame will instigate lying and deception. (See Belief Behind the Behavior, p. 83).

Parents can do many things to encourage a trusting relationship. It begins with an environment of respect, openness, and problem solving. Trust is dependent on parents knowing they cannot control the choices their teens will make. This can be a very scary prospect because of the fear children will make the wrong choice or commit big mistakes with irreversible damage. Instead, parents focus on connecting, mentoring, real life discussions, teaching critical thinking, showing faith, and creating space for teens to feel safe asking for advice or help. The goal must be to teach teens to be responsible for their decisions.

For example, Ahmed and his parents have talked countless times about social events and underage drinking. He clearly knows his parents and his faith are opposed to alcohol consumption, so he chooses not to drink. His parents allow him to attend a friend's party. However, when he gets to the party, he sees his friends have been drinking. Should he stay and hide the fact that there is drinking at the party from his parents? If he is not drinking himself, what is the harm in staying? He is uncomfortable staying at the party and decides to leave, but he needs a ride home. A friend who was drinking offers him a ride. Does he get in the car? Does he believe it is safe to drink and drive? Does he call his parents for a ride? Does he feel comfortable being honest with his parents? If he calls them, will his parents berate him for being at a party with alcohol, or will they be happy that he called for a safe ride home? What consequences can he bear? The choice is his. The choice he makes will depend on weighing the risks of all of the options, and his honesty will depend on the connection he has with his parents.

Academic Performance

There are different factors that contribute to a teen's academic success or failure. Researchers (Masud, Thurasamy, Ahmad, 2014) found that the authoritative parenting style was the most effective in enhancing the academic performance of children. On the other hand, there are various factors that lead to difficulties in academic performance: biological, behavioral, emotional, social, and environmental.

One common problem is lack of proper sleep. Unfortunately,

many teens struggle to develop healthy sleeping habits. Researchers (Asarnow & Harvey, 2013) at UC Berkeley found late bedtimes were linked to worse academic performance and emotional distress. Sleep is critical for all ages but especially for teens as they learn to balance their schoolwork, extracurricular activities, and deal with their changing bodies and emotions.

Students who have not developed good study habits, time management skills, or organizational skills, can also experience academic difficulties. Feeling overwhelmed by the demands of school lead to feelings of failure and inadequacy. Some students react to pressure by avoiding the tasks at hand. Others believe "I can't do it" and avoid studying and completing assignments.

Mental health concerns like depression and anxiety hinder the ability to concentrate and complete schoolwork. A student who struggles with social pressure (like bullying) feels isolated and depressed. A teen who has an undiagnosed learning disability may feel incompetent, stupid, and discouraged.

There are also social factors that impact a teen's academic performance. A home culture where education is not valued sends the message that higher learning is not a priority. Attitudes held by the peer group about education will also impact a teen's involvement at school. Sometimes the family may be going through a crisis (parent diagnosed with a disease, financial difficulties, death of a loved one), which also will have an impact on the teen.

What can parents do when teens are not doing well in school? Parents can encourage their teens to establish healthy sleep patterns by establishing routines and parking electronics in the evening. According to the National Sleep Foundation (Hirshkowitz, 2015), teens need 8 to 10 hours of sleep each day. UCLA researchers (cited in Sifferlin, 2012) found that sacrificing sleep to study was actually counterproductive with students doing more poorly on tests, quizzes, and homework. Students need to exercise time-management to get the proper amount of sleep and thereby be better able to focus in class and do better academically.

Routines are important for teens who struggle with following through on tasks and staying focused. Parents can help with good study habits, if they structure the environment at home so that teens have a set routine for doing homework, a schedule for all other activities (sports, volunteering, jobs, social activities), and a place at home where teens can complete their work. Parents can brainstorm with their teens the additional support available to help them, such as peer study groups, private tutors, and extra help from teachers at school.

If teens are overwhelmed, parents can provide emotional support as well as seek counseling. When psychological difficulties are discovered, collaborating with teachers, school counselors, and psychologists to create a support team is essential. Sometimes it may be necessary to consider alternative schooling options that might be a better fit for the teen's needs.

Parents must remain positive. While education is important and the process of learning is valuable, the relationship between the parent and teen is critical for any progress to happen. Teens must feel valued for more than just their grades and academic performance in school. Failure is a part of the learning process. Teens who are not afraid of failure will actually be more willing to accept academic challenges and less likely to sabotage their own academic efforts. Parents who focus on teens' innate strengths (p. 44) will discover who their teens are and what is important to them.

Parents can connect with their teens by treating them with respect, being genuine in their interactions, and seeking to know them through causal connections (in the car, doing errands, etc.). The day-to-day conversations are opportunities to notice a teen's excitement and enthusiasm about a particular subject or activity. Parents can use the tool Be There (p. 77) to have conversations with their teens that teach, encourage, and empower them to reach their goals.

Teens who feel a strong connection to their parents will feel safe exploring their interests and goals in life. Conversations respecting teens' autonomy will serve to guide rather than control teens as they decide how to proceed academically. Parents who spend too much time talking and lecturing will cause their teens to tune-out and disconnect. Using the tools Listen (p. 113) and asking Curiosity Questions (p. 82) will build trust and respect so that the teen can explore goals for the future. Through the process, parents can learn more about the teens' personal goals. If parents see a misalignment between the teens' goals and actions, an opportunity is created for Problem Solving and re-evaluating.

Curiosity Questions parents can ask.

- What is your assessment of your school performance?
- What do you see are your strengths in school? Your weaknesses?
- What is your plan after completing high school?

- What plan are you using to reach your goals?
- How has your current academic performance caused you problems?
- How important is it for you to improve your academic performance?

When teens respond with, "I don't know!" or "I don't care," a parent can say, "It seems you are not ready to have this conversation. Let's reschedule to another time. I truly believe you and I can collaborate to understand what is going on. I want to help you."

College

The educational path young adults choose is a critical part of their lives. Hence, many families seek to influence and shape their teens' college majors. In the final years of high school, teens begin to explore careers to determine what areas of study they are interested in and what paths to higher education they will pursue. These years are a time of personal growth and exploration as teens gain greater self-awareness and discover their personal and professional identities. Some parent-child conflicts revolve around college majors, university locations, and who will pay for school expenses.

Some parents hold a clear roadmap for their teens' future and feel extremely disappointed when their teens choose majors or careers they dislike or are not aligned with their vision. Parents may see careers in medicine and engineering as respectable professions and pressure their teens disregarding the teens' interests and abilities. When teens choose fields outside the hopes and dreams of parents, conflicts may arise.

Parents who struggle the most at this stage are those who have difficulty accepting their young adult's independence and the choices they make. Some parents, in an effort to regain "control" of their teens, may limit university choices to only a select few they approve of or that are close to home. They may threaten to only pay for university degrees they find acceptable. Some teens succumb to parental demands because of their limited financial resources but the relationship deteriorates as teens feel controlled and imprisoned by the parents' dreams. Other teens choose to pursue their own paths thus rejecting parental demands. Some move out, take loans, and work to support themselves. Helping teens determine the path that is the best for them and in alignment with their strengths and goals will yield better results.

Connected families will discuss their teens' interests, skills, and aspirations throughout high school and early adulthood. They will have a better understanding of their teens' inclinations and driving passions. These young adults will be able to explore and articulate their plans for higher education and how they will pursue employment upon graduation. Some teens chose to take a gap year while others chose to begin working immediately. Every teen will make a choice that makes sense for who and where they are on their academic path.

As tuition costs continue to rise, families will need to discuss finances openly and honestly. Sometimes finances determine the choice of college and career. Some of the key financial points to cover are:

- Family budget.
- Plan for paying higher education costs.

- Financial aid requirements.
- Education loans.
- Teen's contribution to the financial plan.

In my (Munira) practice, I have seen families push their students to attend a particular local university or a "trophy" university without regard for determining what is the best fit for the teen. When teens attend a university that is not a good fit academically, socially, or culturally, they end up having greater challenges to overcome in order to successfully graduate. It is important that families discuss the type of university that would work for their teens: a big research university, a small liberal arts college, a community college, a trade school, etc. Walking on a college campus, sitting in a lecture hall, and talking to current students will help teens decide if they belong on a particular campus. In the end, if the teen's college choice is not a good fit, there will be lessons to learn, which will help them clarify their long-term goals.

Internet Safety & Use

According to the Pew Research Center's report (2015) on Teens, Social Media and Technology, "92 percent of teens go online every day and 24 percent report being online almost constantly." This news is not surprising considering 88 percent of teens have access to smartphones and 91 percent go online, at least occasionally, from a mobile device. Social media platforms are the primary sites that 76 percent of teens visit. As apps, platforms, and technology continue to change and evolve, parents need to be aware of their teens' online presence.

From early childhood, parents monitor and teach children

how to use media responsibly so that when they are teens they are able to self-regulate. Engaging in their online world while respecting their autonomy is most beneficial. Parents should not stalk nor attempt to control what their teens say or post. While most social media platforms require a minimum age of 13 in their terms of use, the reality is many teens establish a social media presence before that age. Accordingly, parents are invited to empower their teens to be Internet safe and media literate (p. 202).

Teens should be educated about the permanence of their online identity and postings. A quick Google search of their names will reveal who they are online. It's critical that they know that some college admission officers and employers may learn about candidates in this way. It may be funny and harmless during adolescence, but their online presence leaves a legacy that may impact their future. A study by McAfee (2012) found that 49% of teens post risky comments. The challenge for teens today is that their lives are happening under the gaze of virtual eyes that document the entire process, including all the mistakes and regrets. When teens choose to post something online, they have to imagine "saying or sharing" that statement on a microphone to the entire world. Their audience consists of not only their friends, but their parents, relatives, friends' parents, teachers, community members, future employers, and others who will hear it and make an assumption about who they are. It is a great responsibility for teens to bear, but it is also the reality of technology. They must choose how to engage with it, as it is here to stay. Every family needs to discuss how best to approach their online use and how to consider the long-term consequences. Ultimately, parents can only model, advise, and recommend safe practices.

Suggestions for Internet use boundaries.

- Use electronics in public spaces at home. No computers and televisions in bedrooms. A teen will be less likely to go to an inappropriate site if someone may walk by at any time.

- Request to have access to your teens' phone or computer to remind them that their Internet use can be shared at any time by you.

- "Park" electronics in the evening. Agree to a time and a place where all electronics are parked in their chargers. Once it is "parked" in the evening, it becomes inaccessible until the morning. If you discover that your children are sneaking out to get their electronics after you sleep, move the Parking spot into your bedroom.

- Limit Wi-Fi access. Create Wi-Fi blackout time zones such as evenings after 10 pm.

- Discuss the amount of time spent on the Internet and begin Problem Solving for ways to balance time online and offline.

- Discuss which Internet sites are safe to be accessed.

- Install parental controls that prevent access to inappropriate sites.

- Agree on what information is safe to be posted online.

- Establish times of the day, days of the week, or even events that will be electronic free. For instance, no electronics at the dinner table or during family gatherings.

Sexting & Pornography

Established guidelines for teens regarding electronic use are vital to prevent problems like sexting and pornography. Researchers

(Martinez-Prather & Vandiver, 2014) have estimated that 1 in 5 high school students have sent a sexually explicit text or photo message (sexting) of themselves. They suggest that sexting is a gateway to sexual behavior in teens. On many high school campuses, sexting has become normalized behavior. It is used to get attention, gain popularity, flirt, or hook up. Some teens do it as a result of peer pressure or as "just a joke." Teens who engage in sexting do not usually fully comprehend the consequences of their behavior. Their impulsive nature and difficulty projecting into the future make it difficult for them to foresee the long-term impact of their immediate "sharing." They also do not grasp the significance of privacy.

Conversations about personal responsibility and online safety encouraging teens to stop and think about what they are posting are ways to empower teens. Emphasizing that messages, pictures, and videos are never truly private or anonymous. With just one click, an embarrassing or humiliating post can become public for anyone to see. Engaging in self- reflection is key. Asking questions like, "How will I be perceived if this goes public?" "Is this something I would want my grandparents to see?" Learning of the potential dire consequences of sexting, like felony charges in some states, may help teens seriously reconsider sexting.

The Internet has made pornography easily accessible on computers and phones. A study by McAfee (2012) found that only 12% of parents think their teens have access to porn online, when actually, 32% of teens have intentionally accessed porn online with 43% on a weekly basis. These statistics highlight the discrepancy between what parents know and what teens are doing. Parents must go further than just saying, "Pornography is *haram* (forbidden)!" End of conversation. It is more effective to discuss personal views and family values about pornography in addition to explaining the negative effects of pornography on the physical, social, emotional, and spiritual dimensions of individuals.

How to talk about pornography.

- Begin by explaining that bodies can be aroused by things the mind may not find appealing. For example, "When people watch pornography they may get turned on by stuff they don't feel good about watching. I don't want you to be in a position where your body reacts to something your head knows is wrong."

- Explain that their expanding brain is making millions of connections and the neural wiring will be greatly impacted by pornographic images. Impress upon them that once neural connections are made in their brain attaching pornography to pleasure, it is difficult to break these circuits. Clarify that such established neural networks are the basis of addiction. Let them know that when these neural circuits take hold, they negatively impact the marital sexual relationship later on in life.

- Discuss the difference between sex and pornography. For example, "Sex is supposed to be beautiful and loving. Pornography shows an offensive and dark form of sex. Pornography is a business where people make money from someone else's degradation. In our family we don't participate in things that exploit other people."

- Connect the negative impact of pornography to their spirituality. For example, "Your eyes are sacred, and the things you see and absorb affect your heart and soul. Negative sexual images can weigh on your self-image and how you see the opposite sex. It makes sex into a vulgar act instead of a beautiful act that Allah encouraged between a husband and wife."

Just as with other uncomfortable topics, parents must continue having conversations (See p. 339) with their teens. The goal is for teens to have correct information, a safe space to dialogue, build self-awareness, and develop personal safety as they grow. If your teen develops an addiction to pornography, guide them to seek counseling.

Sex & Relationships

The values families hold regarding gender relations fall on a wide continuum. While some families will expect complete separation between boys and girls, other families may be comfortable with mixed groups of young people. Still other families may be comfortable with couple relationships. Family values will be determined by a combination of religious beliefs, cultural expectations, and social context. Therefore, what one Muslim family may expect may not be the same in another Muslim family. Accordingly, the topic of gender relations must be discussed specifically within each family unit so that values are communicated clearly about how to behave and engage with people of all ages and genders.

Important areas to discuss with teens.

- The boundaries of intimacy between men and women.
- Family values about hugging, kissing, handshakes, etc.
- Family values about prom and school dances.
- Social activities at school and personal responsibility.
- Family values regarding dating.
- Discussing the purpose and reason why people choose to date.
- Healthy ways of interacting with the opposite sex.
- Self-worth in relation to the opposite sex.
- Group relationships versus a couple's relationship.
- Ramifications of physical and emotional intimacy between two people.
- Value of abstinence before marriage.
- Family values about masturbation.
- Family values about how and when to seek a spouse.
- Family values about religious identity.
- Family values about cultural identity.

Some Muslim parents believe that Muslim teens are not engaging in premarital sexual behavior. Unfortunately, The Family and Youth Institute (2014) found that nearly half of the Muslim college students (both males and females) surveyed had engaged in premarital sex. A study by Heart Women and Girls (2014) found that the most frequently used sources of sex education for teens were media and friends, with parents being the least utilized source of information. Hence, it is paramount that parents openly talk about sexuality to have a better chance of influencing their teens' sexual choices (see Difficult Conversations, p. 339).

Parents who disregard their teen's sexuality and delay conversations about sex until marriage do a huge disservice to their teen. Conversations about sexual activity, sexual health education, body awareness, spirituality, and value of marriage, need to be discussed cohesively and with empathy. Young adults will make choices about their sexual activities, and parents must give them all the information so they are informed of the consequences of their choice and are empowered to make the best decisions. Families who have developed open communication, educated their teens about sexual health, and discussed their expectations will be able to discuss and understand where their teens are coming from as well as influence them to make healthy choices as they continue to grow.

While parents may vary regarding where they stand on these topics, the following messages are clearly defined values within the Islamic context. We invite you to share these with your teens:

- Sexual desire is a natural and normal feeling that Allah has imbued us with. It is nothing to be ashamed or scared of.
- When sexual desire is fulfilled in marriage, it becomes part of divine worship.
- Sexual desire is strong—especially in young people. However, acting on this strong desire outside of the bounds of marriage could lead to unwanted pregnancy, STDs, discontent, and emotional pain.
- Address the assumption teens may hold of their invincibility: "This could never happen to me."

- When the desire is strong and a person is not yet ready to get married, fasting can help ameliorate the pressure.

- No one should ever be pressured to have sex. Saying no, means no.

One common problem found in the Muslim community is an established "double standard" between what is expected of boys versus girls. The thinking "boys will be boys" and they can explore while advocating that girls must maintain their reputation and chastity is an unfair double standard. This message destroys parental credibility with teens because the value they hold is based on a cultural context that teens may find irrelevant. Teaching teens how to exert self-control and respect at all times is most beneficial for both boys and girls. Having a different expectation based on gender can lead to sexism which can further alienate teens as they decide what their personal beliefs and values are. (See Breaking the Shackles of Misogyny, p. 313).

Unfortunately, some children experience sexual abuse. In these situations, it is vital that parents respond with empathy and understanding. Parents must Listen (p. 113) calmly and offer comfort and support. Children may believe the abuse is their fault, be scared of the abuser, ashamed, or worried that parents won't believe them. Parental love and support is necessary for healing. In addition, when parents take the appropriate action against the perpetrator, they affirm that what occurred is absolutely unacceptable. To curtail the psychological scars of sexual abuse, families are advised to seek professional counseling.

Sexual Orientation

One of the facets of development that is processed during the teen years is sexual orientation. While the majority of teens will begin to experience predominantly heterosexual desires, some will experience same-gender sexual desires: lesbian, gay, bisexual, transgender, and questioning youth (LGBTQ). Various studies (cited in Centers for Disease Control and Prevention, 2014) highlight the vulnerability of LGBTQ population. They are at a higher risk than heterosexual youth for violence perpetrated against them, depression, self-harming behaviors, suicidal ideation, and suicide attempts. Most importantly, connection to families and others has been found as a major protective factor against mental health concerns.

Our intent here is not to explain the causes of same-gender sexual attraction nor argue for the Islamic stance on same-gender sexual behaviors. Our focus here is to empower parents with the most appropriate response if teens share they are experiencing same-gender sexual inclinations. The first response, and most critical, by parents is asserting their love. Typically LGBTQ teens are fearful of their parents' rejection. One teen in my (Noha) practice asked his mother if she hated him after sharing that he is bisexual. *Alhamdu Lillah* (all praise to God) the mother being cognizant of both the Islamic stance and the current social pressures was quick to affirm her love. She was able to contain her shock and confusion and validate her son's inherent worth regardless of his sexual orientation.

The second point to emphasize is clarifying the difference between behavior and orientation. I (Noha) have observed that when this distinction is not made clear, some young people feel alienated from Islam believing erroneously that Islam condemns them simply for their orientation. It becomes a losing battle for these teens: they know what they feel and are told (incorrectly) that these *feelings* are sinful. For some, the only way to reconcile the two is by rejecting Islam. Otherwise, these teens go through life with a deep sense of shame and self-loathing. Therefore, it is critical that parents assure their LGBTQ teens that, according to Islamic principles, their orientation by itself does not shame nor condemn them.

The most appropriate way to address this topic would be for parents to share the Islamic etiquette regarding sexual behavior, highlighting the difference between Islam's stance and current cultural norms. The following points are most critical:

- All humans deserve to be treated with dignity and respect regardless of their sexual orientation. Islam prohibits the denigration and discrimination of people.
- Islam highly protects the privacy of individuals. One's sexual activities are private matters regardless of the orientation. No one has the right to question another's sexual orientation or practice.
- Sexuality does not define an individual. It is an integral part of the person but not the defining criteria for worth.
- Marriage in Islam is a contract between a man and a woman.
- Permissible sexual contact is limited to the bounds of marriage in Islam.
- Respecting the Islamic rulings regarding sexual behavior is a submission to Allah.

TEEN YEARS | 267

There will be a need for more than one discussion regarding this issue. However, to be effective, parents are advised to avoid forcing their teens to talk when they are reluctant. Instead, an invitation as follows is more effective, "I am here for you. I know this is a difficult challenge, and I would like to help you in any way I can. So, if at any time you would like to talk to me about it, come find me."

Many parents of LGBTQ teens struggle with the question, "Why is this happening?" Some go back and assess all childhood events trying to find answers. Some blame themselves for having done or having failed to do something critical. Even though we don't have a full understanding of the origins of same-gender sexual attractions, my (Noha) experience in private practice has confirmed it is not associated with something the parents have done or failed to do. Until we know more, we invite you to focus your energy on supporting your teen instead of ineffective self-recrimination and rumination.

While parents guide and teach, the decision—how to live one's life—is an individual decision. Hence, parents are invited to focus on their areas of control in the event their teens choose to act upon their same-gender sexual desires (in the same way they would if it were a heterosexual relationship outside the bounds of marriage). In my (Noha) practice, I have observed various positions when it comes to this issue. Parents go from kicking teens out of the home all the way to fully accepting their sexual relations. The decision about how to react in this situation is a personal one. This particular challenge remains one of the most difficult for parents to deal with. We invite you to seek support from a Muslim therapist.

At a time when secular lifestyles are gaining momentum, abiding by an Islamic sexual lifestyle is tough. It's a life-long struggle. Ultimately, only a strong connection with Allah will empower individuals to practice patience and restraint toward establishing their own personal Islamic lifestyle. Always make *duaa* (supplication) for your teens to have a strong bond with Allah. *Oh Allah, be their constant companion.*

The Question of Faith

During this phase, some teens begin to evaluate their faith. For many teens the question of ideology will be addressed during the college years. However, deep-thinking teens will engage in a critique of their family's faith earlier than others. In general, teens respond to the question of faith in one of four ways:

1. They follow the practices of their parents. Practicing Islam does not become an issue of contention in the family.
2. They maintain the major obligations of Islam (prayers and fasting) but behave in a way that parents do not like.
3. They show signs of wavering faith like missing prayers, resisting reading Quran, refusing to attend Islamic classes, avoiding the mosque or, in extreme situations, rejecting Islam completely.
4. They practice a stricter form of Islam than their parents.

Parents of the first group are generally content to see their children following their path. This is a blessing not to be taken for granted. Gratitude to Allah for His bounty is in order. Parents of the second group may place too much emphasis on the small things and forget the fact that faith is a journey. For these parents, we invite you to be grateful that your child is maintaining the major obligations of Islam. We invite you to avoid nagging your teen about the "small stuff." Certainly make your position clear, but in a respectful and loving manner. Avoid shaming and using your anger as a weapon to manipulate their behavior. Take, for example, a teen who prays and fasts, but loves to listen to music when the parent believes music is forbidden. In situations such as these, we invite the parents to state their position by saying, "I personally follow the school of thought that music is *haram* (forbidden). I have noticed that you are listening to music which I understand is permissible in other schools of thought. I would request that you respect my position by wearing headphones."

For the parents of the third group, we invite you to keep the following two Islamic principles at the center of your interactions with your teens:

- "There is no coercion in religion. Verily, the right path has become distinct from the wrong path" (Quran, 2:256).
- "No soul is beholden for the sins of another" (Quran 6:164; 17:15; 35:18; 39:7; 53:38).

This is an invitation-only phase. Your influence will be more effective and powerful if you shift from coercing and monitoring to observing and inviting. While during the earlier years you may have been more involved in how the child practiced, during the teen years it's advisable to continue reinforcing the habits you had instilled earlier while avoiding confrontations and battles, "I have noticed that you are missing more and more of our group prayers. What is going on? Prayers are important for me personally but they are your responsibility. How can I support you as you figure out what you need to do to maintain your prayers?"

Continue to gently invite your teen to learn and practice. However, stop when these invitations are met with resistance and the rift between you and your teen is widening. Choose your battles. Focus your energy on the important ones. And when you decide what is important, utilize the scale of Islam rather than the scale of social shame. For example, praying the five obligatory prayers supersedes wearing the *hijab* (head covering). If your daughter is struggling with her prayers, focusing on supporting her connection with Allah through prayers takes precedence over demanding she wears *hijab* solely to avoid social criticism.

If your teen overtly refuses to maintain the religious practices they maintained before, and your conversations about the issue do not help, we invite you to be clear about how these obligations are personal responsibilities by saying, "Your prayers are your responsibility. I will continue to call to prayer, but it's your responsibility to decide to join us or not. I would love for you to have a strong relationship with Allah, and I will pray that you will, but you have to decide how you want to develop that relationship." Focus on maintaining your loving relationship with your teens despite your pain over their wavering faith. This attitude will go a long way in easing them back into Islam when they are ready. Seek the Support of Allah the All Powerful, and make *duaa* (supplication) for you and your teen to find Guidance.

The last group of teens are those who practice a stricter form of Islam than their parents. In this category, the term stricter is relative to where the parents are in their faith journey. The spectrum encompasses parents who do not uphold the religious practices and those who assiduously do. I (Noha) was part of this last group as a teen myself and then as a parent of a teen who was stricter in his practice of Islam. Here are my reflections on how to handle the situation:

As a teen, I sincerely appreciated the respect with which my family treated my devotion for Islam. I was not mocked, ridiculed, or disparaged for my practices. I invite you to do the same. When situations arose, my parents would gently share their opinion with me but grant me the freedom to decide how I wanted to proceed. For example, when we were traveling in Europe, I might sense the presence of alcohol in food and refuse to eat it. My father, rather than dismissing my concern, would ask the waiter if, indeed, there was alcohol in the food. And when my assessment was correct, he would have me order something else.

Every family will have its own dynamic. We differed with my son in our opinions over which meat to eat. My husband and I followed the ruling of permitting the meat of the People of the Book while my son chose to follow the opinion requiring the Islamic way of slaughtering. I gently explained our stance to my son with all the scholarly rationale but respected his stance when he chose to follow the other opinion. Collaborating with him, I began cooking with meat slaughtered according to the Islamic tradition. Since my son's increased religiosity occurred in a post 9/11 era, I made it a point to engage him in conversations often to check in with his understanding of Islam.

My experience with my parents was validating, empowering, and respectful. Hence, when my son became stricter in his practice, I engaged with him as my parents did with me—with respect, communication, and space. I invite you to do the same.

Youth Radicalization

Political or religious radicalization of teens, either through peers or online groups, has become a prevalent concern for parents. Radicalization is a grooming process by which people are indoctrinated into a "special club" with extreme ideas. Researchers (Lyons-Padilla, Gelfand, Mirahmadi, Farooq, & Egmond, 2015) found that radicalized youth suffer from feelings of alienation as a result of an intense existential struggle for identity and belonging. Children of immigrants who did not identify with their cultural heritage or their new adopted country were easy prey for radical groups. Certainly, discrimination and prejudice in the adopted countries further fueled the fire of disconnection and marginalization. Youth that gravitate towards groups like gangs, cults, or terrorist groups all have in common the need to belong.

The number one protective factor against radicalization is a strong family bond. Even if you believe the earlier years did not foster such a bond, it's never too late to begin. With teens, focus on spending special time unhindered by lectures and criticism. Follow your teens' requests for what to do and enjoy their company. Teens who feel they belong in their families, with friends, and in their community feel connected to others, which precludes seeking outside groups for validation.

Another protective factor is parental openness to conversations which fosters safe spaces for sharing of all ideas. Opportunities for dialogue within the family where differing opinions and views on Islamic topics are discussed is vital as teens seek Islamic knowledge. Some parents attempt to engage their teens through lectures bent on changing convictions and attitudes.

What is more effective is planting seeds of a more balanced view and practice of Islam. Offer small doses of wisdom and wait. Parents may believe their ideas are falling on deaf ears, but we assure you they are germinating under the surface and will sprout later. As with everything else, if a parent is unclear or unsure about an Islamic issue, they can use it as an opportunity to seek knowledge together, thereby encouraging critical thought and intellectual dialogue.

A third protective factor against radicalization is belonging to a mosque community. A Gallup study (2012) found that attending a mosque regularly is linked to having more tolerant views of people of other faiths and greater civic engagement. Parents can encourage youth to attend the mosque youth group to build strong community connections. They can also encourage teens to join sports teams, participate in community service projects, and interfaith initiatives. Engaging with others who are drastically different is an integral piece of dismantling walls of isolation and prejudice.

A common theme found with radicalized youth was that their actions were unknown by their families. While it is difficult to penetrate the secrecy established by teens, there are strategies that parents can engage in to disrupt the path of radicalization:

- Begin by honestly assessing your own views of other groups (other Muslims, non-Muslims, racial, ethnic, cultural, etc.). Youth radicalization is based on a prejudiced worldview of "us" vs. "them." While talking to your teens, what terms and labels do you personally use to refer to others who are different than you? If your own view of others is based on an "us" vs. "them" paradigm, then work on adjusting this foundation of prejudice and discrimination. Remember that we are not judges.

- Empower yourself with Islamic knowledge. Research and learn to have a strong foundational base for your conversations with your teens. This also leads to a sidebar discussion about monitoring where teens get their religious knowledge and being especially cautious about what they find on the Internet. There is a proliferation of inaccurate information online and teens can be misguided if they are not having conversations about what they are learning.

- Listen carefully to what your teen is saying and doing. Share your knowledge and understanding with regard to those concepts and practices that are on the fringe. If you don't know the ideology of your teen's mentors, find out. When my (Noha) eldest was in college, I attended some of the Islamic study circles he attended to reassure myself of the ideas he was exposed to.

- Share your concerns openly. Say, "I am worried about you. I see you…and I am afraid you may be pulled into a misconstrued understanding of Islam. I worry about you becoming one of the young people we hear about who have joined…"

- Recognize that some of this zeal is part of the psychological growth process. Teens have a difficult time seeing the middle path of ideas. They tend to be all-or-nothing thinkers; so, be gentle and respectful in your discussions.

- When assessing your teen's behaviors, differentiate between those that are cause for concern and those that are real practices of Islam. For example, a teen going to the mosque is not indicative of danger, while a teen who has become more observant, is gone for days, and whose activities are kept secret is a cause for alarm.

- Empower teens by mirroring back their strengths (Innate Strengths, p. 44; Encouragement versus Praise, p. 94; Empowering versus Enabling, p. 90). Youth radicalization is a terrifying reality, but there are numerous ways families can be empowered to disrupt the path of extremism.

Mental Health Concerns

While advances in neuroscience have shed light on mental health disorders, uncertainty about the causes and progression of these conditions continue. Nonetheless, the intense biological changes of the teen years are recognized as possible triggers for certain illnesses. Severe, dramatic, or abrupt changes in a teen's behavior are serious signs for immediately seeking help. However, sometimes symptoms of mental health issues are gradual and subtle. The difficulty for many parents lies in differentiating between normal teen behavior and serious cause for alarm. Here are some red flags:

- Consistent difficulty sleeping or regular insomnia.
- Excessive sleeping (beyond the typical teenage fatigue).
- Serious low self-esteem/poor self-image.
- Dramatic decline in academic performance.
- Excessive anger that is out of character.
- Sudden or intense withdrawal from social interactions.
- Significant weight loss.

- Adamant refusal to eat.
- Extremely loose clothing (hiding cutting marks or extreme weight loss).
- Cutting marks.
- Sadness for days on end.
- Signs of intoxication (slurred speech, bloodshot eyes).
- Unusual passivity and loss of energy.
- Consistent lack of personal hygiene.

The National Alliance on Mental Illness (2013) cites that four million children and adolescents in the United States suffer from a serious mental disorder, with 20 percent of children ages 8 to 15 having a diagnosable mental or addictive disorder. As many as one in five teens suffers from clinical depression. Teens may experiment with drugs or alcohol or become sexually promiscuous to avoid feelings of depression. They also may express their depression through hostile, aggressive, or risk-taking behavior. Teens may try to control feelings of helplessness, anxiety, or pressure through acts like cutting, anorexia, or bulimia. (See When Addictions Rule, p. 331).

Mental illness occurs at similar rates around the world, in every culture, and in all socioeconomic groups. Mental illness is not a choice, character flaw, or moral failing. Rather, mental illness is a condition triggered by the confluence of genetics and the environment. Seeking professional help rather than shaming or denying the problem is vital for the teen and the family.

Signs of Trouble

Parents seeking professional help during the adolescent years are commonly struggling with any of the following challenges:

    Perfect teen.

Parents of these teens may not recognize that anything is amiss until these teens become emotionally overwhelmed. This manifests usually during the sophomore and junior years of high school when the pressure over college choices peaks. Perfectionism usually manifests itself as anxiety about current achievements, future plans, and self-worth. This issue is one of the most difficult teen challenges to detect because the teen appears to be "just fine" and a parent assumes the anxiety is part of the normal stress of doing well in school.

Checking into whether the teen's sense of self is independent of a "perfect performance" helps parents differentiate between normal anxiety and dysfunctional self-worth. Teens focused on *being* perfect rather than on *doing* their best are at risk. Such teens commonly express messages like, "I am a failure," "I am not a good…," "I am nothing," While it's quite normal for every teen to express these sentiments every now and then, it is the pervasive sense of worthlessness and shame that are cause for concern.

To counteract such tendencies, it is critical for parents to be aware of what messages they are sending at home: "Do your best" vs. "You need to be the perfect student;" "You are a failure because you made a mistake," vs. "Oops! You have made a mistake. How will you fix it?" Tragically, the "perfect" teen syndrome is commonly behind teen suicide that is unrelated to drugs or mental health issues.

Rebellious teen.

This is the common stereotype of a troubled teen. Rebellion looks different in each family. Some examples are excessive disrespectful talking back, using drugs, flaunting house rules openly and dangerously, illicit relationships, running away, becoming physically violent with family members, etc. A rebellious teen is a discouraged individual. Acts of rebellion are commonly cries for love, help, and support. There are many reasons why teens rebel. However, based on our observations of families, we believe the main reasons are:

- Ineffective emotional regulation strategies.
- Disconnect from family.
- Lack of self-awareness.

Priorities when parenting teens (p. 236) presents a framework for handling teens in trouble. But that is not enough. When teens rebel, we highly encourage the family to engage the teen in individual therapy while also doing family therapy with another therapist. The earlier therapy is begun and maintained, the better the chances for teens to heal and overcome their rebellious ways.

Depressed teen.

As noted above, several symptoms of mental illness may be observed at this age. Depression is of particular interest because, while there are many reasons a teen becomes depressed, a silent trigger is an intense psychological struggle between what the teen wants to do or be and what the parent is expecting. In some authoritarian homes the parental expectations are so high and unrealistic, they do not fit the teen's innate gifts or personality.

Teens who love their parents and strive to please them may deal with their inner struggle by becoming depressed. When teens believe they are voiceless, depression shifts the focus away from parental expectations and is a silent, passive expression of the teen saying "no."

Another common trigger for depression in teens is the existential angst over the meaning of life. No matter how well parents have taught and guided, the journey of formulating a life theory is an individual journey. For some teens, this journey is intense and overwhelming, culminating in a state of depression that is not relieved until they find answers. Lastly, depression in the teen years could be a symptom of serious mental illness such as bipolar disorder or schizophrenia.

Dual-personality teen.

If teens find it unsafe to express themselves or behave as they would like around their parents, they will go underground. A teen will adopt a home-persona and an outside-the-home-persona. To some extent teens will behave differently around their parents and their friends no matter how good the parent-teen relationship is. However, a dual-personality is a concern where there is a dramatic difference between who the teen is inside and outside the home. Such a gap yields major emotional and psychological problems and may be exhibited through behaviors such as cutting, suicidal ideation, drug use, running away, frequent fickle relationships, etc.

Why is my Teen in Serious Trouble?

Can anyone predict how a child is going to turn out during the teen years? Only Allah can with His infinite knowledge. Humans are not robots that follow a coded script; rather, each individual is unique, idiosyncratic, and unpredictable. This is how Allah Created mankind. In our observations of families, we have come to recognize that a confluence of all the following five factors inevitably explain why teens behave the way they do.

1. Allah's qadar (divine preordination).

In a culture where people unconsciously believe that everything is under their control, it is easy to lose sight of the sixth article of faith: divine preordination. The six articles of faith in Islam revolve around beliefs of the heart: the belief in Allah, angels, divine books, prophets, Day of Judgment, and the favorable and unfavorable qadar (divine preordination). These six articles of faith constitute a framework reminding Muslims of their limitations. Unfortunately, the belief in both the favorable and unfavorable qadar is commonly neglected in daily life.

The path teens decide to take is part of qadar. Parents can implement the best parenting practices and have the best life, but their children can be part of the struggles that Allah Has preordained for them. It can be that teens are addicted to drugs, affiliated with bad company, breaking the law or alienated from Islam. When teens engage in such behaviors, parents experience intense and deep emotional pain. Nonetheless, the fact remains that no matter what a parent does—the best, worst, or something in between—it is part of their qadar.

Invoking the qadar of Allah is not an excuse to renege on the parental duty and responsibility to guide and teach. Allah holds parents responsible for the conscious parenting they did and not for how their children turn out. The belief in qadar is intended to ease the aching hearts of parents struggling with troubled children. In the dark moments of agony over the chosen path of a child, nothing brings more solace and peace as submitting to Allah and seeking His sustenance.

2. Teen's temperament & parenting style.

A recent study (Panetta, et al., 2014) analyzed the impact of temperament and parenting styles on the emotional and behavioral regulation of teens. Teens' temperaments (p. 39) were found to explain almost half their functioning. Parenting styles (p. 31) were significant but less so than children's temperaments. This particular study helps to explain why children from the same family with the same parents turn out differently. The combination of the teen's temperament, genetic disposition, and parents' style is unique to each child.

Scientific literature abounds with studies linking parenting styles to outcomes in children. While specific studies vary in their details, a common theme emerges from the research: authoritative parenting, especially when practiced by both parents, is associated with the best outcomes for children (Panetta, et al., 2014; Fite, 2009). Observations in our work with families support this view. While the parenting style is not the sole factor influencing the effectiveness with which a teen navigates the twists and turns of life, it plays a significant role. Certain life lessons are learned faster and more effectively by children of authoritative parents. Children of authoritarian and permissive parents will take longer and struggle greatly to learn the same life lessons. Sometimes these life lessons are never learned and life becomes a constant barrage of difficulties and challenges.

3. Teen's unique perception.

Children create unique individual theories that explain the world. These theories become the framework by which they perceive themselves, others, and the world at large. According to Adlerian philosophy, this world theory is in place by the time the child is five years old. Certainly the child is unaware of what theory has been internalized. Nevertheless, this early theory of life becomes a strong motivator for behavior or misbehavior. While it is based on events and reactions of others, it is 100% the perception and creation of the child. For example, a toddler who is cute and adorable and is paid a great amount of attention may believe that, in order to thrive in life, one has to be the center of attention. Another toddler may have been commended for being a great helper and thus internalizes the belief that, in order to thrive, one must be of service. The possibilities are endless. However, some theories more than others (people must take care of me; if people don't say I am good, I must be bad; if I am not loved by everyone, something is wrong; life is all about having fun; etc.) lend themselves to trouble during the teen years.

4. Mental health issues.

As previously mentioned, sometimes the challenges experienced have to do with serious mental health disorders (e.g. bipolar, schizophrenia, depression). If a parent suspects mental illness, it is critical to have the teen evaluated. Don't delay. The earlier a teen who struggles with mental illness is assessed and treated, the better the prognosis.

5. Social norms.

Teen social norms play a major role in influencing identity

formation. The cultural context can be different from one community to another even within the same geographical area. Social norms change from one generation to another and are usually reactions and counter-reactions to prior norms. Some examples of trends the Muslim community has experienced in recent decades: increased observance of the *hijab* (head covering), the removal of the *hijab*, focus on religiosity, decrease in mosque attendance, focus on community service, increase in dating, and doing drugs. Teens who are disconnected from their families will follow the cultural trends of their times.

Engaging in Counseling

Typically, parents experience many emotions when their teen exhibits any of the above challenges. For a while, parents ride a rollercoaster of helplessness, confusion, anger, and fear. It is common that they react by attempting to exert control over their teens and the situation. Unfortunately, this strategy backfires every time. Teens do not respond well to coercion and manipulation. They respond best when they are held responsible for their lives and are invited to be collaborators. When the parent-teen bond is strong, parents are able to handle simple teen years' challenges on their own. However, when parents are at a loss, they will seek help and guidance from family, friends, and professionals.

At the early signs of trouble, therapy will help teens adjust faster and more effectively. With all the struggles outlined above, significant coping strategies are missing. It is highly recommended to seek counseling for even a short period of time. A therapeutic setting helps struggling teens shift their perceptions, learn effective ways to deal with life's struggles, and begin to recognize their innate gifts. Therapy also helps parents gain a deeper understanding of what ails their teens and adopt new ways of responding that empower rather than enable. We invite you to overcome any stigma associated with seeking therapy in the Muslim community and focus on doing the best for your teens. We would also like to emphasize that therapy is a process based on time. Challenges will not be overcome in a few sessions. Sometimes years are needed to overcome the difficult struggles. Never give up. Patience and seeking Allah's sustenance are key. *Bil tawfiq* (with divine success).

The teen years are the preparation for the coming parent-child separation in the letting go years. All strategies used during the teen years will be necessary for the next stage in life: parenting young adults. However, a major shift in parental attitudes must take place so young adults can lead their lives independently. In the next chapter, we will cover how parents of young adults can continue to maintain influence while letting go.

CHAPTER 9

ADULT CHILDREN

Most families navigate their children's emerging adulthood with little tension and chaos. However, there are families who will struggle. In this chapter we highlight potential areas of conflict and offer reflections and invitations aimed at fostering connection and understanding.

Letting Go

One of the natural processes of life is the gradual and continuous shifting of responsibility from parents to children. As children become adults they take on more responsibilities for their lives while their parents become observers and mentors. In many traditional Islamic cultures, parents let go of their responsibility for their adult children when the latter are married. However, sometimes, even with marriage, the letting go process does not take place. In some traditional societies the new couple merely become a subset of the larger family, and the older family members continue in their leadership roles. While there are still communities where letting go occurs at the time of marriage, the dramatic changes in the global culture (social, economic, technological, political) are forcing an earlier onset of parent-child separation. Current global cultural norms are influencing adult children still living at home to lead their lives the way they wish despite parental disapproval.

The most difficult letting go occurs when the adult child has chosen to lead a life that does not align with the parent's worldview. I (Noha) encounter many families who are torn apart by such differences. Typically, tension arises over the adult child's choices regarding marital partner, friends, education, career, sexual orientation, or, in the most difficult of situations, religion.

Letting go is a frame of mind. It is actually an Islamically based principle. The premise in Islam is that, "each will come on the Day of Resurrection alone," (Quran, 19:95) and "no soul is beholden for the sins of another," (Quran, 6:164; 17:15; 35:18; 39:7; 53:38). These are Divine principles that parents sometimes fail to remember in their zeal to protect their children from any "wrong." Parents love their children and want what is best for them; however, usually that love is anchored in an expectation that the child will live in accordance with the parent's way of living.

Letting go is not abandoning a child. Letting go is recognizing that the adult child is not you and may make decisions that won't align with your opinions or ideas. Letting go is conversing with your adult child, sharing your concerns and views, while recognizing that they can and will make their own decisions. Letting go is simply stepping aside to let your children lead their lives while assuring them of your continual support and love.

Money, Time & Friends

Some parents of young adults struggle with issues related to money, time, and friends. The financial support parents offer their young adults will vary in each family. Parents will have to clarify financial boundaries. Will they cover tuition and living expenses? Entertainment expenses? Summer travel? Car payments? Giving young adults an allowance for living expenses while in college will help them gradually shift to financial independence as they manage money effectively and seek employment. Setting limits around borrowing money teaches young adults not to expect parents to "bail them out." Expecting adult children to save and pay for their own expenses independently inculcates responsibility and delayed gratification. Lastly, holding back judgments regarding purchases that young adults make with the money they have earned empowers the latter to learn from their mistakes.

When young adults move away, many parents miss the liveliness of having them around. Young adults gradually spend more time at work and with friends than at home. They may or may not call or visit as often as a parent wishes, and this can be difficult for some parents. However, a secure parent-child relationship will still feel connected because the relationship is grounded in friendship and respect. Parents and their adult children can schedule time to talk and visit regularly based on their situation (locations and commitments). Mutual respect and understanding of the shifting priorities of adult children will help ease this transition (Get A Life, p. 105).

Finally, a challenge for some parents is their adult children's friendships. They may not know their adult child's new friends from college and work like they did when they were in high school. Parents no longer have direct influence on their choice of friends. The social life of adult children undergoes growth and change away from the watchful eyes of parents. However, these relationships play a critical role in the emotional development of young adults. It is helpful for parents who do not like their adult children's friends to recognize that these choices are not under their control. Certainly, parents can express their concerns and reservations, but they must trust their young adults to figure their way. Parents can set boundaries if they do not want to welcome the friends in the family home.

The Question of Faith

Whether a young adult aligns with a parent's worldview or not is part of a parent's *qadar* (divine preordination). In *surah al-Ahqaf* (The Wind-Curved Sand Hills Chapter, Quran, 46:15-19; see Appendix A) Allah describes two faithful households. In one, the child follows in the footsteps of the parents. In the other, the child rejects the faith of the parents. The faith of a child is only one of the many areas where the *qadar* of Allah will supersede.

The majority of young adults will seriously contemplate their belief systems during their early twenties. For some, getting exposed to new values while in college either solidifies Islam as their own choice or plants seeds of doubt. There are also young adults who will not consider the faith question during their twenties, directing their energies toward their college majors and careers, instead. As with teens, young adults will fall into one of four groups with regard to their practice of Islam (see Question of Faith, p. 268, and Islam-the-Choice p. 397).

Religiosity in societies goes through waves (Quran, 7:169; 19:59; see Appendix A). At the time of this writing, there is a strong tide of "nones" in the U.S. (Lipka, 2015). These are individuals who do not identify with any religious tradition. According to Pew Research Center, there has been a significant jump in the number of "nones" in the U.S. between 2007 and 2014. Interestingly, this attitude is more concentrated among young adults born in the years 1981-1996. Simultaneously, although unclear if related, there is an upsurge of spirituality seekers through secular practices such as Yoga and meditation. Another current trend is the increase in religious Humanists. These are individuals who believe in the teachings of a religious tradition but without engaging in the ritual practices prescribed by that faith. Many individuals who fall into these categories cite instances of religious intolerance and, in their views, nonsensical beliefs and practices as the root of their disillusionment with organized religion. While these trends are not the majority, there is definitely a strong wave of waning religiosity. Unfortunately, some young Muslim adults have been swept up by this tide. Just as quickly as this wave has gained momentum, a counter wave will be on the rise soon, as has been the pattern of human behavior according to Allah's Will.

If you are a parent who has been blessed with practicing young adults, give deep gratitude to Allah. While you have certainly put effort into teaching and guiding, ultimately their practice of faith is *tawfiq* (success) and *rizq* (provision) from Allah. Be grateful and humble. We also implore you to let go of judging other families whose children are struggling with faith. There are many parents who have taught and guided well, but their young adult children have chosen another path.

For parents whose young adults have chosen a different practice of Islam or have even decided not to follow Islam all together, we invite you to take an approach of "wait and see." We are aware this stance is one of the most difficult for parents. However, unless your young adult has become a staunch adversary of Islam (Quran, 58:22; see Appendix A), we implore you not to sever the relationship. The main reason is Allah's Decree that "there is no coercion in religion" (Quran, 2:256). Any imposition of faith is counter to the free will that is at the foundation of Islamic thought. Faith is a choice, not a forced practice. This core principle of Islam is even more critical during the current era of public renouncements of faith and traditions. Before the advent of the Internet and spread of globalization, individuals who had issues with Islam or the practice of Islam would hide their misgivings because social norms in the past dictated conformity. Social norms today celebrate nonconformity. It is with this understanding that we invite you not to sever ties nor abandon your adult child.

Beyond the acceptance of an adult child's free will in choosing a way of life, there is continual hope. The Quranic narrative in the stories of prophets Nuh, Ibrahim, and Lut (peace be upon them all) are invitations to hope for a loved one's transformation until the end. The clearest example is the story of Nuh and his son. Until the very last minute Nuh continued to invite his son to join the believers. In an age where the conformity of previous eras is no longer the norm, the practice of Nuh, Ibrahim, and Lut serve as guidance and solace.

Physician, philosopher, and prolific writer Dr. Mustafa Mahmud (1921- 2009) of Egypt is the inspiration for the concept of "wait and see." According to his writings, Dr. Mahmud began questioning the existence of Allah at the young age of 13. It took him 30 years to come full circle and believe in Allah again. He described the years of lost faith as years when he worshiped his own intellect and rejected all ideas outside the realm of tangible lab science. The same types of arguments are heard today by young adults questioning their faith.

Following his reversion to Islam, Dr. Mahmud embarked on a journey of education and charity work in Egypt that thrives to this day. The same science he used to deny the Divine Creation became the foundation for his belief in Allah. The legacy Dr. Mahmud left inspires the awe of Allah by highlighting the wonders of His Creation. He successfully bridged the gap between science and Islam in the twentieth century and in the process reassured countless young Muslims of the continued relevance of their faith. This legacy came from a man whose early life followed a different path. His story is one of the reasons that, whenever parents seek advice regarding their lost young adults, we say, "Wait and see, maybe your young adult will be another Mustafa Mahmud."

Let us be clear that giving space and time is not synonymous with crossing critical personal and family boundaries. Just because young adults choose to live in a certain way does not give them the right to force their un-Islamic lifestyle (drinking alcohol, mocking Islam, illicit sexual relations, etc.) into your own home. Be firm about what is acceptable to you within the confines of your home. That is your right. Your adult child may not respond to these boundaries from a position of belief, but accepting these limits from a place of respect for you and your values is something you certainly can communicate and expect.

Sexual Orientation

In my (Noha) practice I have worked with many families of Muslim LGBTQ young adults. Since the Muslim community is yet to discuss this issue openly and clearly, many families are lost and confused. The 21st Century is marked by a global movement to bring LGBTQ issues into the open. In the process, there is pressure to question and challenge religious rulings regarding same-gender sexual activity. There are calls to exhibit pride by publicly proclaiming one's orientation and engaging in same-gender relations. Young Muslim LGBTQ adults are under a lot of pressure. Who do they heed? The value system they were raised with or the new cultural norms?

Muslim parents respond to their LGBTQ young adults in different ways. When parents suspect but are uncertain, some ignore the issue until it's forced upon them while others engage in open discussions with their children. When young adults share their sexual orientation, families in my (Noha) practice have responded in the following ways:

- Love and compassion. Some parents understand the traditional Islamic opinions as well as the current social pressures. This group is able to engage in open discussions about the issue. They disconnect the sexual orientation from spiritual worth. They invite and empower their young adults to focus on their connection with Allah to find guidance on how best to address their orientation within the context of living a virtuous Muslim life.
- Shock and fear with gradual understanding. Some parents never thought this issue would come up in their homes.

After the initial phase of shock and denial, this group seeks help and support from *Imams* (religious leaders) and Muslim therapists. They gradually accept their young adults' sexual orientation while clearly expressing their position on same-gender relations.

• Shock and fear without full understanding. This group resorts to coercive measures, hoping to change their young adults' sexual orientation. Some force their children into conversion therapy, which has been proven to be ineffective. Others force their young adults to marry heterosexual partners in an attempt to avert social stigma while secretly hoping these young adults will be convinced they are actually heterosexual. This is another losing battle.

The most challenging situations are those when LGBTQ young adults have chosen to reject Islamic guidance and engage openly in same-gender sexual relations. Parents then find themselves in a quandary. What takes precedence? Loving Allah by following his prohibition of same-gender sexual relations or loving their children and accepting their choices? What are the limits of a parent's responsibility? It's true that "no soul is beholden for the sins of another" (Quran, 53:38), but what about a parent's responsibility to guide and teach? For these families, we invite you to consider the following:

• Muslims are not morality judges. Allah is the only Judge for "Allah knows and you (humans) don't know" (Quran, 2:216). Also, parents are not responsible for the choices their young adults make. Deal with your young adults with love and compassion. Avoid shaming, demeaning, mocking or ridiculing. Hold your values through your boundaries and not through your judgment.

- Be very clear about limits and boundaries. Some parents, after a major conversation expressing their position, restrict conversations regarding this aspect of their young adult's life. Others draw the line at welcoming sexual partners in the home. "We would love to see you anytime you wish. However, we are not fine with meeting your partner." Every family will determine its stance based on its unique circumstances and values.

- Disconnection needs to be a last resort and only when parents cannot reconcile their own values with behaviors that directly impact them in their own homes. In this drastic way of letting go parents decide that being true to their own convictions is incompatible with maintaining relationships with their adult children. These families would benefit greatly from seeking counseling to find peace in their situation while continuing to send a message of love to their disconnected young adults.

My (Noha) experience in private practice does not cover all parental reactions in the Muslim community. With such a complex topic, it is difficult to address all situations in this writing. This will be a non-issue for Muslim parents who reject the traditional Islamic ruling on same-gender sexual behaviors. They will be comfortable opening their homes to their children and their same-gender sexual partners. However, for the Muslim parents who believe in the traditional rulings governing sexual relations, this challenge is formidable and confounding. Finding a Muslim therapist to work out the specifics of a family's situation would be the best course of action.

One thing is certain though: the practice of knowingly forcing young adults who experience same-gender sexual attraction into heterosexual marriages they did not initiate leads to pain and suffering. These marriages typically exhibit major intimacy issues as the LGBTQ partner displays disinterest or has difficulty engaging in sex. I have counseled many couples who come to therapy for such problems. Typically, the heterosexual partner is unaware of the sexual orientation of the other partner. Problems occur early in the marriage with the unaware spouse sometimes being blamed for the sexual difficulties. In some instances, marriages dissolve without acknowledgment of the sexual disparity, and the heterosexual spouse is left to deal with feelings of guilt and shame. One family's unwarranted shame leads to another family's undeserved shame. This is not to say that LGBTQ individuals cannot marry heterosexual partners. They may—but only if they want to. And to prevent unnecessary pain, I strongly recommend transparency with the prospective spouse from the beginning. The majority of Muslim scholars state that issues kept secret intentionally before the consummation of marriage and which are certain to impact the marital dynamics are strong grounds for the dissolution of marriage (Sabiq, 1983, v. 3).

One final point with regard to sexual orientation: we invite the community at large to drop judgmental attitudes about LGBTQs. We invite the community to distinguish between sexual orientation and the actions related to these desires. We invite the community to invoke the prophetic tradition in dealing with people: sins are between an individual and Allah. We are not morality judges. We deal with all people with respect, love, and compassion despite what we may presume about them or our personal values. "To us our deeds, and to you your deeds. Peace be to you. We seek not (the way of) the unaware. Verily! You guide not whom you like, but Allah guides whom He wills" (Quran, 55-56).

Marriage

Humans seek social connections and intimate relationships during early adulthood. This search for companionship and connection is a meaningful process of personal growth. Young adults at this stage clarify their personal goals in their professional life and seek partners with whom to share their experiences and dreams. Conflicts occur at this stage when young adults contemplate marriage, and parents doubt their readiness for commitment. Conflict also arises if young adults are showing interest in life partners deemed incompatible or unsuitable by parents. Early conversations elucidating the parents' values and expectations will reduce conflict as well as help guide the adult child when seeking a spouse. (See Sex and Relationships, p. 261).

In my (Munira) premarital counseling work with young adults, I have found that 70% of the Muslim couples in my practice struggle with parental interference. For many Muslim families, marriage is a time when the "child" becomes an adult, and this transition can be very messy and confusing when there is poor communication and a resistance to the changing family dynamics. Parents may still see their offspring as children who must obey their advice and recommendation of whom to marry (see Blind Birr, p. 385). Unfortunately, there are families who continue to hold marriage criteria that are based on un-Islamic principles. Disagreements over criteria related to race, ethnicity, culture, and religious practice are common problems in these families.

Many young adults find it difficult to balance their own needs and the expectations of their parents while navigating a healthy marital relationship. They feel conflicted between respecting their parents and choosing their own life path. Many feel strangled by cultural, and religious assumptions and find themselves stagnant and unable to move forward with life partners of their own choosing.

Parents ultimately want to see their adult children happy and successful. This requires letting go of unrealistic expectations and encouraging adult children to form healthy bonds with their spouses. Parents who acknowledge that they no longer "play a starring role" in their adult children's lives will have an easier time with this transition. Parents who cling to their old position and see spouses as a threat, or struggle with feelings of loss and unimportance, will endure further conflicts. Parents who have learned to see their adult children's marriage as a natural extension of their growth will let go and accept their choice and focus on having a positive relationship with the couple. Their adult children are no longer "theirs" as individuals. Rather, the couple is a new family with whom they have the opportunity to share memories and enjoy time as they age.

Parents who encourage and support the unity of the couple as a priority over other relationships will empower their adult children to form healthy marital relationships. The commitment to a spouse is the building of a new family which requires balancing the perspectives of the parents with the couple's goals. Parents can encourage the new couple to seek premarital counseling if they are concerned about their relationship skills. Parents must actively choose not to interfere by establishing healthy boundaries with the couple, for instance, encouraging the couple to solve problems rather than complain to parents. It will be important to build a new relationship with the couple by taking into consideration their relationship dynamic and individual personalities. Respecting the choices the couple makes and not offering unsolicited advice will be vital to maintaining harmony. Parents who let go at this stage and refocus on their own marital relationship will feel the most contentment and success.

Career

Depending on the relationship, adult children may seek their parent's advice about their career paths or the potential jobs they are considering. The career an adult child chooses to pursue may or may not be in alignment with a parent's dreams, but the encouragement and advice a parent offers is a gift. If parents feel that their adult children are aimless or unfocused, they can have a heart-to-heart conversation sharing their concerns and listening to what the young adults are going through. At this stage parents are more effective acting as mentors and observers.

Due to the economic downturn of recent years, many Millennials are coming back home after college while they seek employment opportunities. The "boomerang effect" has changed family norms. The young adult is "independent" yet living with parents which adds a new layer of complexity to the relationship. Establishing clear boundaries and expectations becomes vital for this arrangement to be successful. An adult child must behave as an adult (not an adolescent). Examples include: contributing to living expenses, taking care of their own laundry, helping with meals, caring for the home, etc. It will also be necessary to discuss short and long-term plans for future career paths that lead to independent living. Additionally, parents must establish clear boundaries and expectations around the extent of the support they can offer their adult children.

In this chapter, we covered areas of potential conflict between parents and adult children. When serious disagreements occur, the sagacious advice, "then let them lead their lives," sums up parents' roles during this stage. No doubt it is one of the most difficult things parents can do. However, it is sometimes the only response a parent can have. With this chapter, we come to the end of our exploration of the parenting journey through the lifespan of the child. We pray we have empowered you with new perspectives, practical tools, and deep insights. In the next section, we share with you in-depth essays addressing various parenting topics.

PART IV

PARENT
WISDOM
ESSAYS

God Delivers

By Ahmed Younis

The closest I've ever felt to God is when my wife was giving birth to our daughter.

They were never-ending moments of supplication for her health, for God to alleviate her pain, for her to have the birthing experience that she wants to have. I prayed and I prayed and I prayed. I prayed on the ground like a Muslim, with my hands crossed like a Christian in Church, like Rastas, Hindus, Sikhs, and every other way of being that I could think of. I prayed to God, the God of Jews, Blacks, Women, and the oppressed. I prayed to the beginning before all beginnings and the ending after all ends, the source of beauty, love, and mercy. Despite always starting my public lectures with that sentence, and in that name, I finally understood what it means to recognize a God of mercy and grace.

There are moments when one is truly helpless—as in, you cannot help—when there is nothing that can be done. I mean, yes, some things can be done. But on the meta-level, they really do not rise to the level of the moment. The positionality of a father during birth is reciprocal and corrective to society's normative approaches to gender relations. This, in my judgment, is exactly as it should be.

A father during birth is silenced. For the first time in his life the man does not get the attention but is constructively told to shut up, to sit aside, to recognize the limitations of his knowledge, and to heed the majesty that is present. It is a minor corrective to the misogyny of this life—to the overwhelmingly negative realities girls and women face every day in all places around the world.

Birthing is the first time that a man is told to yield, halt, take caution. If he is smart, he begins to understand that he is helpless.

To be clear, it is not my wife or anyone else who tells her husband these things. It is the totality of the experience both as it is socially constructed and as it is naturally ordained. We each had a role. Our cooperation was effortless.

During the birth of our daughter (may God always bless her), I found the line between the spirit and the intellect to be blurred. I was intimately involved in the physicality of the experience from early contractions to our daughter's birth—rocking, rhythmic dancing, pushing, and every other thing you can imagine, to support my wife. She led in every way—not because of her insatiable appetite for prenatal reading, not because of our classes together, and not because she is a brilliant person. She led from a place of spiritual power that can only induce awe and amazement. Her knowledge was primordial in so many ways. It was a visceral power that no human can muster by choice but can channel only if centered on the occasion. You see, it is not about rising to an occasion. The occasion is the event. We are not the event. We do not rise here. We prostrate in deep humility to the Creator of all things. It is a centering, a calm, strong, hopeful centering, that my wife mastered like the great sages of all time.

There is no experience that I've had that can even be spoken of in the same breath as this one. It is incomparable in every possible way from the banality of life's normalcy.

On that day I felt our midwife was a sage who deeply understood the liminal nature of the moment. We were together "in between" worlds. We were standing between the material and the spiritual, this life and the next, extreme happiness and unbridled fear. Those in the room were all in a liminal state. We were all connected to a power source in different ways. That power source felt as though it was housed deep inside my wife's soul and was coming out to the world as an act of ultimate devotion and sacrifice.

God guides and sustains in such moments the ones that require the most of our capacity. It felt to me as though our team, led by the midwife, understood they played a role in that sustaining. Despite not being of the same faith, we were—on that day in those moments—of the same faith. We were all believers! We believed together in an intangible power that was animating all our actions and every action was pure, aimed at a just purpose, and delivered with great care and love.

I've always attempted to live with purpose and chosen to concern myself with complex social realities that cause individual and systemic oppression in its various forms. One of the issues I've held close and studied with concern is the situation of girls and women around the world. Women's safety, their health, their education, and their employment—these things have always mattered to me. As I explored these ideas and marched into adulthood, I was convinced that marriage and children were not for me. I believed that my life would be dedicated to the work, the travel, the writing, the social entrepreneurship, and the relationships.

Then I met a woman named Yasmine. She blew my mind and overwhelmed my heart. God blessed us with a daughter who is (as of this writing) four months old. In living those three sentences, my whole world and understanding of reality changed. Like birth, marriage is also the process of life begetting life. And like birth, God delivers.

Dr. Ahmed Younis is married to his superstar wife, Yasmine Abdel-Aal., Esq., an expert in entertainment and intellectual property law. Together they have a beautiful daughter. Ahmed is Chief of Operation of the Global Engagement Center at the Department of State. Prior to joining the Obama Administration he served as Assistant Professor and International Ambassador for Global Ethics and Social Justice at The Paulo Freire Democratic Project at Chapman University. Ahmed holds a Ph.D. in the Philosophy of Education (Critical Pedagogy) from Chapman University and a Juris Doctor from Washington & Lee School of Law.

An Attitude Of Gratitude

By Tarek Shawky

When my son was about two years old, my wife and I enrolled in a Positive Discipline course taught by Noha. We were dealing with the usual challenges of raising a toddler and needed to learn quickly some basic parenting skills. I felt anxious and very ill-prepared for the task of parenting. It's a unique anxiety experienced by expectant parents who have only nine months to prep for a job that never stops. Our Positive Discipline course included discussions with other parents sharing our common experiences; it was as therapeutic as it was educational. It was instrumental in turning my perspective as a parent toward focusing on big-picture parenting goals: parenting is about being the person I want my kids to be; so, I have to model the behaviors I want them to absorb.

One of the most valuable lessons that stuck with me from that class is the importance of practicing and modeling gratitude. I now know that so much of parenting is about having the right attitude and perspective you want to pass to your kids.. Simply put, it's focusing on the positive and being grateful for what we have instead of being resentful about what we don't have. Practicing gratitude helps me adjust my perspective during difficult moments and gives me a positive outlook on life, one that I want to nurture in my kids.

I recognize that exercising gratitude is easier said than done.

Any exercise sounds nice in theory, but the implementation can be challenging. Muhammed Ali once said, "Enjoy your children, even when they don't act the way you want them to." I am constantly challenged in my daily interactions with my children. I have come to recognize that there is a fine line between gratitude and resentment. In the midst of difficult situations, it's easier to be pulled into a negative mindset. When my son or daughter completes their artistic masterpiece on the living room wall using permanent marker, remembering to be grateful for the child and everything that comes with childhood is the last thing that comes to mind.

My wife and I are working parents. We actively co-parent. Much of my energy is spent co-parenting our two kids. If you've done it, then I don't need to explain. If you haven't, just imagine clocking into a job and staying on the clock 24/7, 365 days a year, after year. It's a job for at least two, but I recommend a village—especially when your spouse is unavailable and you're parenting solo. The most challenging moments can often trigger negative responses like yelling or spanking. It's easy to lose your cool when you find your older child knocking over his little sister after you told him not to…twice. I try never to spank my kids, but it happens, and I know it's a discipline tool some parents still use. I was spanked as a child, but I prefer not to pass along that experience because I think it's a lazy response that ignores the underlying cause of the behavior that triggered the spanking. When parents lose their patience and reach the end of their rope, that spanking is the emotional response, the quick temporary fix. I admit I've been there.

Many parents find themselves alone at times since having two working parents is no longer the exception, but the norm. My wife is an amazing working mom who sometimes travels; so, I've had my share of single dad experiences, albeit in small doses. When my wife leaves me alone with the kids to pursue her dreams, I am tested. I walk that thin line between gratitude and resentment, and, while I try not to fall off on the side of resentment, it happens. A rough weekend alone with two kids always raises the scepter of resentment about spending days changing diapers, feeding, bathing, and mediating between my kids. But when I am in my gratitude zone, I can see through even the hardest time to the hidden blessings. To be clear, I don't resent my family. I sometimes resent the weight of the responsibility of caring for two young kids from sun-up to sundown by myself. It's challenging. But I consistently agree to do it because I love my wife and kids.

Those short stints as a single dad give me a tremendous appreciation for all the mothers who traditionally have managed the parenting alone. I am also amazed at all the single parents out there who sacrifice their all to raise kids while keeping their sanity and keeping their lives together. I am certainly more appreciative of what it takes to raise children, and I am grateful that I am not alone on this journey.

My wife is a brilliant woman. People who know her often stop and tell me how much they love her and are inspired by her. I always echo the sentiment. I appreciate her even more because, despite the demands of her work, she also pulls more than her share of the work raising two kids. While she's an exceptional mother, that wasn't why I married her. I was drawn to her mind, her tenacity, and her commitment to social justice activism. When I hear her speak to communities around the world, I'm immensely proud, and I appreciate the example she is setting as a smart, confident, outspoken Muslim woman. The best way I know to support her is to give her the space to pursue her dreams. While I know that's the right thing to do, it is still very challenging. Every time she travels, I still get a little nervous because I know that I am the first and last resort for my kids for the duration of her trip. I get no breaks and have no subs. It's certainly a test, and I can choose to be resentful and stress about it, or I can re-focus on the positive.

I see it as my personal responsibility to play a complimentary role so my kids learn the value of a dad who supports mom's work. What sustains me in difficult single-dad situations is knowing that I'm supporting my wife's dream as she inspires others. Being conscious of the fact that she is a stellar role model to our kids who are learning the role of women through her example also eases my struggles. Even more important, I am grateful that she is my daughter's inspiration. My girl sees the world through her mom's eyes. Her experiences include observing her mom at the front of the room, behind a mic and engaging an audience with confidence and compassion. I know there is a positive correlation between a confident successful mother and her daughter. When I do feel frustrated with being alone with two kids, I remember that this time is an investment in my kids as much as it is an investment in my wife. A mom who is a confident educated leader will instill the same values in her daughter, and that's the daughter I want to raise. Those are the types of women I grew up with, and I appreciate the value of such women in society. My job is to affirm the reality my girl sees in her mom and to send a consistent message by supporting her mom every step of the way. I'm tasked with reinforcing gender equality so my daughter never feels inadequate or discouraged by her gender. I also have to make sure my son sees the importance of supporting and respecting his mom and sister so he never falls victim to the misogyny and gender discrimination that only provide his sister with 0.78 cents to her brother's dollar.

To be clear, my wife still spends much more time at home with our kids than I do. I'm doing my part in raising the family, but she spends more time in the trenches. We both value civic engagement, and our lives and schedules reflect that. We chose to raise our kids with the experience of activism and public service with the hope that it becomes natural to them. One of the reasons we are able to do all that we do is because we take our kids along everywhere we go.

One strategy for parents to stay positive and grateful is to find someone that helps relieve the stress and responsibility of parenting. Some of us are lucky to have healthy grandparents who live nearby. They often make the best substitute parents because nobody cares more about kids than grandparents. Aunts, uncles, and cousins are great, too; they're all huge blessings for parents with young kids. We utilize family often, and I'm so grateful for them. We also have great friends and sitters that help us keep our commitments and our sanity as working parents.

Another way to ward off the resentment and negativity of child rearing is to find a balance where both parents contribute accordingly. If I'm not available for a week because of work or meetings, my wife is always there, never complaining, just doing whatever it takes. I feel empowered and supported in my life and work, and so my natural response is to be supportive and empowering right back. That balance is like a solution to a mathematical equation. If you get the numbers right, you solve the equation. But if the numbers are off, so is your life. In addition to supporting each other in our work endeavors, we also make time for personal self-care. That includes exercise, connecting with friends, hobbies, or just clocking out for a few hours. We recognize that personal time gives us the physical and emotional boost needed to continue being a grateful, active, contributing parent, and we prioritize scheduling it.

We all have fine lines to walk. As parents, we have so much to be grateful for and some challenges we may resent. It's important that we always focus on the gratitude even in the tough times. We owe it to our kids to be the example we want them to become so they can make the world a more positive place, full of blessings, full of gratitude.

Tarek Shawky is a dedicated criminal defense lawyer with a passion for justice and equality under the law, serving clients throughout Southern California. He is married to his brilliant wife, Edina Lekovic, and together they are raising their young son and daughter to be socially and politically conscious individuals.

BREAKING THE SHACKLES OF MISOGYNY

By Saleh Kholaki

I am an extremely lucky man. I have been married for 35 years and have been given the gift of a great family: a magnificent wife, two lovely daughters, and two lovely sons.

Immigrating to the U.S. from the Middle East in 1983, my wife and I had too many conflicting ideas about the West. We held the belief that our home is where our fathers are buried and believed that one day, we would go back "home." We worried about raising our children in the midst of a dramatically different culture with another language and set of values. We pondered how we would imprint our children with our own traditions and values while navigating the social pressure of our new adopted country.

I am grateful that we realized early on that our home is where our children and grandchildren will be raised. One thing, though, did not change: the different standards we held for raising boys and girls. Curfew for the boys was different from the girls. Extracurricular trips were generally allowed only for the boys. Restrictions on who rides in the car were reserved for the girls.

Male dominance in Middle Eastern culture is palpable. It stems from a place of responsibility for the family. Fathers and sons are responsible to provide and protect. Girls are overly protected because they need to appear to the community as well-mannered and well-raised worthy brides. This is the mistake we fell into. Or at least I did, because my wife was the most forward-thinking of the two of us.

Thank God we matured in our 30s and 40s, and we recognized that it was impossible to implement our old culture and traditions—the whole package, if you will—on our "American" kids. Thank God that, as life went on, we appreciated our new culture and adapted to our new life. The kids grew, and their needs changed. Through interacting with the larger community at school and at work, a paradigm cultural shift occurred. Unconsciously, we altered the way we raised our kids. Integrating into the larger community around us and belonging to the Islamic Center of Southern California eased our worry. We came to appreciate that whatever happens, the kids will be fine. They won't be a replica of my wife and me but will be their own unique blend of Eastern and Western American Muslims.

Our shift forced us to rethink the way we tried to differentiate between our sons and daughters. We felt we needed to give in to a better way outside our comfort zone. We were empowered to let go of all those decayed traditional ideas that shackled us; we had to completely extract them from our minds. Getting to know Islam without the chains of Middle Eastern culture liberated us to appreciate that girls have equal rights as boys in every facet of our family life.

One day, my daughter needed to be picked up from the Islamic Center after a trip. There was no one available. She asked if a male friend from the youth group (whom we knew very well and were close friends with his family) could drive her home. I had to make a decision quickly. Let her wait or not? At some point, we as parents need to make intelligent and wise decisions on these matters. Why is it ok for a female friend to drive my son home and not ok for a male Muslim friend to do the same for my teenage daughter? In that moment, I made a decision based on trust. I knew how I raised my children. I knew I could trust that my daughter would follow the early guidance we instilled in her.

As parents, we must teach our children this valuable lesson: "The honor of men need not be founded on the degradation of women." God has asked both genders equally to be responsible for their lives, their actions, and their decisions. "The Believers men and women, are protectors one of another: they enjoin what is just, and forbid what is evil: they observe regular prayers, practice regular charity, and obey Allah and His Messenger. On them will Allah pour His mercy: for Allah is Exalted in power, Wise" (Quran, 9:71).

The fact that we are responsible for the upbringing of our children does not mean we own them. Children are a gift and a trust from God Almighty that was put in our hands to nurture according to Islamic and moral values. We cannot overprotect them to the point of suffocation. In fact, we could lose them this way. Eventually, they will grow out of the nest and fly, taking with them the values we planted in the early years of childhood.

This is our formula for success:

1. We worked hard on being an integral part of our children's lives from day one. We gave precedence to their needs over ours. We invested in our children. It's like a chemistry equation: what goes on the left side will come out on the right; nothing goes to waste.

2. We planted our Islamic and family moral values during the first seven years. We believed that these were the foundational years for their character development.

3. We knew who their friends were.

4. We allowed our children equal participation in sporting and artistic activities under our supervision.

5. We let them grow, trusted them, and ensured we were there for them at the time of need.

6. We recognized that they were not growing up in the same era as ours and worked on establishing trust with them.

7. We understood that cultural influences (peer pressure, the Internet, school, entertainment industry, etc.) are inevitable. We trusted that they would make wise decisions in our absence since we raised them well.

8. We PRAYED hard, day and night, trusting God to guide them to the right path.

9. We encouraged them to fly with the wings of love, respect, and Islamic values.

God has given us the responsibility to raise children equally with no difference between genders. They both need to guard themselves and behave responsibly. Islam's unique message for all family members is to take responsibility for actions and stand corrected if needed. No culture will over-rule God's word.

Dr. Saleh Kholaki was born in Damascus, Syria, and immigrated to the U.S. 33 years ago. He graduated from Damascus Dental School and went on to receive his DDS from UCLA. Dr. Kholaki currently runs a private practice in Southern California and is serving on the California Dental Association Board of Trustees. He is the father of four children and has been married to his lovely wife, Lina for 35 years. He was the past Vice Chairman of the Islamic Center of Southern California and Chair of the interfaith committee.

Single Parents

By Munira Lekovic Ezzeldine

Parenting is a tough job, but single parenting is an even tougher challenge as one parent tries to fulfill the roles of both mother and father to their child. Single parenting is highly demanding physically, emotionally, and financially. There can be numerous reasons and circumstances for single parenting such as divorce, a spouse working abroad, a child born out of wedlock, or the illness or death of a parent. Sadly, the Muslim community often alienates and ostracizes single parents and is often selective regarding which single parent "deserves" compassion based on the reasons they are single. Such a judgmental attitude does not encourage single parents to be the best parents possible to their children. Compassion and support from the community are necessary to help single parents on their challenging journey. This article seeks to offer constructive support to single parents as they seek to raise their children.

Numerous examples exist in the Islamic tradition of single parents who successfully raised children to become strong individuals. These individuals then left a legacy for humanity that shines more brightly. Hajar, the mother of Prophet Ismail (pbuh), Maryam, the mother of Prophet Isa (pbuh), and Amina, the mother of Prophet Muhammad (pbuh), all raised their sons alone due to different circumstances. They put their trust in Allah and worked hard to be the best parents they could be to their children.

Also, the mothers of Imam al-Shafi, Imam Ahmed, and Imam Bukhari raised their sons alone, and all of them became renowned figures who had major impacts on the world. The reality is that single Muslim parents do exist today. They need support as they strive to raise resilient Muslim children for the future.

Children raised by single parents thrive in homes where stability, safety, love, and consistency exist. A single parent who is committed to providing loving discipline will create an environment in which the child can truly flourish. Raising secure and successful children requires single parents to confidently implement the following parenting skills.

Discipline.

Sometimes single parents may feel guilty or overwhelmed by their parenting duties; so, they resort to weak enforcement or bending of rules in order to make their child happy and reduce conflict. Some parents may compensate for the absence of the other parent by being permissive in their parenting style. Single parents must be careful not to allow children to dismiss rules or become their friends. Setting boundaries for children creates much needed structure in all households (single and dual) because children want to know that their parent has rules and has set limits and expectations. Boundaries also create a sense of safety because the roles of the parent and child have been clearly established. Parental limits teach the child to respect the parent and solidify their role in the family.

Consistency.

Children dealing with a divorce or a death will crave stability as they adjust to their new life with one parent. Establishing routines, schedules, and traditions are important when adjusting to a new family dynamic. A child wants to know what to expect and look forward to on a daily basis. Consistency in everyday routines gives the child a feeling of security and stability. Creating morning routines, weekly schedules, and having dinners together are small ways that establish constancy for children. Availability by the parent in terms of attention and physical presence will assure the child a sense of belonging. Also, creating new traditions and memories during holidays and special occasions reaffirms the new family identity.

Emotional Support.

Single parents and their children may struggle with various feelings and emotions surrounding their new family structure. The parent and child may struggle with changes and upheavals in their lives, and may share with one another the challenges of the new family structure. Parents need to listen and truly hear their child when they share their thoughts and feelings. Parents must not make disparaging comments about the other parent as a means to gain the sympathy of the child. Despite common stress, parents must not turn to their child for emotional support nor burden them with the personal struggles they encounter. Parents must turn to their social circles and confide only in other adults and friends. Confiding worries or complaining to a child is inappropriate, regardless of the level of maturity of the child. It is extremely detrimental to children to absorb the thoughts and feelings of their parents. Children need to remain children and should not become a friend or therapist to the parent. Parents who feel stressed, depressed, anxious, or lonely should seek professional guidance or support from other adults as they adjust to single parenthood.

It Takes a Village.

Single parents will need help and support with the endless tasks and responsibilities of raising the child. This requires being comfortable asking for help from family and friends. Seeking support with childcare (carpooling, help in case of emergencies, or schedule conflicts at work) will benefit single parents when they are stretched in multiple directions. Creating a teamwork environment at home where the child has chores and responsibilities is also important so that the child understands their role in the family and feels like a capable contributor.

Take Care of Yourself.

Single parents work hard to care and provide for their children. They neglect themselves many times or may feel guilty taking time away from their children. However, it is necessary for parents to take care of themselves physically, emotionally, and spiritually. Giving without replenishing will limit a parent's ability to be their best. Scheduling time for hobbies and enjoyable activities like reading, watching a movie, or having coffee with a friend are ways parents can find personal fulfillment. Creating time to exercise, eat properly, and focus on prayer and connection to God will reduce stress. Developing a social network of close friends or other single parents will also empower parents so they do not feel alone in their journey. Strong support systems can enable single parents to share and feel accepted by other adults who understand their context. Ultimately, the child's emotional well-being is affected by the parent's healthy and balanced lifestyle.

Single Muslim parents who have a positive attitude and express resiliency will model strong character to their children. Single parents must be kind to themselves and focus on doing their best. They will not be "perfect" nor will they be able to fill the shoes of the second parent. Being the best parent is being present and connected with your child in a manner that is loving and encouraging every day. These are the most important things you can do as a parent, single or otherwise.

Essay originally published at www.virtualmosque.com.

Our Journey With Autism

By Dina Eletreby

I do not know exactly when I felt that something was different about my beautiful son, Kareem, but I instinctively knew something was different well before his first birthday. I remember religiously reading the *What to Expect When You Are Expecting* book and any other articles that could prepare me for, not only my pregnancy, but for parenthood. My background in education drove me to be as well-prepared as possible for pregnancy and parenthood—both new experiences for me since Kareem was my first child. In hindsight, here were the signs that made me worried:

- He never gazed into my eyes while nursing.
- He was more mesmerized by the mobile over his crib than our faces.
- He was too independent—did not look to us for confirmation, comfort, or connection—and he had no interest in other children.
- He lacked simple language—no 'mama', 'dada', 'wawa'—not even to point to indicate what he wanted.
- He loved to see things pour or spill—water, juice, uncooked rice, a box of plastic spoons - without regard to our reaction.
- He used to use our finger as a 'tool' to open something or turn something on—our hands were instruments to him.

By Kareem's second birthday, I was worried enough about his language delay and his idiosyncratic behavior to begin to search for answers online. I came across the diagnostic checklist for autism and realized that Kareem exhibited many of the characteristics. During Kareem's two-year well-visit, I asked his pediatrician if he thought Kareem had autism. He looked at me quizzically and said, "He can't have autism because he is sitting calmly in your lap." I assumed the pediatrician would know, and, in cases like these, a mother wants to be wrong. I shared my concerns for his language delay which took us down the medical path of making sure that Kareem's hearing was intact. I remember the pediatrician also encouraging me to enroll him in a daycare since he may not be benefitting from a language-rich environment with just he and I at home. I took the doctor's advice and, after assurances that Kareem's hearing was just fine, I was gifted by his daycare provider, Tina, saying to me one day, "There's something different about Kareem." When I asked if she thought it was autism, she said she wasn't sure because Kareem was also different from another boy she knew with that diagnosis. That did not really matter because what Tina did was give me the assurance that I was not imagining my son's differences. They were real, and I trusted her observations since her work revolves around two and three year olds.

The diagnosis finally came after visiting a pediatric neurologist and filling out a questionnaire. Within 10-15 minutes of sitting with me and my husband and observing Kareem, he asked the question, "Have you ever heard of autism?" I had the strangest combination of feelings—relief and grief—over the confirmation of his diagnosis. By then, I had also delivered our daughter, Kenzie; and her first years of life were a blur of tagging along on doctors' visits, speech therapy, and other special services for Kareem that were originally provided by the regional center and then by the school district.

This was the late 1990's and all the services were based in behaviorism. Behaviorism is the theory that human and animal behavior can be explained in terms of conditioning without appeal to thoughts or feelings, and that psychological disorders are best treated by altering behavior patterns. Behaviorism is the foundation for animal training. You get a dog to roll over by giving him a treat because he has done what you commanded. The focus is on 'fixing' the autism by changing the child's behavior without regard to understanding what is behind the child's behavior. Unfortunately, ABA (Applied Behavior Analysis) was the only approach to which West Coast professionals prescribed, at that time, to 'treat' autism. Its technique are adult-directed and reward-centered. Tasks are broken into small steps and taught in a repetitive manner. For instance, if Kareem was lining up toy cars, he would be redirected to sit at a table and do some other task. If Kareem refused, he would be forced to do it, hand over hand, and then he would be praised and given a candy. This approach went terribly wrong for Kareem. He did not like being forced to do tasks that had no meaning for him, and he fixated on getting the candy. I saw Kareem tantrum and self-abuse for the first time in his life after just a few sessions. I felt at my lowest around this time. I was angry with the world and felt the sting of injustice. Why me? Why my son? Why my family?

The year was 1999 and there was a fundraiser being held at a friend's house for a new Islamic school opening in Orange

County. I rarely went out because I was still hiding my son's diagnosis from the community in case he was "cured" before anyone could notice. During this fundraiser, the speaker asked the audience what we wanted for our children and the audience answered: happiness, a good career, financial security, a loyal life partner. The speaker said, "Yes, all of these things are good and, of course, we would want these for our children. But a true believer knows that this life is fleeting and the Hereafter is eternal, so the first thing a parent should want for their child is that they attain Heaven." In those few sentences, my grief unraveled and disappeared. Children who are disabled are unaccountable for their behavior. So, he will not be judged. So, Kareem is guaranteed Heaven. And, not one other parent in that room could guarantee their child's place in Heaven. Instead of seeing his disability as a burden, in that instant I saw Kareem as an angel gifted to me by God, and my only responsibility was to care for him until he or I returned to God. I began looking for a more naturalistic approach to working with my son and that is when I stumbled upon Floortime.

Floortime is a technique developed by Dr. Stanley Greenspan and was used primarily on the East Coast. Unlike ABA, Floortime was much more humanistic, completely child-centered, and incorporated the social, emotional, and cognitive aspects of the child. In this model, if Kareem was lining up toy cars, the therapist or I would get on the floor and line up cars with him until he noticed. If Kareem did not notice, then we could disrupt his car line by taking one or turning them upside down in order to connect with Kareem and elicit a response. The goal of Floortime was connection and meaningful interactions. Sounds similar to

Positive Discipline, right? I was hooked! I again went into my reading frenzy, trying to learn as much as I could about Floortime and even traveled to the East Coast to learn directly from Dr. Greenspan and his associates.

Kareem is 21 years old at the time of this writing and one of the happiest people I know! He is still significantly language-impaired and will likely need care his entire life, but there is not a person who meets Kareem without loving him. He is gentle, has a sense of humor, and carries a perpetual smile. When people hear that I have a son with autism, I get the wrinkled, upturned brows while they say, "Oh, I am so sorry." But I quickly tell them that we are lucky, he is amazing, and he's been a blessing in our lives. Kareem means "generous" in Arabic, and he has been true to his name. He has brought our family so much in patience, acceptance, love, and understanding. I truly feel blessed to be his mother!

That Islamic school fundraiser that changed my family's life was for a school in Irvine called New Horizon. I have been the Head of School there for twelve years, not only because I feel grateful and compelled to give back, but because I want to share the wisdom and experience I have gained with other families in our community. New Horizon School, Irvine, has adopted Positive Discipline schoolwide and has promoted Positive Discipline among hundreds of American Muslim families in southern California.

For parents who may be feeling the challenges of raising a child with a disability, here are a few things to keep in mind:

- Believe in and develop your instinctual and empathetic skills. Your child may not be able to express how he or she feels, so it is important to step into their bodies, observe how they process their senses (sounds are too loud, lights are too bright, food textures are too soft or strong), and see the world through their eyes. Think about how role-playing in Positive Discipline helps you see another person's perspective and attempt to role-play with your child to learn what he or she needs.

• Set realistic expectations and celebrate even the smallest accomplishment. If your expectations for your child's behavior are too far beyond their age or capabilities, you may set yourself up for disappointment and set your child up for stress and anxiety. Think about the smallest gain from where your child is now and work towards a small incremental growth from there. When Kareem did not speak, I worked with him to choose what he wanted by pointing to a picture of two choices—one that I knew he wanted and one that he did not want. In the beginning, I accepted him just looking at the picture he wanted as his answer to me and I would point to the picture and say, "Oh! You want the french fries!" Over time, months and months, Kareem eventually pointed to his picture of choice—and then months and months after that, he actually said "fa-fa" for French fries—his first intentionally communicative word ever! Honestly, it took almost a year, but the day he said "fa-fa" was one of the happiest days I can remember.

• Choose friends wisely and find other parents and siblings with similar circumstances for support. No one can truly understand what you are going through like another parent who faces similar challenges. I had a harder and harder time sitting among friends who were unaware/insensitive enough to complain that their child was not reading above his or her grade level or did not get played long enough on their sports team when mine was struggling to say 'mama.' My friendship circle changed after Kareem's diagnosis depending on how comfortable or uncomfortable other people were around him or how they treated him. Kenzie would also choose friends based on the same criteria. She welcomed those into our home who were the most comfortable around Kareem and distanced herself from those who were not.

• Have a sense of humor! Some of the most horrifying things that Kareem has done have turned into our favorite stories to remember and share with friends: Kareem jumping into a pool fully clothed at a friend's birthday party; Kareem pouring the entire bubble bath bottle into the tub creating a mountain of bubbles; Kareem going into the neighbor's home, uninvited, to get the mint chip ice cream from their freezer. All of these stories could have ended with us yelling at Kareem or punishing him for his lack of impulse control. Instead, they ended with us apologizing to any offended party, explaining to Kareem that this was not a good choice, but internally enjoying the sheer humor of the moment.

My final advice would be to stay optimistic and realistic at the same time. Try to see every circumstance as 'the cup half full, not half empty' so you never look at your child through a lens of deficit. Do not try to 'fix' your child; rather, recognize God's Perfection and Wisdom in selecting you as this child's parent. There must be something extraordinarily special in you for God to choose you for this important role!

Dr. Dina Eletreby has been an educator since the late 1980s. She is the Head of School at New Horizon School in Irvine, CA and has presented papers at numerous state and national conferences on such topics as Self-Determination, Critical Pedagogy and Culturally Responsive Research Methodology. She is an American Muslim of Egyptian descent who was raised in two religiously and culturally different worlds of home and school. She brings with her a unique perspective that allows for new insights into teaching and research as it relates to being a Muslim youth within the context of the United States.

WHEN ADDICTION RULES

By Metra Azar-Salem

"The world finally came to a crashing halt. Everything and anything I had felt all of a sudden stopped. Not only was my pain gone but I felt a sense of calm. I could sleep. I could stop thinking and life just slowed down a bit. Nothing had ever stopped the chaos I was feeling like that first pill I took. I knew immediately after it wore off, that I needed more."

This is how Zack (not his real name) described his entry into the world of addiction. He had dropped out of his community college, was living with his mom, and was experiencing days of high and low energy and sleep. Zack's mom arranged to see me, a Muslim therapist, because she felt I would better understand what her family was going through.

The all too common journey of Zack and his mother highlights the difficulties parents face when helping youth struggling with addiction. The cultural and religious context of my client's life impacted how his addiction was labeled, the lens through which the family understood the problem, and how they responded to the challenge. Initially, both Zack and his mother felt deep shame and embarrassment driven by the idea that Zack was committing a sin. His addiction shocked her because she believed such behaviors occurred only in "bad families." Her son was a "good boy." He was always respectful, sensitive to others, and willing to help. It's true that he was struggling academically and isolating socially, but he was a "good boy!" She also lamented her destiny, "How could this happen to us? Why me? What did I do wrong? Is

Allah punishing me for something I have done? I don't deserve this!" As is common in many families, both mother and son blamed the addiction on others and life circumstances. In Zach's case his father was absent most of his life, and theirs was an immigrant family trying valiantly to adapt in a new country while maintaining their cultural identity. Complicating the situation was the enormous social and cultural pressure they both felt to hide his addiction. In their culture protecting the "good name" of the family was paramount. Zack's mother was, in effect, a single parent. She felt alone and did not feel safe sharing her problem with others in her community. She felt depressed, angry, and helpless.

Traditionally, addictions have been viewed as a morally wrong act conducted by an individual. The current conceptualization has shifted to acknowledge that addiction is a process that occurs as a result of many risk factors. It is no longer attributed only to the "wrong" choices an individual makes. Addiction should be treated like a disease. Many families would take on a more supportive role if their children were suffering from a disease. Conceptualizing addiction in this model will help parents find support rather than blame and shame the adolescent as they go through the recovery process.

According to the National Institute of Drug Abuse (www.drugabuse.gov), researchers have identified the following risk factors for addictions in young people. It is critical to note that these factors don't determine addictions. They only contribute to increased vulnerability which, when coupled with lifestyle choices, can lead to addiction.

- *Biology.* The genes that individuals are born with account for about half of addiction vulnerability. For example, gender plays a role; males are more susceptible to addictions. Family history of addiction is also considered a risk factor because of the inherited vulnerability.

- *Mental Disorders/Learning Disabilities.* Individuals struggling with any mental disorder or learning disability are at a higher risk for addictions: ADHD, bipolar, depression, mood disorders, anxiety, information processing disorders, auditory processing disorders, and language/reading disorders. Children with undiagnosed learning disabilities tend to quit school earlier, which is another risk factor for addiction.

- *Environment.* An individual's environment includes many different influences: family, friends, socioeconomic status, and quality of life. Experiencing difficult family situations (marital problems, parental addiction, abuse, domestic violence, displacement of child from home) leads to disconnection from the primary support group and may increase the risk of addiction. Other factors such as lack of parental supervision, peer pressure, social isolation, and ineffective stress-response strategies can greatly influence the occurrence of drug abuse and the escalation to addiction.

Tips for parents:

- If your teen has one or more of the risk factors listed above, focus on establishing a strong connection and nurturing healthy stress-management skills. Even if your child is not exhibiting addictive behavior, seeking preventive counseling goes a long way toward mitigating the impact of risk factors.

- Engage in the free resources you have within your child's school district if you suspect any educational, mood, and/or behavioral challenges.
- Start early. Avoid waiting for the problem to resolve itself.
- Seek family/couples therapy early if you are experiencing increased tension at home.

The National Institute of Drug Abuse (www.drugabuse.gov/family) invites families to ask the following questions to assess the family dynamic. Any question that is answered in the negative is a call to action for changing parenting strategies.

- Are you able to communicate calmly and clearly with your teenager regarding relationship problems?
- Do you encourage positive behaviors in your teenager on a daily basis?
- Are you able to negotiate emotional conflicts with your teenager and work toward a solution?
- Are you able to calmly set limits when your teenager is defiant or disrespectful?
- Do you monitor your teenager to assure that he or she does not spend too much unsupervised time with peers?

Not only did Zack have others in his family that were also struggling with addiction, but his environment, family life, and mental health issues further complicated the problem. Zack was an impulsive child who had many behavioral problems growing up. He came from a low socio-economic background. He had a difficult relationship with his father who was rarely around while Zack was growing up. He hit developmental milestones later than his siblings. His mother reported concerns about his fluctuation of moods that were never evaluated.   She suspected that he struggled with some mental health issues especially during his adolescent years.

Zack: She will never understand me....I am 23 and she still treats me like I am four.

Mom: That is not true, I love you and you don't know what this is doing to our family.

Zack: All you care about is your family name, not the members of your family...go ahead tell everyone your son is an addict....one son is married with 3 kids and the other an addict.... just as your husband was a secret alcoholic...leave me alone...GET OUT or I will leave this room!!!

Mom: I will leave, but please know (to therapist) he is lying. I am a good mother, we are a good family. He was just in pain and took some meds and it's messing him up inside...and his girlfriend.... she is driving him crazy...

Therapist: Let me walk you out.... I understand your dilemma...I know you are a good mom...let me try and figure this one out...thank you for being here...(walks mom to hallway.)

Mom: I feel like a failure. May God help bring Zack back to me.... I am dead inside, but I know this is all his girlfriend's fault My son is a good boy...

Therapist: Thank you, I will call you later.

Zack: Is she gone?

Me: Yes.

Zack: You know she is right, she is a good mother, it's my fault not hers.... she doesn't deserve the shame and heartache I am giving her.... I just don't know how to stop.... can you help me....(Zack starts crying.)

Through counseling Zack's mom learned what she could do to help her son in a more productive way. She came to realize that her son's health and her own sanity depended on letting go of her guilt, the need to please others, and the pressure to cover the addiction. She was able to build a support system. She also worked on developing an adult relationship with her son, which helped her recognize that it was ultimately his choice to get help. More importantly, she accepted that his addiction relied heavily on her financial support and took measures to put an end to it.

Tips for parents:

- Keep your child engaged in a relationship. This is key to recovery. Even brief conversations are better than none. If your child is not responsive to you, find a friend or family member they feel closer to and help them stay connected to him/her. A parent does not need to be the only source of emotional support for an addicted child.

- Forgive yourself and the addict because holding onto blame does not help the situation. Blaming, shaming, and using guilt only pulls addicts into a more stressful state that can lead to more substance abuse as a coping mechanism.

- Take an addict's statements with a grain of salt. Remember that you are now dealing with a person under the influence of a substance. Don't personalize anything they say.

- Establish support for yourself. A group of friends and family that can help you cope are critical in this process.

- Financially supporting an addict without accountability will enable the behavior. Meeting with an addiction therapist and setting up a financial plan that establishes responsibility is critical. It is highly recommended that parents buy essentials for their children who are addicted rather than giving them money.

- Attend to other family members: siblings, spouse, others living in the home.
- Trying to figure out what could have been done differently will not help you solve the problem because no reason will be sufficient to justify why your son/daughter is going through this. Be OK with not being able to solve this problem, and seek help from a professional.

Zack's family was of utmost importance to his recovery process. Zack and his mom were able to develop a positive relationship. Zack's mom learned to rely on the strength of their relationship and allow Zack to make choices that he would have to live with. Giving him this autonomy and parenting from a place of connection allowed for trust to be built again in their relationship. Our four months of therapy culminated with Zack enrolling in a rehab center. However, as is common with people who are addicted, Zach went in and out of the facility many times before he finally decided to stay. Two years later, I saw Zack at an event I was attending, and he looked healthier. I did not approach him nor did he approach me. A glance and a smile were all we exchanged and that was enough for me to realize he was at least on the road to recovery.

Dr. Metra Azar-Salam is an adjunct professor at Bayan Claremont College where she teaches about minorities' mental health issues, identity formation, spirituality in therapy, substance abuse, parenting issues, PTSD, ADHD, and children of minorities who suffer from autistic spectrum disorders. She is a Marriage and Family therapist and has worked with children and families in school and private practice.

DIFFICULT CONVERSATIONS

By Munira Lekovic Ezzeldine

Having conversations with children about difficult topics like sex, drugs, death, terrorism, disasters, racism, and divorce are often anxiety-provoking subjects for parents. Many parents don't know what to say about these topics or are personally uncomfortable themselves, so they are reluctant to talk to their children about these issues. Dumas (1997) found that 90 percent of children, especially those between 8-12 years old, want their parents to talk to them about today's toughest issues. At the same time nearly half of 10-12 year olds "try to avoid talking about these subjects with their parents" and "feel uncomfortable when a parent brings up one of these subjects." This is the nature of difficult topics: children want to know and parents want to educate, but it still feels awkward and uncomfortable for many.

Children who have early conversations with their parents are more likely to continue turning to their parents as they become teens. When children don't feel their parents are approachable, they will reach out to friends, relatives, teachers, or the Internet. The connected relationship between the parent and child will be foundational for difficult conversations to happen. Jafar al-Sadiq, an 8th century scholar, reminded Muslims, "Endeavor to converse with your children, in case others who transgress and disobey get to them before you." Adolescents want a caring adult in their life with whom they can ask questions and explore difficult issues.

Parents have a responsibility to educate their children by sharing accurate and relevant information. A parent's goal is to educate and inquire—not scare or lecture children. Throughout childhood, parents continuously build on information with multiple conversations about various difficult topics. It should never be just one BIG talk.

Parents must first explore their own attitude about a difficult topic. How did you learn about the topic? What was your relationship like with your parents? What do you feel now as a parent? It is okay to admit to your child that you are uncomfortable. You could say, "You know, I'm uncomfortable talking about... because my parents never talked to me about it. But I want us to be able to talk about anything so please come to me if you have any questions. If I don't know the answer, I'll find out." Reflect on your emotional response to difficult conversations. Are you anxious? Embarrassed? Confused? Angry? Your emotional temperature will impact how your child receives the information you share with them. It is not unusual for parents to report feeling caught off guard when a child brings up a difficult topic. Breathe and keep your composure. A parent can say, "That is an important question, and I want to talk to you about it. Let me finish what I am doing and I will talk to you about it in a few minutes."

How does a parent approach a difficult topic? Start early to initiate conversations with your child in order to create an open environment in the family where a child is comfortable asking and discussing all topics. It is important that a parent be honest with answers from the start in order to build trust. The process of difficult conversations largely entails listening to a child's questions, curiosities, and fears without creating an atmosphere of shame or guilt. Parents have an opportunity to communicate their values and views on a topic while being open to hearing other viewpoints and opinions. Conversations that occur in casual settings where the child feels comfortable are most effective. A parent may not be able to eliminate all awkwardness, but using everyday opportunities, like driving in the car or going for a walk, will create a natural space in which to talk. Also, it is advisable that parents have a private conversation with one child at a time rather than in a group setting with siblings so that each child is comfortable asking personal questions.

Refer to the Positive Discipline tools of Understand the Stage of Development (p. 52), Effective Communication (p. 87), Be There (p. 77), and Connection before Correction (p. 80, for more tools when navigating difficult conversations.

Sex

The Prophet Muhammad (pbuh) said, "There is no shyness in matters of religion." His wife, Aisha, shared, "Blessed are the women of the Ansar, shyness did not stand in their way of seeking knowledge about their religion." These prophetic teachings highlight that knowledge in all topics of faith, including sexual relations, is a duty for all Muslims. Parents must be the primary source of sex education for children. The Family and Youth Institute (2014) found that 76 percent of Muslim youth received their information from public schools and 4 percent from the mosque. Teens were primarily exposed to sexual information from media and friends. However, the study found that sexual education that included a parent and child reduced a teen engaging in risky sexual behavior.

Discussing the topic of sex requires parents to consider their child's maturity level and to share more details as the child gets older. Since each child is different and each is exposed to different issues, it is important that parents address each child's questions as they come up and discuss issues casually as the child continues to grow. Below are general guidelines about the topics children should be familiar with at different ages.

2-5 years old.

Young children should understand that their bodies belong to them, and there are private areas that no one is allowed to touch or see besides their parents or a doctor. A parent helps a child wash and dress and a doctor, in the parent's presence, checks the body to make sure it is healthy. Empower children to feel in control of their bodies and advocate for themselves if anyone ever makes them feel uncomfortable. Teach children that "no means no" and this statement should be respected by everyone. Encourage children to share their thoughts and feelings about their bodies.

6-8 years old.

At this age it is important that children understand the correct terms for their body parts and body functions. Many families like to use nicknames for private body parts, but it is important that a child also knows the correct anatomical names. Parents can explain to a child that it is inappropriate to have conversations about body parts with friends or younger siblings because each child should talk to their parent about these private topics. It is important to answer a child's questions honestly and to listen clearly to what is being asked. At this age it is also important that parents establish Internet safety, set up parental controls on the computer, and caution their children about inappropriate images on the Internet. Remind children that if they have questions, it is best to talk to their parents rather than search on the Internet to find their own answers.

9-12 years old.

At this stage, it is important that children are aware of the approaching changes in their bodies (e.g. wet dreams and menstruation). Explaining these natural body changes is an opportune time to discuss human reproduction and the normal process that all of God's creations go through. A parent can say, "All of God's creatures reproduce and have babies. This is a natural part of life. When two adults get married, they may have a baby and this is how people reproduce." Using biological terms when explaining reproduction will help a child understand the science of how the body works and how babies are born. Books can help a parent explain the biological aspects of human development. Parents can begin to explain the social aspect of marriage as a path to building a family. Many children will still be confused at this age as to why sex is important. Parents can explain that one of the purposes of marriage is reproduction which occurs through sex. A parent can say, "As your body continues to grow and change into adulthood, you will develop natural feelings of attraction and one day, you will want to be intimate."

13-18 years old.

At this stage a child needs to have a clear understanding of sex biologically, socially, and emotionally. It is vital parents provide sex education to their children before entering middle school. The American Academy of Pediatrics recommends that, by middle school, teens know all the following aspects of sexuality:

- Expectations and values
- Correct names for sexual organs
- What sex is and how women get pregnant
- Sexual practices
- STDs and HIV / AIDS
- Menstruation
- Masturbation
- Sexual Orientation

Discussing the social pressures of relationships will be at the forefront of a teen's mind. Discussing media images of sexuality, body image, beauty, etc. will uncover a deeper understanding of sexuality in the public sphere. Parents must share their expectations of marriage, their value of abstinence, and how they expect their teen to engage with peers and friends. Many parents who are uncomfortable speaking about sex will expect the school or mosque to educate their children about these topics. Children's primary source of information about sex, contraception, masturbation, pornography, homosexuality, sexual practice, pregnancy, and relationships should be from their parents. The school and mosque can act as a reinforcement of the message the parent conveys, as the child's knowledge will inevitably be supplemented by secondary sources like their peers, teachers, and religious figures. What is most important is that, when children learn information from a secondary source, they will not be surprised by what they hear. If they hear something they are unclear about on the soccer field or in a youth group, they will know they can talk to their parents about what they heard since the parents were honest and open about the topic in the first place.

Drugs

Researchers at the National Council on Alcoholism and Drug Dependence found that the main reason children don't use drugs is their parents. A strong parent-child relationship where the child does not want to disappoint the parents acts as a protective factor against drug use. Parents who have ongoing discussions with their children about drugs will be aware of their growth as they have new experiences in school and meet different people.

2-5 years old.

Beginning conversation early about drugs is important because this is when the parent has the greatest influence. Young children may see family members or strangers who engage in smoking or drinking alcohol. Children may ask questions like, "What is that person doing? Why is there smoke? What is that smell?" Short and simple statements by a parent that are repeated often will clearly communicate the parental values about drugs. A parent can say, "In our family, we don't smoke or drink alcohol." Sharing family expectations and values will help children internalize the message about drugs as they grow older. It is also important for parents to explain to a child that ingesting or inhaling anything like glue or cleaning products is very dangerous. Teaching children to respect their body and what they put into it is a life-long goal. Engaging in role-play with children so they practice how to respond if they are offered drugs will serve to empower them in their social experiences.

6-8 years old.

At this stage parents can explain what drugs are and how they change a person's behavior and thoughts. Begin by explaining there are two types of drugs. One type is what doctors prescribe which are helpful to the body when recovering from an illness. Many children associate prescription drugs with a delicious flavor. Remind children that taking the same prescribed drug when a body doesn't need it would be dangerous and a very poor choice. Another type of drug that people take are those that are not prescribed by a doctor, but people can buy them in a store (like alcohol, tobacco, and pills). These drugs actually hurt a person's body and a Muslim is not respecting their body when they ingest drugs. For example, smoking hurts a person's lungs and alcohol hurts a person's liver. These drugs do not help people live healthier lives.

Children are usually curious as to why people take drugs, and it is important for them to understand the common reasons. A parent can say, "Drugs make people feel and think differently, and people take drugs because they like the feeling they get. When people take drugs, they feel better about themselves and their life. But, this feeling is only temporary which is why people have to keep taking the drug because they want to get the feeling again. Relying on a drug to feel good can cause people to become addicted so they feel like they can't live without it." It is important to use Curiosity Questions (p. 82), by asking, "Why do you think God prohibits Muslims from using drugs? What would you do if you saw a close friend of yours taking drugs?" Have continuous and open conversations about the effects of drugs and your values about taking them.

9-12 years old.

A child at this stage should know that people not only buy drugs from the store legally, but also buy drugs from drug dealers illegally. Children should be familiar with common names of street drugs like weed and pot, as well as other drugs like heroin, cocaine, inhalants, and prescription drugs. Parents need to be familiar with current trends of drug use in their community since drug names and methods of use change. Teens also may have misinformation like, "Pot isn't bad for you, like alcohol," or "I can't get addicted." Parents can check in with their teen about myths around drug use and discuss the effects of drug use on the brain and body. Encouraging conversations about views on drugs and how teens choose to respond to drug use around them is vital.

13-18 years old.

Some teens at this stage experiment with drugs while others abstain. Abu-Ras, Ahmed, Arfke (2010) found, in a survey of American Muslim college students, 47 percent consumed alcohol and 70 percent began drinking before entering college. The primary motivation given for teens consuming alcohol was curiosity, peer pressure, having a good time, and decreasing stress. Parents can empower teens with what to say and do if they feel pressured to consume drugs at school, parties, or on a sports team. "No man, that's not for me." "That ain't cool, bro." "My mom would kill me if I tried that!" Encouraging teens to come to parents for help, even if they've made a mistake, is important.

Parents can guide a teen away from drugs by helping them identify their long and short-term goals. Discussing how drugs can interfere with their plans may persuade a teen to abstain from doing drugs. Parents can say, "It sounds like you have many great plans ahead of you. Taking drugs closes doors of great opportunity. I hope you focus on accomplishing your goals." A positive and connected relationship between parents and teens is the greatest prevention to drug use. If a parent is concerned their child is using drugs, it is advisable to seek counseling or professional help.

Scary News Stories

Discussing the topic of terrorism and violence locally and globally is a sad reality that parents wish they did not have to address. News of terrorism and violence evokes feelings of fear in parents as well as children. The initial shock of scary news can be terrifying for children as they seek to understand local and global events from their parent's response. Children primarily need reassurance of their safety since they are still at a stage where they are concerned with how scary news affects them and their family.

Turning off the television and reducing repeated exposure to an event is an important step in limiting the traumatic effects of violence and terrorism. Younger children should not be exposed to violent images and news stories at all because the images can be overwhelming for them and are developmentally inappropriate. Exposing children to excessive violence and disturbing images can be psychologically damaging because children have more difficulty understanding and processing the images they see. For older children who may watch news stories with their parents, it is important to discuss the images and stories they see and/or read so they can process the news and ask questions. Children may not be able to move on from scary news stories as quickly as adults. So, it may require multiple conversations to process their feelings and thoughts.

When discussing violence and terrorism, parents can follow their child's lead and continue the discussion based on what the child knows or heard. Parents will need to listen to what children are asking and listen beyond their questions to understand how they are feeling about what they are learning. A parent can focus on listening to a child's feelings about the news to help them make sense of the events and reduce their fears and anxiety. Parents must keep their language simple and use concepts the child can understand. Parents must also be careful about sharing their own theories or ideas about events. The way a parent interprets violent acts can either sow the seeds of fear, blame, and pessimism or the seeds of hope, faith, and resilience in humanity. A child will see the world the way the parent sees the world. So, the political and spiritual lenses the parent wears must be adjusted and clarified with wisdom.

Discussing natural disasters and accidents are opportunities for children to understand deeper issues like global connectedness, charity, and reliance on God. Sharing the facts about a disaster or accident, while assuring children of their safety, will allow them to share their concerns and fears about the incident. Again, limiting repeated exposure to the event via television and the Internet is critical. When a disaster or accident happens, parents can empower their children by devising a plan for what the family can do if a disaster is near their home and how they could react to ensure safety. Parents can also use the incident to show empathy and compassion for those who have suffered and encourage children to help others through acts of service or charity for those affected. The lack of control people have when disasters and violence occur can also be an opportunity to teach children about reliance on God in difficult situations. In these moments, focusing particularly on their connection to God will be vital to help them cope and recover emotionally from any trauma.

Racism

Children understand and experience racism differently depending on their context: where they live, who they go to school with, and their own racial identity. The U.S. is one of the most diverse societies in the world and discrimination is prevalent for minority groups. In the U.S., being a member of a marginalized minority group is challenging because the emotional impact of hostility weighs on a child and/or family.

While talking about race can be difficult, some parents avoid talking about it with children because they believe their children are "color-blind." These parents worry that an open discussion about racism may cause them to notice race in a way they did not before. The fact is that children do notice differences between people, and they make sense of it on their own as part of their theory about the world. Children develop attitudes toward others, which are molded (either directly or indirectly) by those around them. By the middle school years, a child develops a complete set of stereotypes about every racial, ethnic, and religious group.

Racism stems from fear and ignorance. Discussing similarities between people will reduce fear and teach empathy and compassion for all human beings. Before speaking to children about racism, parents should reflect on their own biases, stereotypes, and beliefs about other people. How do you feel about racism? Do you harbor certain prejudices about other people? Have you experienced racism yourself? Understanding your own views and beliefs will help you approach the topic of racism with your children in a meaningful way. It is important that parents who have experienced racism do not perpetuate prejudice toward other groups but, rather, teach empowerment and peace.

Parents who model inclusive relationships with people of all backgrounds will help their children develop tolerance and empathy for all people. Children learn compassion, justice, and respect by the implicit and explicit messages they receive from their parents, teachers, peers, and community. These views will shape children's beliefs and how they choose to interact with others. Minority children may have experiences with discrimination themselves which they can reconcile by talking to their parents to receive support. In situations where children have witnessed or experienced racial insults, parents can help them learn how to protect themselves and how best to respond.

As with all difficult conversations, casually discussing race shows a child that all topics are open for discussion. Parents can take opportunities like cultural awareness weeks, national holidays, and news stories to discuss topics of diversity, race, and social disparity. Children may make inappropriate comments about people without understanding that such comments are racist or because they heard someone else say them. A parent can use these opportunities to teach values by saying, "We don't use somebody's identity as an insult." Racism is an unfortunate part of the human story beginning with Iblis (devil) not bowing down to Adam. As God mentioned in the Quran, "He said, 'What prevented you from bowing down when I have commanded you?' He said, 'I am better than he; You created me from fire and You created him from mud'" (7:12). Hence, conversations about race and equality are wonderful teaching opportunities for parents to guide their children's moral compass. Encouraging children to resist engaging in feelings of arrogance and superiority will help them embody a prophetic character that treats all human beings with respect and compassion.

Divorce

Discussing the dissolution of a marriage can be a very difficult topic for children. Younger children may initially have many questions and, ultimately, just want to know how it affects them personally. News of a divorce between relatives or family friends can be difficult for children to understand because it impacts family interactions and gatherings. Parents may generally explain the changing family dynamics when loved ones divorce and how it may impact them directly. Parents can say, "Aunt Mona and Uncle Faris got divorced, so they aren't living together. When we visit your cousin this weekend, we will go to her mom's house. You and your cousin will have plenty of time to play together."

Obviously, the most difficult divorce for children to understand is that of their own parents. Often end of a marriage comes after many years of unhealthy family functioning to which the child has become accustomed. Yet, the finality can still come as a shock to the child. A child needs a basic understanding of why the parents are divorcing. Children tend to process the divorce through their egocentric lens. Accordingly, they may assume they are the reason for their parents' divorce. It is important that children have a clear understanding of the parents' narrative for the divorce so they can come to terms with their changing family dynamics and accept that they are not the reason the parents divorced. Parents can say, "Mommy and Daddy have been trying to work out our problems for a long time. We now realize we can't do this and have decided to get a divorce. Our problems are about each other and not about you or your siblings. This has been a very difficult decision and we are sad about it. We both love you very much and we will continue to take care of you, but it will be from two separate homes. We won't ask you to pick sides or carry messages back and forth. We want you to have a good relationship with both of us always."

Children will have many thoughts and feelings about their parents' divorce, and the process will affect each child differently. Allowing a safe space for children to share their feelings will help them heal and cope with the divorce. Seeking family counseling to understand the changing family dynamics will help children and their parents resolve problems and find peace with the decision.

Death

Discussing death can be a very difficult experience for parents, especially if they experienced the death of a loved one and are struggling with their own grief. While parents mourn a death in their own way, their children may experience the news of the death differently and grieve in their own manner. Parents must be honest with their children about the sad news. Allow children to share their own thoughts and feelings about death and answer their questions honestly. A parent can explain that the feelings of grief are normal and when a person feels sad is a great time to utilize the reliance on God as a way to cope. This will help children understand the physical and spiritual aspects of death.

Taking into consideration the age and maturity of the child, parents can explain death through experiences like the loss of a pet or the death of a distant relative or friend. These early experiences of how the family copes help shape a child's view of death. The simplest approach to explaining death to a child is by describing the basic biological facts of death: the body stops working; a person stops breathing, moving, and talking. This basic explanation helps young children understand what it means to die and many children will ask what happens after. God reminds in the Quran, "Indeed we belong to God, and to Him we will return" (Quran 2:156). Parents can say, "When someone dies, their soul returns to God and *insha Allah* (God willing) we will be reunited in heaven together." Many children find solace and acceptance when they understand the existence of a soul and afterlife. It is normal for children to ask questions and speak about death more than an adult might. This process is how children make sense of death and how they discover their thoughts and feelings about the death of a loved one and their own existence.

Some families want to protect their children from the "truth" and don't want to speak frankly about death. However, children need to hear the news from their parents to find comfort. Knowing how and why someone died helps a child feel the sadness and begin to live without the loved one. A parent can say, "Her body was so injured/full of disease that it stopped working. The doctors tried the best they could to help, but she died today." Attending funerals and understanding the process of death will make death less obscure and help children move to acceptance. Young children who experience the death of people close to them, like a parent or sibling, will certainly have a difficult time processing the death. Seeking professional support from a counselor will be beneficial for families struggling with grief. As children grow and reach new milestones, they may re-grieve and reflect on their loss. This is a normal process. Teaching children healthy coping skills like prayer, reading Quran, crying, talking, or journaling feelings can all help to deal with the process of death.

BUILDING RESILIENCY

By Munira Lekovic Ezzeldine

Resilience is an ability to bounce back from adversity. When a person is resilient they think to themselves, "I am capable of getting through this." Resiliency is a skill that helps a person get through life when things don't go well. Many times it is referred to as grit, perseverance, or growth mindset. Resiliency develops and changes over time with life experiences. In cases where children suffer from a trauma, resiliency plays an important role in their healing process as it contributes to their personal growth. Resiliency is built through learned behaviors and thoughts. God reminds in the Quran, "Seek help with patience, perseverance, and prayer, for God is with those who patiently persevere" (2:153) and "truly with hardship there is ease" (94:5). Encouraging optimism and gratitude through life experiences teaches children coping skills and positivity in times of adversity and calm. The process of building resiliency involves both internal factors, like a person's cognitive ability and personality, and external factors like parents and caring adults.

The primary factor in resilience is having caring and supportive relationships within the family. Strong relationships create love, trust, encouragement, and reassurance, as well as provide role models, all of which can bolster a child's resiliency. Parents must examine how they model resiliency to their children through their own words and behavior. Parents who struggle with resiliency themselves will need to reflect on ways to change their own mindset in order to raise children who are resilient. Resiliency is like a muscle that needs to be exercised in order to develop properly.

According to Edith Grotberg of The International Resilience Project (1995), there are three sources of resiliency for a child: environment, self-esteem, and social skills. Parents impact all three domains through their parenting practice which helps exercise a child's resiliency. An environment of trusting relationships, structure at home, role models, and encouragement for autonomy and independence help a child develop resilience because the child knows what to expect from caretakers and feels encouraged to develop into a mature adult. A child who feels loveable and has an appealing temperament will also feel proud of becoming more autonomous and independent. Finally, a child with strong social skills who is able to communicate, problem solve, and manage feelings and impulses will have better personal connections and will seek to be in trusting relationships.

The authors of *Raising Resilient Children* (2002), found that parents can do six specific actions to help children manifest resilience:

- Teach and convey empathy.
- Actively listen and effectively communicate.
- Teach decision making and problem solving.
- Recognize and focus on their strengths.
- Connect and love their child for who they are.
- Use mistakes as opportunities to learn.

These six behaviors are in complete alignment with the Positive Discipline tools outlined in this book. Unfortunately, many parents undermine their child's development of resiliency through behaviors like being overprotective or expecting perfection. Well-intentioned parents who are overprotective seek to prevent anything bad from happening to their children and so unwittingly encourage their children to become fragile. When children are not allowed to experience negative emotions like disappointment, fear, and sadness, they do not learn the necessary skills to tolerate and negotiate adversity in life. When children are protected from experiencing the consequences of their actions, they do not learn personal responsibility for their behavior. Children who are constantly protected may develop into adults who feel entitled and are prone to blame others for mistakes they make.

When children receive the message they must be perfect at everything they do, they fear making mistakes and feel like failures. This fear paralyzes children and may cause them to procrastinate when they don't feel confident, give up, or not even try new things because they don't want to fail. The worry of what their parents may think, if they make a mistake or fail, will limit their drive and personal capability. Children who seek to please their parents by being perfect also may view their performance as a measure of their self-worth. They will only feel good about themselves when they are perfect and feel extremely discouraged when they are not. Children who don't experience moments of failure may develop into adults who crumble emotionally when they experience failure in life (which will inevitably happen) as well as feel inept at recovering and moving forward.

Encouraging resiliency in children is a gift that parents give to their children throughout the process of parenting. As children become resilient, they will see life as challenging and ever changing; but, at the same time, they will believe they can cope with those challenges. Children will be able to view mistakes and weaknesses as opportunities to learn. They will believe they can influence and even control outcomes in their lives through effort and skill. Resilient children will focus on what they can do rather than on what is outside their control; and so they will find great purpose and meaning in life and relationships.

Peaceful Families

By Munira Lekovic Ezzeldine

Peace begins with the individual. Dr. Tariq Ramadan, the renowned European Muslim scholar, said, "If you are not at peace with yourself, you cannot spread peace." Having a sense of peace and personal contentment will transcend the environment of the home. A peaceful family begins with the marital relationship between husband and wife as the couple sets the tone for their family culture. Strong families are able to create and promote a peaceful and happy family home for all members.

In 2000, the Family Strengths Research Project of Australia identified the following eight characteristics in strong families: communication, shared activities, togetherness, support, affection, acceptance, commitment, and resilience.

Communication

Families benefit from open communication that is loving, understanding, and patient. Ways that families can develop open communication are:

- Be honest with one another.
- Listen to each other with full attention.
- Stay in contact with each other.
- Reassure each other of their love through affirmative words, hugs, and making time for each other.
- Share thoughts and feelings without censoring or criticizing

each other.

- Encourage positive behavior.
- Allow the appropriate expression of negative as well as positive emotions.
- Work together to solve problems and conflicts.
- Laugh together.

Sharing Activities

Peaceful families share activities. Ways that families can build shared experiences are:

- Make dinnertime an opportunity for family discussions.
- Play together.
- Go on regular family outings.
- Create family traditions by deciding together how to celebrate birthdays, anniversaries, and religious holidays.
- Plan vacations the whole family will enjoy.

Togetherness

Children need to be involved in some of the decision making if they are to feel like a worthwhile family member. Peaceful families share a feeling of togetherness and this happens when:

- Share a common sense of belonging.
- Share beliefs and values.
- Enjoy the place called home.
- Celebrate together.
- Share memories.

Support

Peaceful families feel a sense of support and encouragement for their goals and dreams. Ways they show support for one another are:

- Look out for each other.
- Share the responsibilities of chores.
- Be there for each other in good times and times of difficulty.
- Encourage each other to try new things.
- Take an active interest in each other's hobbies.

Affection

Peaceful families love one another unconditionally and show their affection for each other. Ways that families can express their affection are:

- Tell family members, "I love you."
- Show love for each other through hugs and cuddling.
- Consider each other's feelings.
- Care about each other's wellbeing.
- Do things for each other.

Acceptance

Families are made up of different individuals with different needs and, sometimes, different values, and beliefs. Strong families are able to show acceptance of these individual differences when:

- Accept the differences.
- Give each other space.

- Respect each other's points of view.
- Be able to forgive each other.
- Take personal responsibility for actions.

Commitment

Peaceful families have a genuine commitment to each other and focus on maintaining positive connections with one another. Ways families reaffirm their commitment are:

- Trust each other.
- Keep promises.
- Do things for the community.
- Have rules.
- Feel safe and secure with each other.

Resilience

Peaceful families are resilient and flexible in their approach to life. Ways that families develop resilience include:

- Talk things through.
- Change plans when necessary.
- Learn from the tough times.
- Keep each other hopeful.
- Pull together in a crisis.
- Discuss problems.

The researchers also found that unhappy families that do not function well have certain traits in common. These include:

- Unfair power distribution, such as one parent ruling the

household.

- Problems with maintaining peaceful conflict negotiation.
- Lack of respect for each other as individuals.
- Not talking or listening to each other.
- Refusing to acknowledge or accept other points of view.
- A tendency to rely on negative forms of communication such as yelling, criticizing, or sulking.
- Use of physical punishment such as smacking or hitting.

All families are different, and they each have strengths and areas of growth. One way to determine your family's strengths is by taking the Family Strengths Assessment (2001) available on our website www.positivedisciplinemuslimhome.com.

Through this inventory you and your family can assess your areas of strength and discuss areas you would like to improve upon. This tool can lead to conversations about the views and beliefs each family member holds about your family dynamics and culture.

Nurturing Spirituality

By Hina Khan-Mukhtar

I was recently mentoring a despondent young man regarding a major crisis in his life when I sincerely urged him, "You need to turn to Allah completely and beg Him for help." He looked at me with bloodshot eyes, a blank expression on his face and said, "How do I do that?"

His question broke my heart and reminded me of what a respected scholar had told us just this past Ramadan: "The orphan isn't the one who doesn't have a mother or father; the *real* orphan is the one who *has* a mother and a father yet doesn't know anything about Allah, his religion, or how to deal with the ups and downs of life."

As a Muslim, you can believe there are many reasons for teaching your children Islam—they should know their Creator; they should understand the real purpose of life; they should be taught Truth (with a capital T). However, as a parent and an advisor of many young people, I have come to realize another important and practical benefit of learning one's religion and spirituality—it gives one the tools to properly deal with life's circumstances, especially when the chips are down.

This particular young man in his twenties was lost. He needed help but didn't know where, nor towards whom, to turn. When the other men stood up for the congregational prayer, he wandered aimlessly around the room, waiting for them to finish so he could return to sit with them, his depression a dark cloud hanging over his head.

In a separate conversation, he alluded to some "major sins" that he had committed in his teens. "I messed up big time," he told me, without explaining his specific lapses. I didn't ask him to elaborate, either. When he continued by proudly claiming that he was grateful for the choices he had made—even his bad ones— because they had allowed him to learn some crucial life lessons, I couldn't stop myself from asking him, "But, what about avoiding certain behaviors simply because they were displeasing to Allah?" He looked startled. "I never really thought of it that way," he confessed.

We all know how to teach our kids the-how-to of prayers; but, how does one inculcate in children the desire to actually have an ongoing personal relationship with their Creator? How do we teach them not just religion but spirituality?

Remember Him and Mention Him...Often

Our sons and daughters benefit when they hear us talking about Allah and His Messenger (upon whom be peace) often and with reverence, love, and respect. It becomes their "normal." After all, Allah Himself tells us in a hadith qudsi: "I am with My slave when he thinks of Me, and I am with him when he mentions Me." When our kids confide in us that they desire something special or fear something frightening, we can encourage them to pray for whatever it is they covet and to ask Allah to protect them from whatever they fear. We should point out the hidden blessings in their daily lives and remind them to give thanks whenever they witness their prayers being answered or the sources of their fears being proven baseless. When they feel remorse and regret for any of their mistakes, they can be taught at that time the various steps for *tawba* (repentance). Children also thrive when they are taught the *sunnah duas* (prophetic supplications) and daily *awrad* (litanies) to recite as part of their everyday routines. We need to help our kids develop the habit of having regular conversations with Allah.

Teach Taqwa (God-Consciousness)

When our sons and daughters ask us, "Where is Allah?" tell them, "He is with you." After all, that is actually what Allah tells us—that He is with us as long as we are remembering Him and mentioning Him. Kids need to know that Allah Sees and Hears all and is with them at all times. They should be taught early the nuances of what is pleasing to Him as well as what is displeasing. If your son serves you a glass of water, it behooves you to thank him and then remind him that Allah loves those children who serve their parents and who quench others' thirsts. If your daughter leaves her room in an untidy state, you can remind her of the hadith (saying of the Prophet) that tells us "Allah is Beautiful and He Loves beauty." Young Muslims grow spiritually when they are taught to think about Allah in everything they do, including the minutiae of life.

Give Them the Tools to Succeed

All children need to learn the *fiqh* (sacred rulings) of their religion. They will not know how to live a life that is pleasing to Allah if they aren't even aware of the basics of what is prohibited, what is permissible, what is encouraged, and what is discouraged.

Along with the do's and don'ts, children can be set up for success by being taught the numerous steps one can take to draw closer to God. These steps include the *adab* of *dua* (etiquettes of supplication) and regular reliance on supplemental prayers like *salaat-ul-istikhara* (prayer of guidance), *salaat-ul-haajah* (prayer of need), *salaat-ul-shukr* (prayer of gratitude), and *salaat-ul-tawba* (prayer of repentance). It is crucial that all children are taught their *aqeedah* (creed) early so they don't grow up having an erroneous perception of Allah. A child who knows his/her aqueedah will be better equipped to handle life's ups and downs. And it is our hope that kids who are taught about Allah, the angels, *Shaytan* (Satan), and the *nafs* (ego) will be able to get a better handle on their impulsive thoughts once they are able to recognize and identify the various sources of those same thoughts.

Provide Role Models

A friend's daughter once told her mother that she was deeply impressed by the leisurely and mindful way her teacher moved through the different positions of prayer. "She seems to really enjoy her *salah* (prayer)," she murmured in awe. "She never rushes through it."

One of my own teachers regularly tells us, "Well-done is better than well-said." Children learn more from what they witness than from what they hear. So, it is very important to be the example that we want them to follow. We are hopeful that having our kids be around adults and older friends who are not ashamed to regularly reference God will give them the confidence to really "own" their relationship with the Creator as well, *insha'Allah* (God willing).

Get Comfortable with the Seerah and Sunnah

The ultimate role model for our children is the Prophet Muhammad (peace be upon him). This blessed guide was sent to mankind to teach us about our souls and how to earn salvation, both in this life and in the next. He was a man who definitely functioned in the worldly realm, but his heart and mind dwelled in the spiritual realm. There is no one better from whom our children can learn their spirituality than the final Messenger of Allah (upon whom be peace) himself. In order to achieve that end, our children should be encouraged to study his *seerah* (biography) where they can learn about his advice and his admonitions.

Kids whose practice of the *sunnah* (way) of the Prophet (upon whom be peace)—like which hand one uses to eat food or which foot one uses to enter the house—is imbued with intention, mindfulness, and purpose are kids who are more likely to practice their faith with spirituality. Such children are less likely to become mindless beings just bouncing along from day to day.

One of the greatest gifts a parent can try to give his/her child is a connection with the Divine. While this desire to know one's Lord is part of our *fitra* (primordial nature), we all need help figuring out how best to develop our relationship with God. If we are going to be successful at this most important relationship, we will need to bring to it what we bring to *all* beneficial relationships—time, attention, priority, mindfulness, and tools for success. But most important of all, we must bring our *duas* for *tawfiq* (supplications for success). As Allah Himself has promised us in a hadith qudsi: "Take one step towards Me, I will take ten steps towards you. Walk towards Me, I will run towards you." May we all joyfully rush towards our Lord and join with Him in the most beautiful of unions. And may our children be leading us in that race. *Aameen* (Amen).

Hina Khan-Mukhtar is a mother of three boys and one of the founders of the homeschooling co-operative known as ILM Tree in Lafayette, California, which now serves over 35 homeschooling families in the East Bay. In addition to teaching Language Arts to elementary, middle school, and high school students, she has written articles on parenting and spiritual traditions for children and is involved in interfaith dialogue.

Teaching Children Love Of Allah

By Ohood Alomar

In his book, *Madarij as-Salikeen*, the famous 14th Century theologian Ibn al-Qayyim said:

> *"The heart on its journey towards Allah - the Exalted - is like a bird. Love is its head, and fear and hope are its two wings. When the head is healthy, then the two wings will fly well. When the head is cut off, the bird will die. When either of the two wings is damaged, the bird becomes vulnerable to every hunter and predator."*

What would he have said if he were to see how parents are connecting their children with Allah today? One day as I sat in the masjid (mosque) waiting for my son to finish his Quran class, I noticed a young boy sitting in the corner, engulfed in his own fear. His mother told him that Allah was going to punish him because he refused to pick up some papers that he threw in the masjid. Her words were "I am not going to punish you. I'll leave you to Allah to take care of your punishment." This awful scene prompted reflections on the way many Muslims choose to raise their children today. It is unfortunate that some parents unintentionally inflict serious damage on a child's relationship with Allah - the Exalted - with their irresponsible words and actions.

Many Muslim children are being raised with a "fear factor." Some parents believe that if they scare their children by focusing on Allah's punishment early in their lives, they will grow up to be good obedient Muslims. Although scaring the child might temporarily inhibit any wrongdoing, it has a huge negative effect on him emotionally and spiritually. According to Professor Suhaylah Zain, a member of the National Society for Human Rights, "The discipline that depends on scaring the children constantly from Allah will eventually produce hatred in their hearts toward religion, in addition to some other serious psychological damage."

So what is the solution?

The Prophet (pbuh) raised a great generation by first instilling the love of Allah—the Exalted—in the hearts of the people, including children. He did so with love, patience, compassion, and kindness. He was loved by the companions who were eager to learn from him about Allah and His guidance. With love began the story of creation as we read the narrative in Quran, 2: 30-38. Allah—the Exalted—honored and loved Adam (pbuh) by doing the following:

- Created him with His own hands.
- Gave him a mind and freewill.
- Taught him useful and essential knowledge for his survival in this life.
- Made the angels bow to him.
- Created him in the best form that allowed him to practice his role in life efficiently.
- Subjected the heavens, the earth, and what is in them for him and his offspring and provided them with the powers and abilities that they will need in this life.

- Entrusted him with the *amaanah* of creation (obedience to Allah—the Exalted—in fulfilling His commands and refraining from what He forbade) that all the other creations of Allah declined to carry.

Allah—the Exalted—also taught Adam how to love Him back and how to totally submit to His will by doing the following:

- Showed Adam the true manifestation of His magnificent Names and Supreme attributes.
- Decreed that Adam and his wife live in *Jannah* (the garden).
- Provided Adam with complete guidance to protect him and his offspring from their first enemy, Satan.
- Promised forgiveness to those who repent sincerely.

So how do parents apply the above guidelines when teaching children to love Allah—the Exalted? Here are some important recommendations to keep children connected to Allah.

1. Maintain a positive relationship.

The parent is the connection between the child and Allah. Since the parent is the primary connector, if the child has negative feelings toward the parent, then he will have negative feelings toward Allah, as well. For parents to maintain a positive relationship with the child, they must focus on the following:

- Maintain the child's dignity. Parents must abandon practices that destroy the child's dignity which may turn the child away from Allah. Examples include: screaming, criticizing, punishing, ridiculing, comparing siblings, excessive preaching, and threatening. Children who grow up in households that use these practices may become adults who have no genuine love for Allah even if they appear to follow His commands.

- Give the child freedom. Giving children room to think, say, or do what they want within reasonable limits will foster a very strong relationship between the child and the parent. When children are not afraid of reprimands and criticism, they will be empowered to speak the truth and defend their beliefs and values.

- Align actions with words. Children emulate behaviors, not words. If a parent embodies their love for Allah in actions, the child will pick up on the actions, too. For example, if a father prays every time he hears the call to prayer, his children will be encouraged to pray regularly and on time.

2. Teach about Allah's manifestation in the world and within.

The best way to do this is by taking advantage of teachable moments that direct their attention toward Allah's great wisdom, mercy, and power. Allow them to explore nature and encounter Allah's creations so that they may see for themselves how Allah is the One who guided them to the best ways to survive in this world.

3. Teach critical thinking skills.

The best way to do that is by engaging in simple dialogues with children about Allah—the beautiful things He gave us in life, and how He created everything for us to benefit. Ask them, "Who gave you eyes, ears, and noses? Why do you think Allah gave each one of us two eyes but He gave us only one mouth? What would happen if we walked on four feet instead of two?" Ask them to close their eyes and imagine what would happen if everybody looked alike or if the sun was a little bit closer to earth.

4. Teach the love of the Prophet (pbuh).

"Say [O Prophet, to the people]: 'If you love God, follow me [and] God will love you and forgive your sins; for God is much - forgiving, and Merciful" (Quran, 3:31).

5. Start early with Quran memorization.

The Prophet (pbuh) informed Muslims that memorizing the Quran at an early age will make it stay firm in the child's body and mind. Abu Hurayrah (may Allah be pleased with him) said that the Prophet (pbuh) said: "Whoever learns the Quran at an early age, then Allah will mix it with his flesh and blood."

6. Teach the virtues of giving.

Establish a charity box at home and teach children to put money in it from their own allowance. You can also teach your child to collect their old toys and clothes that are in good condition and give them to charity. Or you can take the child to a homeless shelter to help feed the poor and needy.

7. Teach Arabic, the language of the Quran.

Teaching Arabic to the young Muslim generation grants direct access to the Quran. This, in turn, empowers them to understand Allah's commands and guidance and stay connected to Him.

8. Teach dependence on Allah, seeking His help and protection.

The best way to do that is by teaching the child simple supplications. Narrating stories, especially of young Muslims who depended on Allah, is inspiring. Abdullah bin Abbas (may Allah Be pleased with him) reported: "One day I was riding behind the Prophet (pbuh), when he said, 'Young man, I will teach you some words. Be mindful of God, and He will take care of you. Be mindful of Him, and you shall find Him at your side. If you ask, ask of God. If you need help, seek it from God. Know that if the whole world were to gather together in order to help you, they would not be able to help you except if God had written so. And if the whole world were to gather together in order to harm you, they would not harm you except if God had written so. The pens have been lifted, and the pages are dry'" (Hadith, Tirmizi).

We must teach our children to love Allah first because it is the driving force toward success in this life and the hereafter. Balancing the love of Allah with the fear of His wrath is important. But, instead of beginning with fear, let's begin with love just as Ibn al-Qayyim stated. May Allah Grant you *qurat ain* (serenity and contentment) in all of your children.

Ohood Alomar is the Director of Al Kawthar Learning Center in California, which offers students Arabic Immersion Language, Dual Immersion (English/Arabic), and Quran Memorization and Interpretation Programs. She is passionate about teaching Arabic so students can understand Quran and apply its teaching to their daily lives. She has over 25 years of experience teaching Arabic, Islamic Studies, and Quran to children and adults. She holds a Master's degree in Islamic Education from the American Open University in Washington D.C.

SPANKING IN THE ISLAMIC CONTEXT

By Noha Alshugairi

An often quoted hadith with regard to teaching children to pray is, "Command your children to pray at the age of seven, spank them for neglecting prayers at the age of 10, and separate them when asleep." This hadith has engendered much debate and discussion in recent decades as global parenting styles shifted from a focus on physical punishment to a more collaborative discipline method. What follows is a simplified and succinct overview of the hadith's position in the Islamic tradition as well as some recommendations for how to reconcile its message with the current abhorrence of physical punishments.

From an authenticity perspective, this hadith is narrated through four main chains of narrations. Two of them are accepted and two are rejected. The two accepted chains of narrations are reported in three of the seven main books of Hadith: Masnad Ahmad bin Hanbal, Sunan Abu Daoud, and Sunan al-Tirmizi. Significantly, this hadith is not included in either Sahih al-Bukhari or Sahih Muslim, the two most revered authentic collections of hadith according to scholars. In addition, hadith scholars differ in their assessment of this hadith with some rating it as *daeef* (weak authenticity) while others rating it as *hasan* (moderate authenticity), which is the second best level of hadith authenticity after *sahih* (high authenticity). Accordingly, the hadith cannot be rejected based on its authenticity.

This hadith was not a cause of concern in earlier times. Using physical punishment as a means of discipline was a common practice across religions and cultures. Today, people struggle with this hadith because of the shift in social and cultural norms. It has triggered a moral and intellectual dilemma for Muslims who revere the authority of the Hadith tradition and, at the same time, loathe the use of physical punishment. Efforts at reconciling the hadith with changing norms have led some to outright reject it, citing its weak authenticity by some of the scholars as mentioned above. Others have resorted to interpreting the word spank (ضرب) to mean guidance or separation instead of actual physical punishment. Muslims who do not find solace in rejecting the hadith nor in reinterpreting the meaning of the word (ضرب) may find the following reflections helpful.

It is unfortunate that lay people quote and apply the hadith literally without full knowledge of the scholarly traditions associated with the hadith. What is even graver is the propagation of this hadith by *imams* (religious leaders) without fully disclosing the Islamic limits on using spanking. After a thorough research of the body of scholarly commentaries regarding this hadith, one cannot but marvel at the wisdom of earlier scholars.

While some scholars extrapolated this hadith as mandating parents to spank their children at the age of 10 if they neglect their prayers, others posited that the hadith merely allowed for the action, if necessary. One view mandates, the other merely permits. Supporting the latter view are other Islamic traditions: "There is no coercion in religion," (Quran, 2:256); "The Prophet (peace be upon him) never struck anyone with his hand; no woman and no servant," (Muslim); Furthermore he stated, "He is not amongst us who does not have mercy on children" (Hadith, Tirmizi).

Another critical point is that *sharia* (Islamic law) revolves around goals (مقاصد). If a specific goal is not attainable via a specific mean, then the mean is no longer utilized. In this case, the goal is training children to maintain prayers. If physical discipline to train children for prayers is producing negative results (as seen in many families today) then the means (physical discipline) is forbidden. At no point in the Islamic tradition do the means supersede the goals.

For those who are reluctant to discard physical discipline as an option, understand that *sharia* has limited its use. If you insist on utilizing physical discipline, you must observe the Islamic rules governing physical discipline. These rules established by Muslim scholars centuries ago are not contemporary rules; yet, as a therapist reading these Islamic rules, it felt as if I was reading the current California laws and ethics guidelines for using spanking. It is unfortunate that the limits understood by Muslim scholars about the use of physical discipline were not taught side-by-side with the hadith. Such practices led to a literal application of the hadith beyond permissible *sharia* limits.

Islamic rules governing the use of physical discipline.

- Scholars agree that, if at any time, spanking leads to graverer consequence, it must be abandoned.
- It must be light. It is forbidden to strike, hit, or beat. It is forbidden to cause injury or sickness. It is forbidden to break the skin as a result of any physical discipline.
- It is used as a last resort—only if reminding, coaxing, and warning do not work.

- It must avoid the face and other sensitive areas of the body: "If you spank, avoid the face" (Hadith, Abu Daoud). It is allowed only on areas that can take the spanking without causing injury.

- Spanking must be done in calmness with an intent to discipline, and not in anger to take revenge.

- Scholars agree that, if a person uses spanking for discipline excessively, that individual is liable for legal punishment by the authorities.

- Many scholars limit the spanking to a maximum of three strikes. They also restrict spanking to be done by the hand or light objects such as the *miswak* (thin flexible stick that is used for brushing teeth). Objects prone to cause injury are prohibited (belts, thick sticks, heavy shoes, etc.).

How many parents can honestly say they spank their children with calmness and not anger? I have not yet met a parent who can claim they spank with full self-control. I myself acknowledge that, when I spanked my children, I did it in anger. I was never calm. I did not follow guideline #5 for spanking according to *sharia*!

As a therapist, I assure you that using physical punishment to train children to pray (or for any other purpose) will backfire for many reasons. First, the global trend is moving toward abolishing such discipline methods. Hence, in many countries excessive physical punishments can be grounds for investigation and even loss of parental rights. Second, while children in earlier times saw physical punishment as a right of their parents, today children believe that it is their right not to be punished physically. Third, most children used to know instinctively that behind spanking there was deep-seated love. Currently, spanking is causing a disconnection between parents and children. Fourth, in a global culture that is emphasizing individuality and uniqueness, spanking children to conform is pushing them out of the family unit and out of the community. I implore you not to spank!

In the end, accepting this hadith as part of our rich tradition does not obligate us to utilize physical punishments as a way of discipline. Our social norms have curtailed the effectiveness of such methods. Hence, according to our *sharia*, we need to find discipline alternatives that align better with our goals for our children. This is where Positive Discipline comes in.

BLIND BIRR

By Noha Alshugairi

Throughout human history, cultural social norms have defined when children take charge of their lives. It is certainly a process that occurs gradually over time. In very general terms, parents tended to let go of their children earlier in previous historical eras simply because life demanded participation from children at an earlier age. One such example is of the story of Anas bin Malik, who, at the age of 10, became the servant of the Prophet Muhammad (pbuh) and was reported to have served him for 10 years. In that era, it was the norm for a child to engage in the adult activities of life. It was not perceived as child labor, but as an opportunity for children to contribute to life according to their abilities and talents. Today, this practice of having children work before the age of 15 is considered unacceptable.

Beginning in the nineteenth century, the Industrial Revolution altered social dynamics. Gradually, over the next century, children were shielded from work activities and were expected to focus on their education as preparation for adulthood. The demarcation between childhood and adulthood was no longer biological (puberty), but was distinguished by social and cultural time limits that restricted the activities and abilities of children. Currently, in developed countries, the age of 18 has become the official entry into adulthood aligned with certain educational attainments that are perceived to be necessary for adulthood.

In addition to social norms, the emphasis on revering one's parents in Muslim communities has also impacted the process of letting go. The duties of children toward their parents, called *ihsan* (excellence), is mentioned seven times in the Quran (2:83; 4:36; 6:151; 17:23-24; 29:8; 31:14-15; 46:15, see Appendix B). In five of these verses, the command to treat one's parents with *ihsan* comes immediately after the command to worship none other than Allah. Therefore, scholars placed the obligation toward one's parents as an immediate second to worshiping Allah. Unfortunately, this noble commitment has been gravely misunderstood and misapplied. In some situations it has led parents to expect blind obedience from their children.

Ihsan is a state of pursuing excellence or going the extra mile. It's beyond covering the basics. It's a state of doing one's best with effort but not with extreme hardship. In the Islamic tradition, *ihsan* is the highest form of worship; a state of being conscious of Allah all the time: "to worship Allah as if you see Him; for if you do not see Him, He Sees you" (Hadith, Muslim). When the Quran uses the word *ihsan,* it denotes an invitation to a realm completely governed by divine principles but within the realistic abilities of the person and the situation. *Ihsan* is not an angelic state with no mistakes. *Ihsan* is a full and intentional striving for Allah despite shortcomings, limitations, and blunders. This is why Allah uses the word *ihsan* to describe a child's obligations toward parents. It is an invitation to extend oneself with parents while being cognizant of the fact that there is no one formula for all. The circumstances of any given situation will determine what *ihsan* is for that particular family.

While the Quran uses *ihsan* to describe the duty to parents, Muslim scholars use *birr al-walidain* (revering and caring of both parents) to denote the same concept. *Al-walidain* means both parents, while *birr*—which is also mentioned in the Quran (2:44; 2:177; 2:189; 3:92; 5:2; 58:9, see Appendix B)—encompasses acts of worship (such as prayers and fasting) as well as all good deeds related to social interactions. *Birr* is an expansive word just like *ihsan,* and it also expresses an extension of oneself beyond the minimal or average.

It's clear from reading the Quranic verses regarding filial obligations that Allah is commanding *ihsan*: extend yourself in interacting with your parents. Nowhere does it say in these verses that children must blindly obey their parents. However, some scholars interpreted the verses (Quran, 29:8; 31:15, see Appendix B) renouncing obedience to parents when they command what is against Allah's ruling as an indication that parents must be obeyed in all other areas. Other scholars posited that parental emotional pain caused by their children's life choices is counter to *ihsan,* and, hence, have prohibited such choices. Consequently, tradition and culture over the centuries have distorted the meaning of *ihsan* toward parents, or *birr al-walidain,* to reflect complete blind obedience. This is what I call the *Blind Birr* phenomenon.

In many Muslim communities, blind obedience from children toward their parents is the expectation. This total obedience is inoculated by a heavy burden of guilt when the child deviates from parental choices and wishes. I have met many clients whose parents have waived the spear of, "Allah's favor is contingent upon my contentment with you! You better do as I say!" These clients, who are striving in their paths to Allah, find themselves stuck when their wishes conflict with those of their parents because they were taught—erroneously—never to disobey.

Ihsan toward parents or *birr al-walidain* is not total blind obedience. So, then, how should Muslim children treat their parents? The Quranic verses (17:23-24, see Appendix B) are very clear about two key components: respect and mercy. Both are a must in interacting with parents generally; but they become even more critical when parents reach old age. Observing older people illuminates the need for these two significant elements. With aging, there is a gradual decrease in the acuity of senses, physical dexterity, and mental agility. In addition, older people's psychological energy needed to deal with life events depletes quickly. This translates to the sometimes unfathomable stubbornness and impatience of old age. Compounding matters is young people's lightning-speed ability to respond and act. The end result is that younger people struggle to relate to their elders as the gap in abilities and faculties between the two groups widens.

With such understanding in mind, it becomes evident why Allah would prohibit the utterance of "uff"—as trivial as it may be—because it's easy to become frustrated and irritated with the marked changes of old age. Dealing with older people requires patience and compassion, and the beautiful Quranic description of humbling oneself in mercy and respect toward one's parents alludes to this state. It is difficult to translate the Arabic verses while maintaining their original poetic beauty. The words used in Arabic evoke the image of a strong young bird kneeling in front of the older weaker parent bird while holding its wings to its side in a sign of humility and respect. The image prescribes a reversal of roles affirmed by the ending *duaa* (prayer), "My Lord, be merciful to them as they have brought me up in my childhood" (Quran, 17: 23-24). If the paltry utterance of "uff" is denounced, then anything stronger in words or actions is definitely forbidden. Again, this is not to be confused with the state of blind obedience. One can disagree with the utmost respect, humility, and mercy. What is forbidden is disrespect, humiliation, and neglect. Affirming this is the Quranic invitation to "address them with respectful speech" (17:23).

Ihsan is goodness in actions and words, not blind obedience as some parents believe. Accordingly, I invite parents to let go of this misunderstanding when raising your children. If you expect your children to blindly obey you, you will certainly experience deep pain and anguish as adult children progressively choose their own path. If, on the other hand, you recognize that your role is that of nurturer and guide who ultimately lets go, you will have a stronger bond with your adult child. Furthermore, that bond will secure your continued influence in their life.

Omar bin al-Khatab, the second Caliph, wisely said, "Help your children in their efforts to extend *birr* to you." His formula for that is simple: treat children well, forge strong connections, and, finally, allow them space to make their adult decisions. Following his formula will certainly ensure their heartfelt *birr* filling a parent's heart with contentment and peace. *Bil tawfiq* (with divine success).

Fragile Adult Syndrome

By Noha Alshugairi

The first time I heard of this phenomenon was in 2010. The late Dr. Maher Hathout (may Allah Have mercy on his soul) was addressing a group of young college students about life after the MSA (Muslim Student Association). Life in the real world! Dr. Hathout was a keen observer of the development of the American Muslim community. His life experience in Islamic activism, coupled with his wisdom and deep understanding of Islam, empowered him to call for a vision of the American Muslim community that was years ahead of others. On that day, Dr. Hathout shared hopes and concerns. His goal was always to expand the horizons of his listeners beyond rigid and restrictive world views.

Among the beautiful messages he shared, I was struck by his description of the current generation of young American Muslims as "soft." He went on to give examples of how such enthusiastic and sincere young adults had difficulties dealing with criticism and failure. Simple comments about how to improve procedures turned into "emotional traumas" with dramatic effects. Constructive criticisms became personal rejections of epic proportions. Dr. Hathout lamented the loss of a safe space where elders could give honest, pertinent feedback to young adults. He noticed that only positive feedback was welcomed and anything construed as negative was repelled.

Dr. Hathout's comments resonated with my own observations as a therapist in the community. His words crystallized what I sensed but had not yet framed in my consciousness. His reflections were actually documented by social science researchers. It turns out that this "softness," or what I call "Fragile Adult Syndrome," is the product of several cultural changes in the U.S.

During the last few decades of the 20th century, there was a gradual increase in several social trends: individualism, materialism, and narcissism (Twenge, et al., 2008). All three trends have led to a self-centered view of the world that revolves around self-gratification through achievements, possessions, and self-image. With such a "me" view of the world, it's easy to understand how minor, innocuous social exchanges become major traumatic wounds.

Social scientists attribute some of the increase in the narcissistic tendencies of young people to what is called the self-esteem movement of the 1980s (Twenge, et al., 2008). This campaign focused on bolstering self-esteem through empty praise. It was one of those fads that came and went. There is no doubt that it did sound plausible when introduced in the late 1980s because the premise was simple: let's focus on *telling* children that they are special and unique; celebrate every little thing they do with words and trophies; validate their feelings and they will certainly become confident. Advocates erroneously believed that self-esteem can be bestowed. However, it quickly became apparent that these attitudes resulted in anything but self-assured children. This well-intentioned movement led to young people whose egos were inflated with grandiose, imaginary perceptions of self. Within a decade, there were calls to denounce the self-esteem movement (Colvin, 1999). Unfortunately, while scientists have shifted from empty self-esteem strategies, parents and teachers are slow to follow.

Self-esteem is simply perceiving oneself as capable and having mastery over life. A life filled with good-enough successes and failures is the bedrock of rich life lessons that seed a positive self-concept. Failures and successes are both instrumental. Without facing the pain of failure and mistakes and transforming them into life lessons, individuals won't cultivate the resiliency necessary to handle difficulties. Without being successful in some endeavors, individuals won't believe in their abilities to contribute and be meaningful. Self-esteem is not being perfect—quite the opposite. It is recognizing one's shortcomings and learning how to contain them, thus bolstering one's strengths. Self-esteem is both day and night, positive and negative, good and bad coming together for a beautiful unique mix that is empowering and productive.

Accordingly, the empty self-esteem movement of the 1980s failed because it focused on "infusing" rather than providing space for children to learn through life. By shielding children from any negative life situation—feeling anger and sadness, rejections, mistakes, constructive criticism, etc.—children were crippled. They could not develop their emotional muscles to handle life's difficulties. They became a generation with Fragile Adult Syndrome.

Signs of Fragile Adult Syndrome:

• Impulsivity.
• Difficulty making decisions.

- Anger if needs and wishes are not met.
- Life revolving around instant gratification.
- Difficulty working hard to achieve a goal.
- Oversensitivity in social interactions.
- Blaming others rather than focusing on what can be done.
- Depending on others to solve problems.
- Entitlement .
- Addictions.
- Anxiety and depression.

The antidotes to this phenomenon are 3 primary Positive Discipline tools:

- Encouragement (p. 94).
- Mistakes as Opportunities to Learn (p. 119).
- Empowerment (p. 90).

Another antidote is training children to take responsibility for their emotions. A debilitating aspect of the self-esteem movement was focusing on reflecting back a child's feelings without teaching the child how to effectively express and contain emotions. The end result was children who felt helpless, took on victimization attitudes, and waited for others to rescue them. Validating feelings is not enough. There needs to always be a follow up: "How would you like to take care of yourself?" "What would help you calm down right now?"

Ultimately, Fragile Adult Syndrome is preventable. Families that begin implementing Positive Discipline early in their homes will raise adults who are responsible, independent, capable, empathic, collaborative, accountable, honest, critical thinkers, and so much more.

ISLAM THE CHOICE

By Noha Alshugairi

Shaikh Jamaal Diwan, co-founder of Safa Center (www.safacenter.org), describes the process of being born into Islam and then intentionally adopting Islam as the transition from *Islam-the-Habit* to *Islam-the-Choice*. Parents are obligated to train children in the habits of Islam. This is what parents do no matter what faith tradition they follow. Prophet Muhammad (pbuh) said, "Every human is born by his mother in a state of *fitra* (pure blank state), his parents afterwards shepherd him into Judaism, Christianity, Zoroastrianism. And if his parents are Muslims, then Islam" (Hadith, Muslim). However, simply teaching or training a child in the parents' tradition does not guarantee a child's lifelong commitment to that faith. While parents have control over Islam-the-Habit in early childhood, Islam-the-Choice is not under their control. Parents teach. Allah guides.

If Islam-the-Habit follows Allah's social process in creation, Islam-the-Choice is the manifestation of Allah's bestowal of freewill on humans and *jinn* (unseen beings): "There is no coercion in religion" (Quran, 2:256). Islam-the-Choice is an individual journey—when it happens, how it happens, or what form it takes. All of humanity submits to the law of free choice. No one is excluded, no matter who they are. If there were exceptions, it would have been with the son of Prophet Nuh (pbuh) whose story is described with stirring details in Surat Hud (Quran, 11:42-47, see Appendix C). The passages paint an agonizing scene for the hearts and minds of parents. Nuh's son did not follow the faith path his father adopted, and their story is a poignant reminder that Allah's decree of freewill supersedes all considerations.

Certain Quranic verses tug at my heart whenever I read them. The story of Prophet Nuh (pbuh) is one of them. It never fails to bring me to tears because I am thrown in the midst of Nuh's humanity and Allah's Divinity. Nuh (pbuh) the Prophet is also Nuh (pbuh) the father. Nuh (pbuh), the Prophet, worked diligently for 950 years to spread the message of Allah the One God. Nuh (pbuh), the father, could not help but wonder how his son was not destined to be amongst the saved people from the flood. This exquisite yet painful story is the balsam for every parent who was and is tested in the way of Nuh (pbuh). It is a reminder that our life is a constant oscillation between our humanity and our striving for the Divine—a struggle that never ceases until the moment of death.

This story is the archetype for the eternal shuffle between parents and children in the journey of faith. The divine principle of freewill manifests in the disparities of faith journeys seen in humanity. Nonetheless, when the dissonance occurs between parent and child, the struggle is personal, agonizing, and for some a powerful instance of submission to Allah. For some, the dissonance leads to a spiritual emotional seesaw.

I have spent long hours reflecting on these verses. They hold a personal meaning for me. As a young mother, I naively believed that my children's journey with faith was dependent on my teaching and guidance. I believed in the sequence, "I teach them, train them, and, of course, they will be practicing Muslims!" That was my goal of *tarbiyah* (raising children). I dedicated myself and my life toward this noble goal. Having shared with you how deep this goal of mine was, you can imagine my shock when my youngest decided to take off her *hijab* (head covering) as she was entering college. While taking off the *hijab* is not on the same level as leaving Islam, nevertheless, my pain was deep. There are no words to describe my feelings of sorrow and sadness. For a week, I was living in a state of numbness where I did not feel anything except this very deep seated agony. A flurry of feelings and thoughts kept swirling through my mind and heart as I tried to come to terms with my shattered dream. I was going through the motions of life, doing everything I was used to, but I was shell-shocked. This was the shuttering of a lifelong goal and expectation.

I reacted the way we all react when our framework of the world crumbles: shock, turmoil, grief, and then, slowly, resolution. My lifelong dream of my children being practicing Muslims the way I taught them no longer sustained me. I needed to tweak my dream to reflect my reality. And since Islam is my guiding light, I searched for answers in our beautiful tradition. With a heavy heart I turned to the story of Nuh (pbuh) and his son. Believe me when I tell you these verses come alive in an indescribable way when you are the one who is tested as Prophet Nuh (pbuh) was.

In Nuh's (pbuh) conversations with Allah, I found solace. I heard the echoes of what I felt and experienced when my daughter renounced her *hijab*. First there was the shock that, after a lifelong dedication to the divine cause, Nuh's own son glibly chose a different path. Faith operates through choices at critical moments in life. With mountainous waves surrounding them, boarding the ship and staying ashore were both avowals of divergent creeds. For Nuh (pbuh), boarding the ship was an emphatic submission to Allah while his son's arrogant, "I will seek protection in a mountain," (Quran, 11: 43) epitomized a human's pseudo sense of control when the heart has not submitted to Allah.

After the shock comes questioning. Nuh's (pbuh) pain-filled inquiry as to why his own son was not amongst the saved resonated with me. It's the same question asked by every parent who was intentional about guiding their children to Islam, and is shocked when their offspring chooses another path or chooses to live Islam differently. It's a wakeup call like no other regarding the limits of our human control. Our own flesh and blood with whom we spent years nurturing, protecting, loving, guiding, and instructing are not a reflection of us. They are not an extension of us. In the words of Gibran, "You may house their bodies but not their souls, for their souls dwell in the house of tomorrow."

In anguish, Nuh (pbuh) called upon Allah saying, "My son is of my family and your promise is true" (Quran, 11:45). He was wondering how it could be that Allah's earlier promise of saving his family did not include his son. But Allah's laws apply to all regardless of someone's privileged position. His son had to earn his place among the saved that day and his father, the Prophet, could not intercede for him—a compelling reminder for all parents.

Allah responds to Nuh's (pbuh) inquiry with, "It's an impious deed and don't ask me about what you don't have knowledge of"

(Quran, 11:46). Most scholars interpret "impious deed" in this verse as referring to the deeds of Nuh's (pbuh) son. These scholars posit that, in this verse, Allah reminded Nuh (pbuh) that his son did not submit and hence his son was not one of Nuh's (pbuh) family of believers. I hear a different echo in this exchange. I know at the time of my daughter's decision, I wondered: Why did Allah test me this way? Where did I go wrong? What did I do in my raising of her to get to where we were at that moment? I hear the same from a multitude of parents: "We have done everything in our power to live, teach, and guide to Islam! How can our own children choose a different path or a different practice?" Perhaps the "impious deed" is this inevitable questioning we parents do when our own children do not follow in our footsteps. If the "impious deed" is the questioning of Allah, then the next verse teaches us what to do. Nuh (pbuh) leads us to do *istighfar* (asking forgiveness) and submit to Allah for He knows and our knowledge ultimately is miniscule, "My Lord, I seek refuge with You that I should ask You something of which I have no knowledge. If You do not forgive me and do not show mercy to me, I shall be among the losers" (Quran, 11:47).

My readings of this very beautiful and personal exchange between Allah and Nuh (pbuh) eventually brought me peace. And that is when I felt Allah's love in the midst of anguish. We are told that in every Quranic story there is a lesson to be learned for all humanity. With Nuh (pbuh), one of the earliest prophets, Allah teaches humans to surrender the question of faith to Him, but only after we do our part in nurturing and guiding our children. We teach; He Guides. Where would I have found my serenity if Allah did not share with us the details of this story in

Surat Hud?

Lastly, Nuh (pbuh) taught me that with acceptance also comes hope. To the last minute, Nuh (pbuh) continued to invite his son to board the ship. I see it as a metaphor for us parents never to give up on our children who are struggling with their faith and may have lost their way. And, just as he invited and did not coerce, we need to invite and leave the rest to Allah, remembering that sometimes the best invitations are the silent ones.

The story of Nuh (pbuh) and his son is a universal story for all parents who hold faith as their life priority. It brings solace for those whose test is the test of Nuh (pbuh). In the end, we are reminded that, "You don't guide whomever you wish for, but Allah Guides whomever He wills" (Quran, 28:56). We train in Islam-the-Habit and we pray fervently that our children end at Islam-the-Choice. May Allah grant you *qurat ain* (serenity) in your spouses and children.

Pulling It All Together

Parenting is work. However, we believe that, if you are intentional about how you relate to your children, the journey will be smoother and more joyful. What follows is a simplified summary of the book that we hope will help pull all the information presented together. A parent will never reach perfection during the parenting journey, even if they implement all the parenting tools outlined in this book. Reliance on Allah and making *duaa* (supplications) on a regular basis is foundational when raising children. Remember that your goal is to inoculate your child with gifts for life. Remember that mistakes are wonderful opportunities for both you and your child to learn.

You need to know yourself to know how to best interact with your child. Take care of your physical, emotional, and spiritual health in order to be present and loving with your child. Growth is a lifelong process. It is never too late to change, learn, and implement better ways of interacting with your child. Reflect on your parenting style and understand key ways to be more effective.

Authoritarian parent: Listen more. Give space to the child to make decisions and have input. Understand that you cannot mold them into what you want them to be. They are different than you.

Permissive parent: Be firm in structures, routines, and rules. Know that you will not harm them by being firm in critical situations. You may actually cause them harm by giving in to their demands.

Authoritative parent: Stick to your values. Just because your child does not see your perspective does not mean you do it their way. Pick your confrontations wisely.

Continue to discover who your child is becoming and seek to learn about their innate strengths and their areas of growth. Are you nurturing their strengths or focusing on their shortcomings? Observe their likes and dislikes, and work with them. Discover your child's temperament and continue to learn and adapt to your child's stage of development.

- What is the crisis of the stage they are at?
- Are you aiding in resolving the crisis successfully?
- What is the child's strategy in gaining mastery over his/her life?
- What can you do to help your child use effective and healthy strategies?

Focus on connecting with your child in a kind and firm way. The fine balance of kindness and firmness is achieved through the following:

- Create and maintain Routines and rules of life.
- Be consistent with Family meetings.
- Listen and mirror back what you hear your child saying.
- Use Curiosity Questions to learn more about what is going on with your child. Avoid asking "why" questions.
- Give limited choices instead of asking yes or no questions.
- Be firm when you need to and use "no" in important situations.

- Focus on encouraging your child and avoid empty praise.
- Empower your child. Avoid taking on their responsibilities at home and school. Avoid bailing them out when mistakes occur.
- Focus on solutions to problems rather than punishments or rewards.
- Focus on what you have direct control over rather than attempting to control your child's behavior or feelings.
- Refer to different Positive Discipline tools when feeling stuck.
- Refer to the parenting challenges in each specific age group for further empowering ideas.

We have come to the end of our journey together. We pray we have succeeded in sharing, with you, ideas and concepts that will empower you in your parenting journey. May Allah grant you *tawfiq* (divine success) and *qurat ain* (serenity and contentment) in your children.

Further Resources

To follow Jane Nelsen, go to: www.positivediscipline.com. For more information about the Positive Discipline philosophy, check out: www.positivediscipline.org.

If you would like to stay connected to the global Positive Discipline in the Muslim Home movement, visit our website at: www.positivedisciplinemuslimhome.com and our Facebook page at: www.facebook.com/PositiveMuslimHome/

If you are interested in watching a full 7-week parenting class that complements this book, go to: www.gumroad.com/sakina. Additional related videos are available at Sakina Counseling YouTube channel.

To get a PDF of all the tables and figures in this book, contact us a www.positivedisciplinemuslimhome.com.

Appendix A:

Quranic References for Adult Children

Quran; 46:15-19

"And We have enjoined on man to be dutiful and kind to his parents. His mother bears him with hardship And she brings him forth with hardship, and the bearing of him, and the weaning of him is thirty months, till when he attains full strength and reaches forty years, he says: "My Lord! Grant me the power and ability that I may be grateful for Your Favor which You have bestowed upon me and upon my parents, and that I may do righteous good deeds, such as please You, and make my offspring good. Truly, I have turned to You in repentance, and truly, I am one of the Muslims (submitting to Your Will)." They are those from whom We shall accept the best of their deeds and overlook their evil deeds. (They shall be) among the dwellers of Paradise — a promise of truth, which they have been promised. But he who says to his parents: "Fie upon you both! Do you hold out the promise to me that I shall be raised up (again) when generations before me have passed away (without rising)?" While they (father and mother) invoke Allah for help (and rebuke their son): "Woe to you! Believe! Verily, the Promise of Allah is true." But he says: "This is nothing but the tales of the ancient." They are those against whom the Word (of torment) is justified among the previous generations of jinn and mankind that have passed away. Verily, they are ever the losers. And for all, there will be degrees according to that which they did, that He (Allah) may recompense them in full for their deeds. And they will not be wronged."

Quran; 7:168-170

And We divided them on the earth as separate nations. Some of them were righteous, while others were less than that. And We tested them with good and bad decrees, so that they might return. Then, after them, came a generation that inherited the Book, opting for the mundane stuff of this world and saying, "We shall be forgiven." But if there comes to them similar stuff, they would opt for it (again). Was not the covenant of the Book taken from them that they should not say anything but the truth about Allah? They learned what it contained. Certainly, the Last Abode is better for those who fear Allah. Won't you reflect?

Those who hold fast to the Book and establish *Salah* (prayer), We shall never let the reward of (such) righteous people to go to waste."

Quran; 19:58-60

Those are the people whom Allah has blessed with bounties, the prophets from the progeny of Adam, and of those whom We caused to board (the Ark) along with Nuh, and from the progeny of Ibrahim and Isra'il, and from those whom We guided and selected. When the verses of The Rahman were recited before them, they used to fall down in *Sajdah* (prostration), while they were weeping. Then came after them the successors who neglected *Salah* (prayer) and followed (their selfish) desires. So they will soon face a bad end. Except those who repent and believe and do good deeds, and therefore they will enter the Paradise and will not be wronged at all."

Quran; 58:22

"You will not find those who believe in Allah and in the Hereafter extending themselves to those who fight Allah and His Messenger, even though they may be their fathers or their sons or their brothers or their clan. They are such that Allah has inscribed faith on their hearts, and has supported them with a spirit from Him. He will admit them to gardens beneath which rivers flow, in which they will live forever. Allah is pleased with them, and they are pleased with Allah. Those are the party of Allah. Be assured that it is the party of Allah that are the successful."

APPENDIX | 409

Appendix B:

Quranic References for Blind Birr

Quran, 2:83

"And We took a covenant from the children of Israel: worship none but Allah; treat with kindness your parents and kindred, and orphans and those in need; speak good to the people; maintain prayer; and give *Zakat* (charity). then you turned away except a few among you, rejecting (the covenant)."

Quran, 4:36

"Worship Allah, and do not associate with Him anything, and be good to parents and to kinsmen and orphans and the needy and the close neighbor and the distant neighbor and the companion at your side and the traveler and to slaves owned by you. Surely, Allah does not like those who are arrogant, proud."

Quran, 6:151

"Say "Come, and I shall recite what your Lord has prohibited for you: Do not associate anything with Him (as His partner); and be good to parents, and do not kill your children because of poverty - We will give provision to you, and to them as well - and do not go near shameful acts, whether they are open or secret; and do not kill a soul whom Allah has given sanctity, except with rightful reason. This He has enjoined upon you, so that you may understand."

Quran, 17:23-24

"And Your Lord has decreed that you worship none but Him, and do good to parents. If any one of them or both of them reach old age, do not say to them: uff (a word or expression of anger or contempt) and do not scold them, and address them with respectful words. And submit yourself before them in humility out of compassion, and say, "My Lord, be merciful to them as they have brought me up in my childhood."

Quran, 29:8

"We have enjoined on man kindness to his parents. And if they insist upon you that you should ascribe partners to Me, then do not obey them. To Me is your return; then I shall tell you what you used to do."

Quran, 31:14-15

"We have enjoined on man (kindness) to his parents. His mother carried him (in her womb) despite weakness upon weakness, and his weaning is in two years. (We said to man,) "Be grateful to Me, and to your parents. To Me is the ultimate return. And if they force you to ascribe partners to Me about whom you have no knowledge, then do not obey them. Keep their company in this world with goodness, but follow the way of the one who has turned himself towards Me. Then, towards Me is your return, so I shall tell you what you had been doing."

Quran, 46:15

"And We have enjoined upon man to do good to his parents. His mother carried him with difficulty and delivered him with difficulty. And his carrying and his weaning is thirty months, until when he attains his maturity and reaches forty years, he says, "My Lord, grant me that I offer gratitude for the favor You have bestowed upon me and upon my parents, and that I do righteous deeds that You like. And set righteousness, for my sake, in my progeny. I repent to you, and truly I am one of those who submit to You."

Quran, 2: 44

"Do you enjoin right conduct on the people and forget (to practice it) yourselves and yet you study the Scripture? Will you not understand?"

Quran, 2:177

"It is not righteousness that you turn your faces towards East or West; but it is righteousness—to believe in Allah and the Last Day and the Angels and the Book and the Messengers; to spend of your substance out of love for Him, for your kin, for orphans for the needy, for the wayfarer for those who ask and for the ransom of slaves; to be steadfast in prayer and practice regular charity; to fulfill the contracts which you have made; and to be firm and patient in pain (or suffering) and adversity and throughout all periods of panic. Such are the people of truth the Allah-fearing."

Quran, 2:189

"It is no virtue if you enter your houses from the back; it is virtue if you fear Allah. Enter houses through the proper doors and fear Allah that you may prosper."

Quran, 3:92

"By no means shall you attain righteousness unless you give (freely) of that which you love; and whatever you give, Allah knows it well."

Quran, 5:2

"Help you one another in righteousness and piety, but help you not one another in sin and rancor: fear Allah."

Quran, 58:9

"O you who believe! when you hold secret counsel, do it not for iniquity and hostility, and disobedience to the Messenger; but do it for righteousness and self-restraint; and fear Allah, to whom you shall be brought back."

APPENDIX C:

QURANIC REFERENCES FOR ISLAM THE CHOICE

Quran, 11:40-48:

"At last, when Our command came and the Tannur overflowed, We said, "Take into the Ark a pair of two from every species, along with your family, except those against whom the Word has already been pronounced and (also take into it) those who have believed." And there were only a few who had believed with him. He (Nuh) said, "Embark it. In the name of Allah it sails and anchors. Surely, my Lord is Most-Forgiving, Very-Merciful." And it was sailing with them amidst the waves like mountains. And Nuh called out to his son, who was at an isolated place, "O my child, come on board with us, and do not be in the company of the disbelievers." He said, "I shall take shelter on a mountain which will save me from the water." He said, "There is no protector today from the command of Allah, except to whom He shows mercy." And the waves rose high between the two, and he was among those who were drowned. It was said (by Allah), "O earth, suck in your water, and O heaven, stop." And water subsided, and the matter was over. It (the Ark) came to rest on the Judi, and it was said, "Away with the wrongdoers." Nuh called unto his Lord and said, "My Lord, my son is a part of my family, and surely Your promise is true, and You are the greatest of all judges." He said, "O Nuh, he is not a part of your family. Indeed, it is an impious deed. So do not ask Me something of which you have no knowledge. I exhort you not to be among the ignorant." He said, "My Lord, I seek refuge with You that I should ask You something of which I have no knowledge. If You do not forgive me and do not show mercy to me, I shall be among the losers." It was said, "O Nuh, disembark in peace from Us and with blessings upon you and upon the peoples (springing) from those with you. And there are peoples whom We shall give some enjoyment, then a painful punishment from Us will visit them."

REFERENCES

Abu-Ras, W., Ahmed, S., Arfken, C. (2010). Alcohol use among U.S. Muslim college students: Risk and protective factors. *Journal of Ethnicity in Substance Abuse, 9*(3), 206-220.

Ahmed, S., Abu-Ras, W., & Arfken, C. (2014). Prevalence of risk behaviors among U.S. Muslim college students. *Journal of Muslim Mental Health, 8*(1).

Ahmed, S., & Amer, M. (2011). *Counseling Muslims: Handbook of mental health issues and interventions.* Abingdon, United Kingdom: Routledge.

al-Ghazali, A. (n.d.). كيمياء السعادة [The alchemy of happiness]. Retrieved March 10, 2016, from http://arareaders.com/books/details/360

Alwan, A. N. (1981). تربية الأولاد فى الإسلام [Raising children in Islam]. Aleppo, Syria: Dar al-Salam.

Asarnow, L., Harvey, A., & McGlinchey, E. (2013). The effects of bedtime and sleep duration on academic and emotional outcomes in a nationally representative sample of adolescents. *Journal of Adolescent Health, 54*(3), 350-356.

Baumrind, D. (1967). Child care practices anteceding three patterns of preschool behavior. *Genetic Psychology Monographs, 75*(1), 43-88.

Berndt, T. J. (2002). Friendship quality and social development. *Current Directions in Psychological Science, 11*(1), 7-10.

Brooks, J. (2011). *The process of parenting* (8th ed.). Mountain View, CA: Mayfield Publishing.

Brooks, R., & Goldstein, S. (2001). *Raising resilient children: Fostering strength, hope & optimism in your child.* New York: McGraw-Hill Education.

Colvin, R. (1999, Jan 25). Losing faith in self-esteem movement. *Los Angeles Times.* Retrieved July 12, 2015 from http://articles.latimes.com/1999/jan/25/news/mn-1505

Corey, G. (2005). *Theory and practice of counseling and psychotherapy.* Belmont, CA: Brooks/Cole -Thomson Learning.

Covey, S. (1997). *The seven habits of highly effective families.* New York: Golden Books.

Cowden, J. D. (2016, May 23). Behavioral interventions for infant sleep training: Effective and not harmful. *NEJM Journal Watch.* Retrieved May 30, 2016 from http://www.jwatch.org/na41417/2016/05/23/behavioral-interventions-infant-sleep-training-effective

Crary, D. (2007). College students are narcissistic! *Boston.com News.* Retrieved Mar 4, 2015 from http://www.boston.com/news/education/higher/articles/2007/02/27/

DeFrain, J. D., & Stinnet, N. (2008). *Creating a strong family: American family strengths inventory.* University of Nebraska-Lincoln Extension. Retrieved June 10, 2016 from http://digitalcommons.unl.edu/cgi/viewcontent.cgi?article=1052&context=extensionhist

Dishion, T., Kavanagh, K., Schneiger, A.K.J., Nelson, S., & Kaufman, N. (2002). Preventing early adolescent substance use: A family centered strategy for the public middle school. *Prevention Science 3*(3),191–202.

Dumas, L. S. (1997). Kaiser Family Foundation and Children Now. *Talking with Kids about Tough Issues.* [Booklet]. Retrieved August 17, 2016 from http://www.unitedactionforyouth.org/Health-pdf/talking%20with%20kids%20about %20tough%20issues%20handbook.pdf

Faisal, S. A. (2015). What does the research say? That Muslim youth need sex education. *Heart Women & Girls.* Retrieved May 31, 2015 from http://heartwomenandgirls.org/2015/05/18/what-does-the-research-say-that-muslim-youth-need-sex-education/

Ferguson, C. (2015). Parents, calm down about infant screen time. *Time.* Retrieved February 7, 2015 from http://time.com/3693883/parents-calm-down-about-infant-screen-time/

Gardner, H. (1999). *Intelligence reframed: Multiple intelligences for the 21st Century.* New York: Basic Books.

Glasser, W. (1999). *Choice theory: A new psychology of personal freedom.* New York: HarperCollins Publishers.

Granju, K. A., & Kennedy, B. (1999). *Attachment parenting: Instinctive care for your baby and young child*. New York: Pocket Books.

Hijazi, O. A. (2008). التربية الاسلامية بين الأصالة والحداثة [Islamic parenting between the old and the new]. Beirut, Lebanon: al-Maktaba al-Assrya.

Hirshkowitz, M., Whiton, K., Albert, S. M., Alessi, C., Bruni, O., DonCarlos, L., et al. (2015). National sleep foundation's sleep time duration recommendations: Methodology and results summary. *Sleep Health: Journal of National Sleep Foundation, 1*(1), 40-43.

Hulbert, A. (2004). *Raising America: Experts, parents, and a century of advice about children,* New York: Vintage Books.

Kolbert, E. (2012). Spoiled rotten: Why do kids rule the roost? *The New Yorker.* Retrieved February 12, 2014 www.newyorker.com/magazine/2012/07/02/spoiled-rotten

Lenhart, A. (2015, April 9). *Teens, social media & technology overview 2015.* Retrieved December 20, 2015 from Pew Research Center Web site: www.pewinternet.org/2015/04/09/teens-social-media-technology-2015/

Lipka, M. (2015). *A closer look at America's rapidly growing religious 'nones.'* Retrieved July 1, 2015, from Pew Research Center Web site: http://www.pewresearch.org/fact-tank/2015/05/13/a-closer-look-at-americas-rapidly-growing-religious-nones/

Lyons-Padilla, S., Gelfand, M. J., Mirahmadi, H., Farooq, M., & van Egmond, M. (2015). Belonging nowhere: Marginalization & radicalization risk among Muslim immigrants. *Behavioral Science & Policy, 1*(2).

Lyubomirsky, S. (2008) *The how of happiness.* New York: The Penguin Press.

Martinez-Prather, K., & Vandiver, D. M. (2014). Sexting among teenagers in the United States: A retrospective analysis of identifying motivating factors, potential targets, and the role of a capable guardian. *International Journal of Cyber Criminology, 8*(1), 21-35.

Masud, H., Thurasamy, R., & Ahmad, M. S. (2014). Parenting styles and academic achievement of young adolescents: A systematic literature review. *Springer Science and Media.* Retrieved on November 2, 2014 from http://www.academia.edu/9440149/Parenting_styles_and_academic_achievem ent_of_young_adolescents_A_systematic_literature_review

McAfee for Business. (2012). *Press Release: 70% of teens hide their online behavior from their parents, McAfee reveals what U.S. teens are really doing online, and how little their parents actually know.* Retrieved December 15, 2014 from http://mcafee.com/us/about/news/2012/q2/20120625-01/aspx

National Alliance on Mental Illness. (2013). *Mental illness facts and numbers.* Retrieved on December 5, 2015 from www2.name.org/factsheets/mentalillness_factsheet.pdf

National Center for Education Statistics. (2013). *Fast Facts.* Retrieved December 5, 2015 from https://nces.edu.gov/fastfacts/display.asp?id=719

Nelsen, J. (2006). *Positive discipline.* New York: Ballantine.

Nelsen, J., Erwin, C., & Duffy, R. (2007). *Positive discipline for preschoolers.* New York: Three Rivers Press.

Nelsen, J., & Lott, L. (1997). *Positive discipline in the classroom: Teacher's guide.* Orem, UT: Empowering People Books.

Newman, B. M., & Newman, P. R. (2003). *Development through life: A psychosocial approach.* Belmont, CA: Wadsworth/Thomson Learning.

Novotny, A. (2014). Students under pressure. *Monitor on Psychology, 25*(8), 36.

Olsen, G., & Fuller, M. L. (2011). *Home and School Relations: Teachers and parents working together* (4th ed.). New York: Pearson.

Sabiq, S. (1983). فقه السنة [Jurisprudence of Sunnah]. Beirut, Lebanon: Dar al-Kitab al-Arabi.

Shabbas, A. (2006, February). *The Arab World and Islam.* Colloquium presented at California State University, Fullerton.

Sifferlin, A. (2012). Study or sleep? For better grades, teens should go to bed early. *Time.* Retrieved January 26, 2014 from healthland.com/2012/08/21/study-or-sleep-for-better-grades-students-should-go-to-bed-early/

Spock, B., & Parker, S. (1998). *Dr. Spock's baby and child care* (7ᵗʰ ed.). New York: Dutton.

Summers, J. (2014). *Kids and screen time: What does the research say?* Retrieved September 23, 2014 from http://www.npr.org/blogs/ed/2014/08/28/343735856/kids-and-screen-time-what-does-the-research-say

Szalavitz, M. (2012). Why the teen brain is drawn to risk. *Time*. Retrieved May 12, 2015 from https://heathland.time.com/2012/10/02/why-the-teen-brain-is-drawn-to-risk/

Taylor, J. (2012). How technology is changing the way children think and focus. *Psychology Today*. Retrieved January 23, 2015 from https://www.psychologytoday.com/blog/the-power-prime/201212/how-technology-is-changing-the-way-children-think-and-focus

Transition Year. (n. d.). *Emotional health and your college student*. Retrieved on June 10, 2015 from http://www.transitionyear.org/_downloads/parent_pdf_guide.pdf

Twenge, J. M., Konrath, S., Foster, J. D., Keith Campbell, W., & Bushman, B. J. (2008). Egos inflating over time: A cross-temporal meta-analysis of the narcissistic personality inventory. *Journal of Personality*. 76(4), 875-902.

Whiteman, H. (2013). Technology in kids' bedrooms disrupts sleep patterns. *Medical News Today*. Retrieved January 7, 2015 from http://www.medicalnewstoday.com/articles/264095.php

Whiteman, H. (2013). Bad bedtime routines early in children's lives may stunt later brain power. *Medical News Today*. Retrieved March 28, 2016 from http://www.medicalnewstoday.com/articles/263010.php

Wills, T., McNamara, G., Vaccaro, D., & Hirky, A. (1996). Escalated substance use: A longitudinal grouping analysis from early to middle adolescence. *Journal of Abnormal Psychology* 105,166–180.

INDEX

ABOUT THE AUTHORS

 NOHA ALSHUGAIRI, M.S., is a licensed marriage and family therapist in private practice in Newport Beach, CA. She frequently facilitates trainings and workshops on a variety of topics for mental health professionals and the community at large. Her strong foundation in Islamic sciences guides her work in helping families integrate faith and culture. She received her B.A. in Zoology from Rutgers University in 1986, and her M.S. in Counseling from California State University, Fullerton, in 2007. Since becoming certified as a Positive Discipline Trainer in 2008, she has conducted numerous trainings for parents and teachers. She has been married for 32 years, and has four adult children and two grandchildren.

 MUNIRA LEKOVIC EZZELDINE, M.S., is a professional college and career counselor. She loves helping young adults gain self-awareness to prepare for higher education and beyond. She has written extensively for various Muslim publications and websites on issues of parenting, family, and marriage. She is the author of *Before the Wedding: Questions for Muslims to Ask Before Getting Married*. She holds a B.S. in Economics from UCLA and M.S. in Counseling from California State University, Fullerton. In addition to being a certified College Counselor she has certifications as a Premarital Counselor and Positive Discipline Educator. She lives in Southern California with her husband and three children.